WASTELAND

BOOK 09

A THOUSAND LIES

AN ONI PRESS PUBLICATION

PUBLISHER JOE NOZEMACK
EDITOR IN CHIEF JAMES LUCAS JONES
DIRECTOR OF PUBLICITY JOHN SCHORK
DIRECTOR OF SALES CHEYENNE ALLOTT
PRODUCTION MANAGER TROY LOOK
SENIOR GRAPHIC DESIGNER JASON STOREY
EDITOR JILL BEATON
EDITOR CHARLIE CHU
ADMINISTRATIVE ASSISTANT ROBIN HERRERA

Oni Press, Inc.
1305 SE Martin Luther King Jr. Blvd, Suite A
Portland, OR 97214 USA
www.onipress.com

ONIPRESS.COM
FACEBOOK.COM/ONIPRESS
TWITTER.COM/ONIPRESS
ONIPRESS.TUMBLR.COM

www.thebigwet.com

Previously published as issues #46–51 of the Oni Press comic series *Wasteland*.

FIRST EDITION: MARCH 2014
ISBN: 978-1-62010-118-6
eISBN: 978-1-62010-119-3

1 3 5 7 9 10 8 6 4 2

Library of Congress Control Number: 2013954581

WASTELAND

BOOK 09
A THOUSAND LIES

WRITTEN BY **ANTONY JOHNSTON**
DRAWN BY **JUSTIN GREENWOOD**

COVER ART BY **CHRISTOPHER MITTEN**

LETTERED BY **DOUGLAS E. SHERWOOD**

EDITED BY **JAMES LUCAS JONES**

DESIGNED BY **ANTONY JOHNSTON**

CREATED BY **JOHNSTON & MITTEN**

ONE HUNDRED AND ONE YEARS
AFTER THE BIG WET.
SOMEWHERE IN AMERICA...

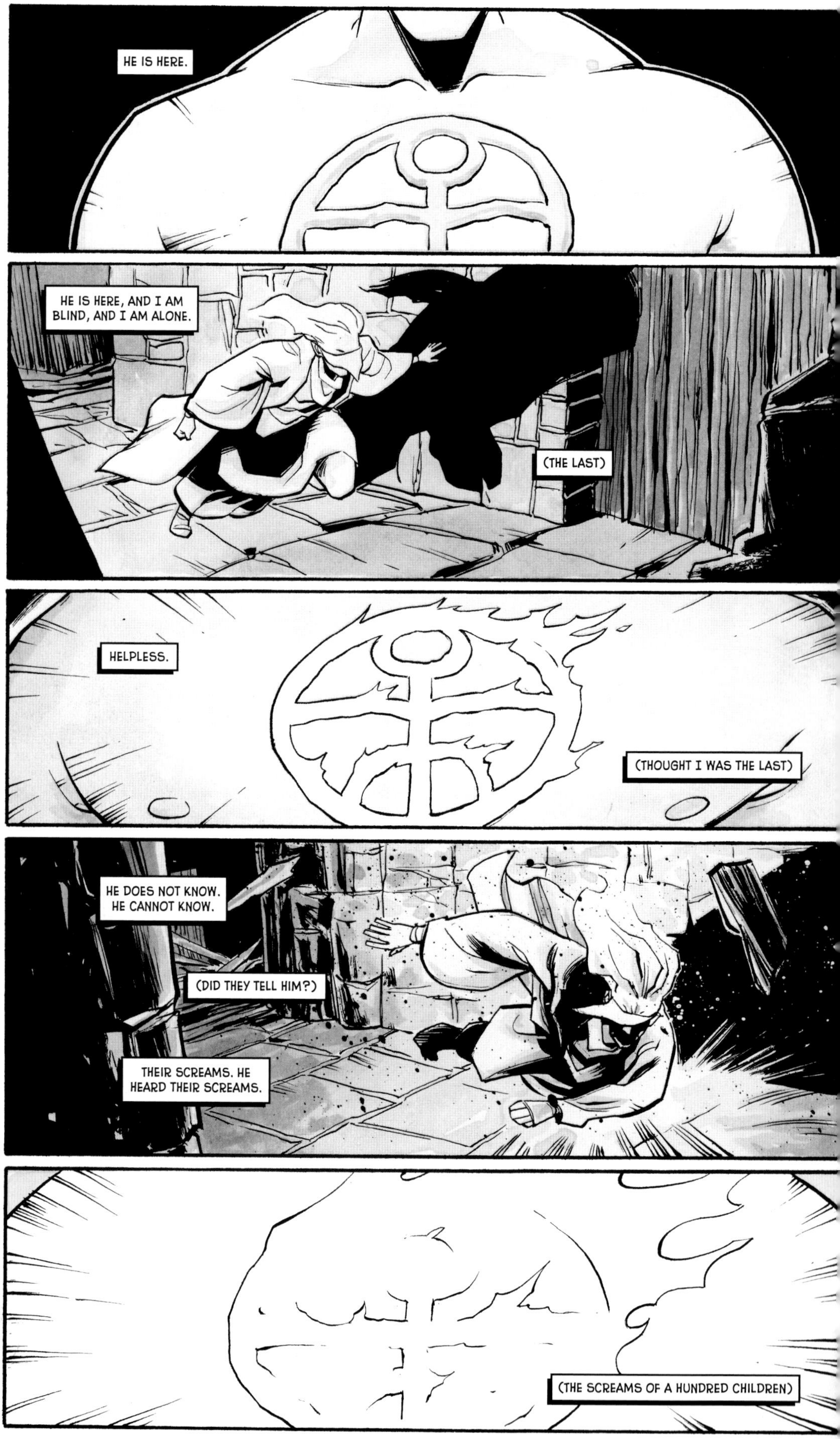
HE IS HERE.
HE IS HERE, AND I AM BLIND, AND I AM ALONE.
(THE LAST)
HELPLESS.
(THOUGHT I WAS THE LAST)
HE DOES NOT KNOW. HE CANNOT KNOW.
(DID THEY TELL HIM?)
THEIR SCREAMS. HE HEARD THEIR SCREAMS.
(THE SCREAMS OF A HUNDRED CHILDREN)

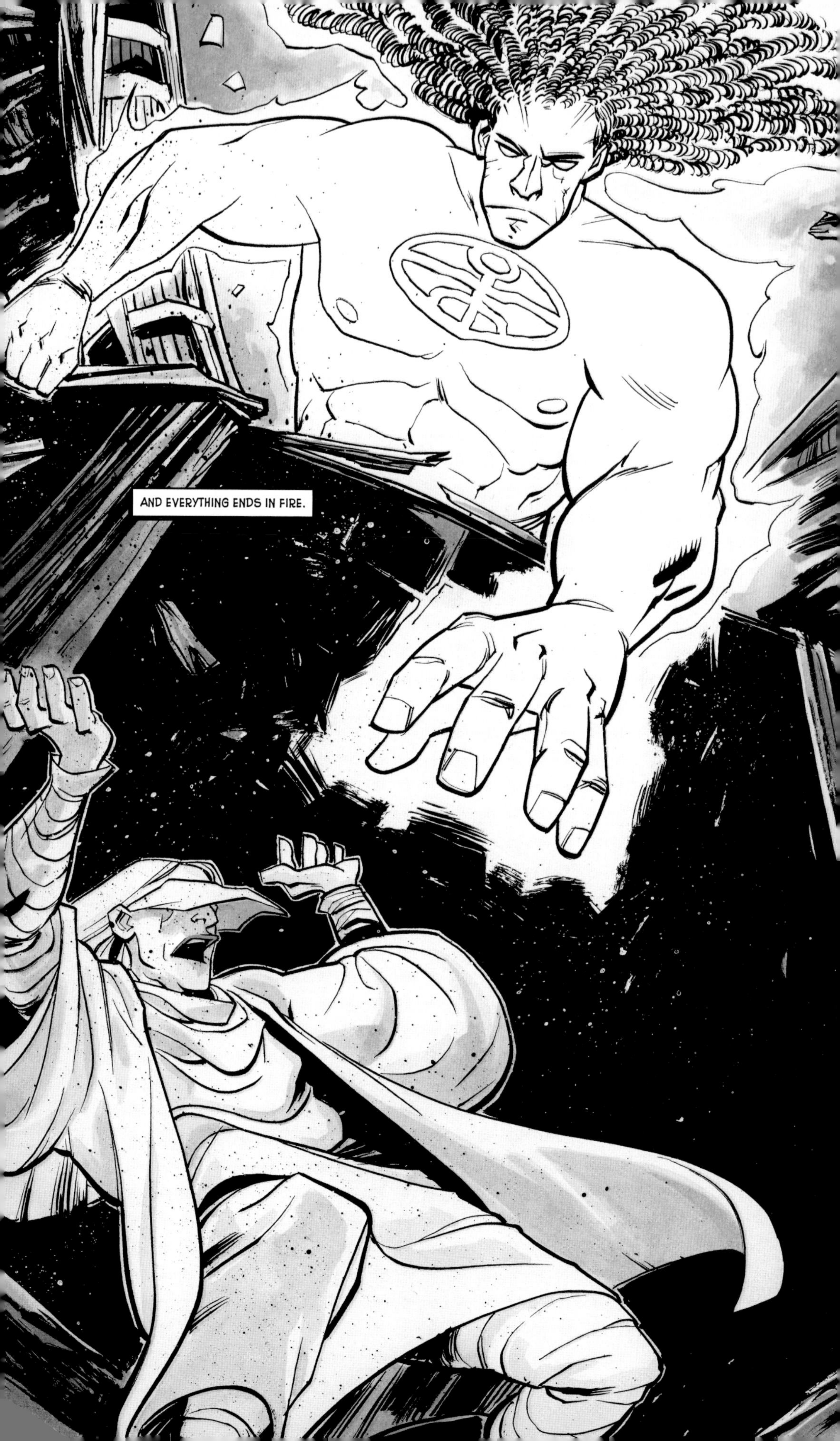
AND EVERYTHING ENDS IN FIRE.

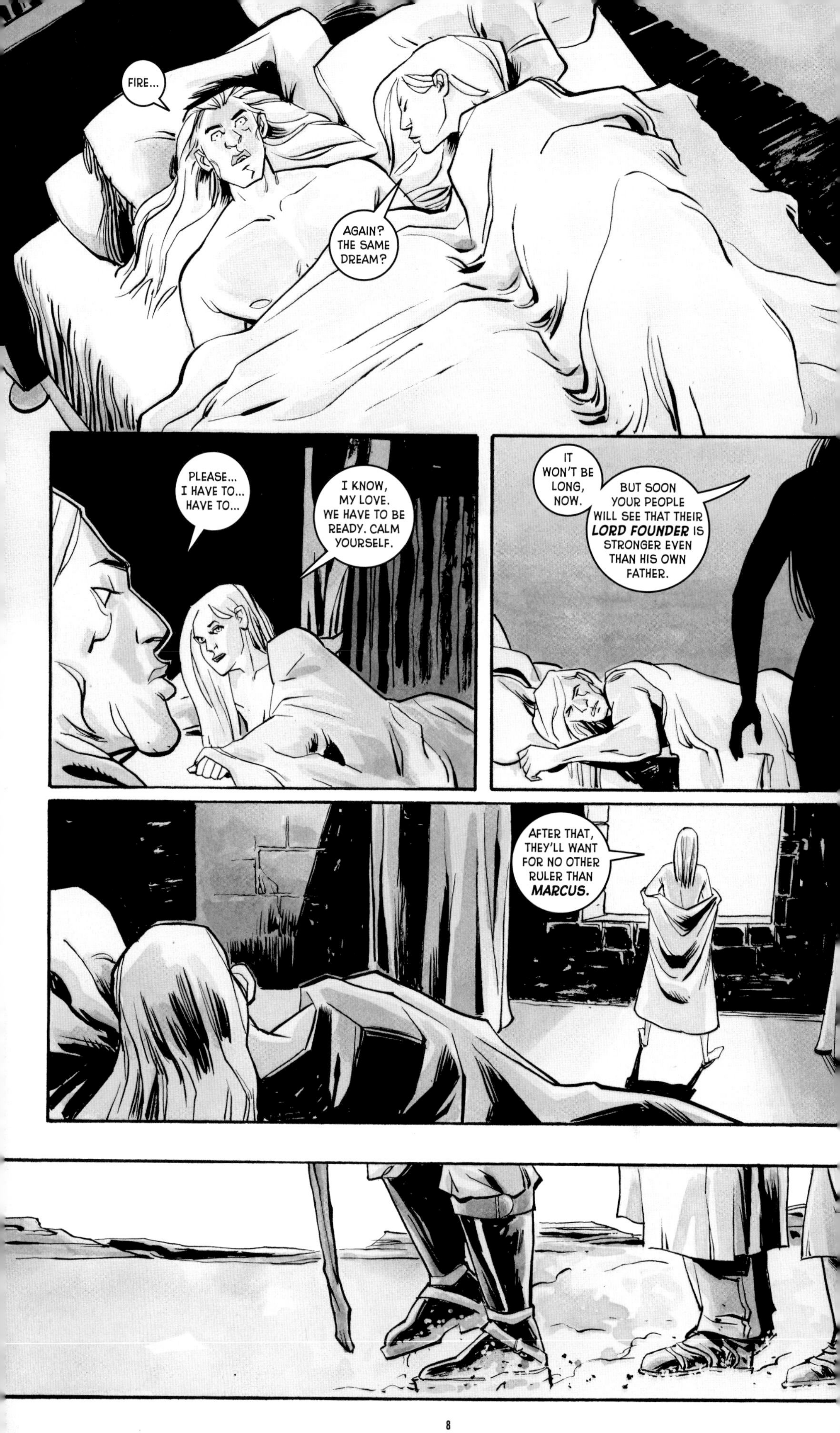
FIRE...
AGAIN? THE SAME DREAM?
PLEASE... I HAVE TO... HAVE TO...
I KNOW, MY LOVE. WE HAVE TO BE READY. CALM YOURSELF.
IT WON'T BE LONG, NOW.
BUT SOON YOUR PEOPLE WILL SEE THAT THEIR **LORD FOUNDER** IS STRONGER EVEN THAN HIS OWN FATHER.
AFTER THAT, THEY'LL WANT FOR NO OTHER RULER THAN **MARCUS.**

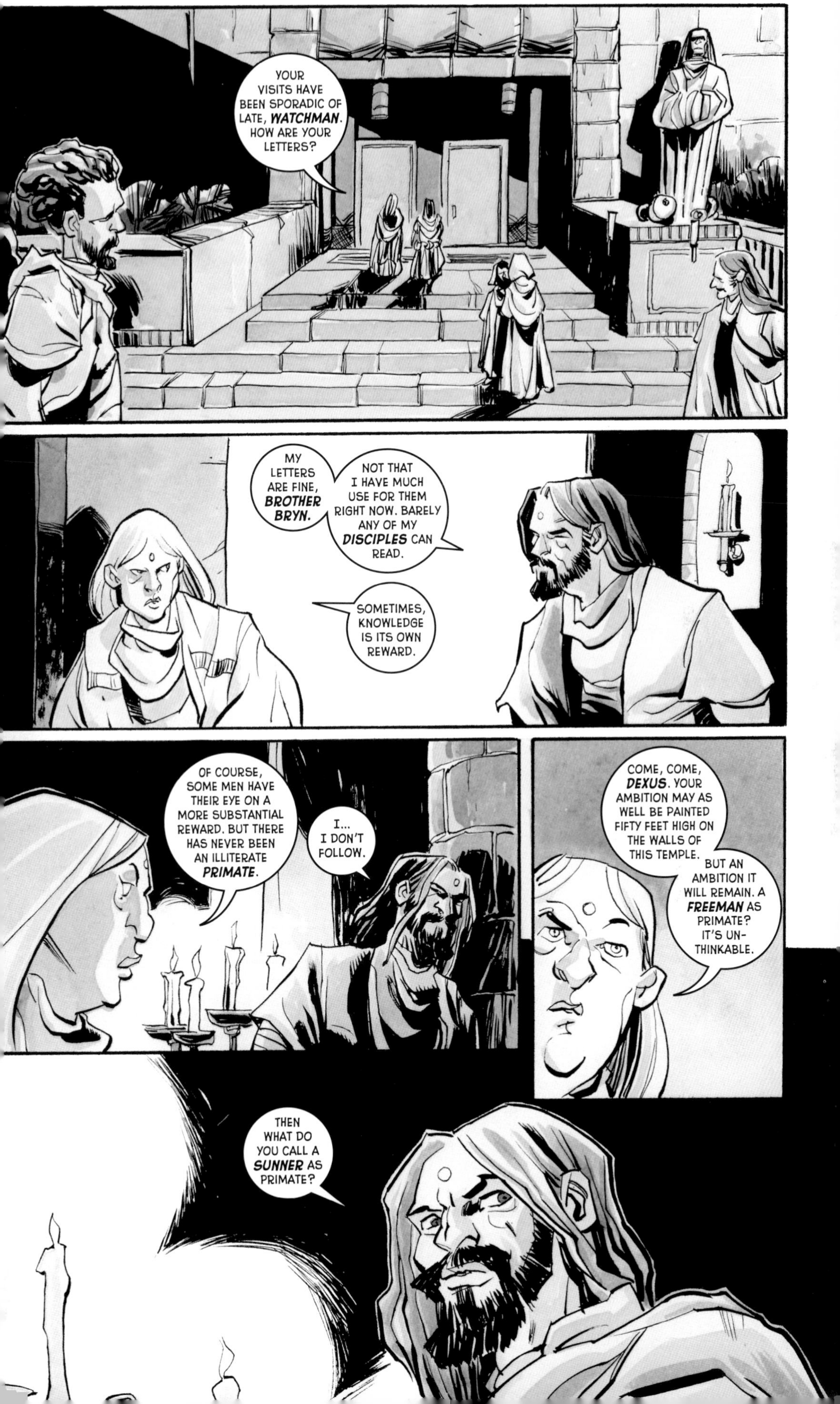
YOUR VISITS HAVE BEEN SPORADIC OF LATE, WATCHMAN. HOW ARE YOUR LETTERS?
MY LETTERS ARE FINE, BROTHER BRYN.
NOT THAT I HAVE MUCH USE FOR THEM RIGHT NOW. BARELY ANY OF MY DISCIPLES CAN READ.
SOMETIMES, KNOWLEDGE IS ITS OWN REWARD.
OF COURSE, SOME MEN HAVE THEIR EYE ON A MORE SUBSTANTIAL REWARD. BUT THERE HAS NEVER BEEN AN ILLITERATE PRIMATE.
I... I DON'T FOLLOW.
COME, COME, DEXUS. YOUR AMBITION MAY AS WELL BE PAINTED FIFTY FEET HIGH ON THE WALLS OF THIS TEMPLE.
BUT AN AMBITION IT WILL REMAIN. A FREEMAN AS PRIMATE? IT'S UN-THINKABLE.
THEN WHAT DO YOU CALL A SUNNER AS PRIMATE?

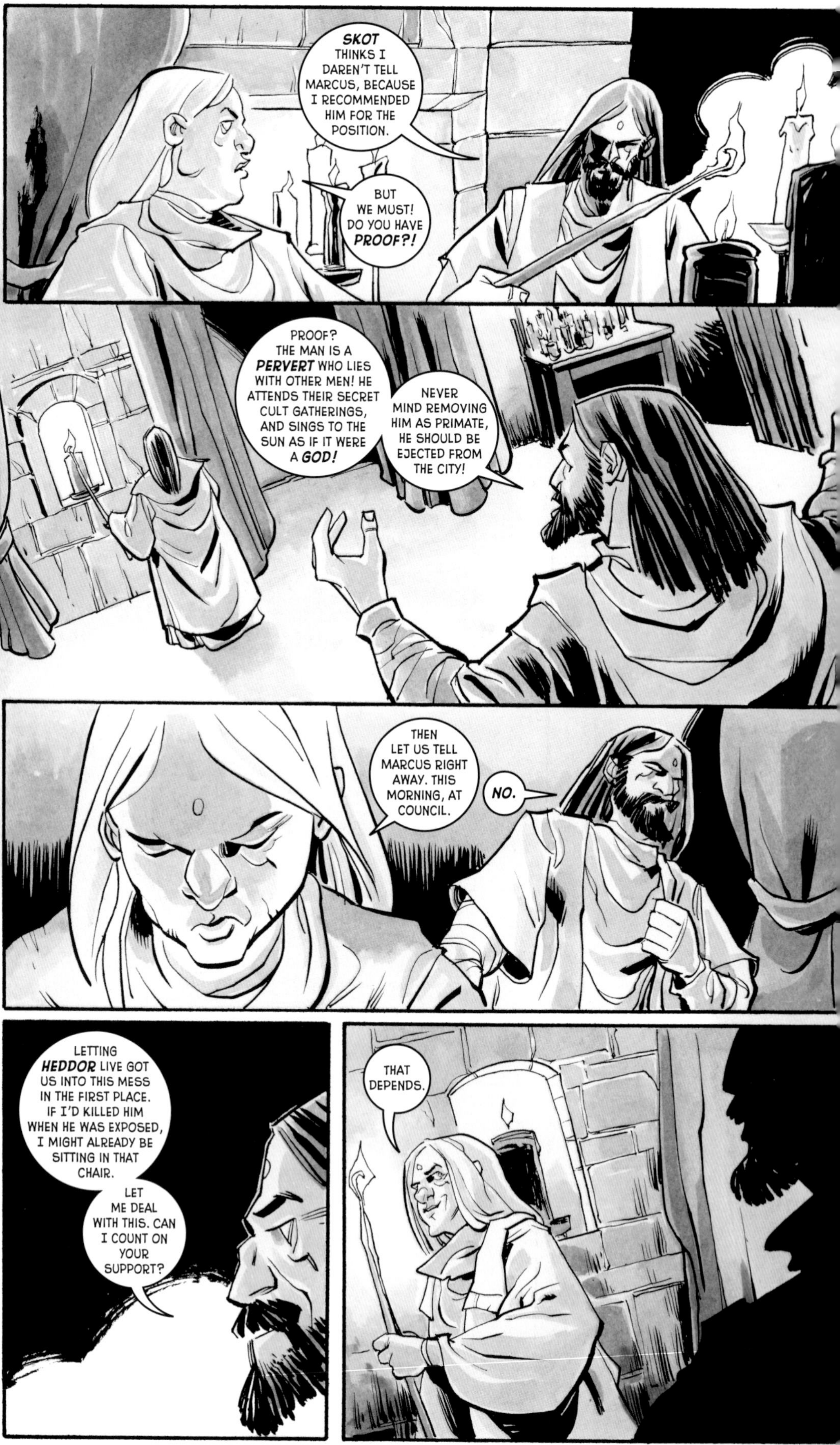
SKOT THINKS I DAREN'T TELL MARCUS, BECAUSE I RECOMMENDED HIM FOR THE POSITION.
BUT WE MUST! DO YOU HAVE PROOF?!
PROOF? THE MAN IS A PERVERT WHO LIES WITH OTHER MEN! HE ATTENDS THEIR SECRET CULT GATHERINGS, AND SINGS TO THE SUN AS IF IT WERE A GOD!
NEVER MIND REMOVING HIM AS PRIMATE, HE SHOULD BE EJECTED FROM THE CITY!
THEN LET US TELL MARCUS RIGHT AWAY. THIS MORNING, AT COUNCIL.
NO.
LETTING HEDDOR LIVE GOT US INTO THIS MESS IN THE FIRST PLACE. IF I'D KILLED HIM WHEN HE WAS EXPOSED, I MIGHT ALREADY BE SITTING IN THAT CHAIR.
LET ME DEAL WITH THIS. CAN I COUNT ON YOUR SUPPORT?
THAT DEPENDS.

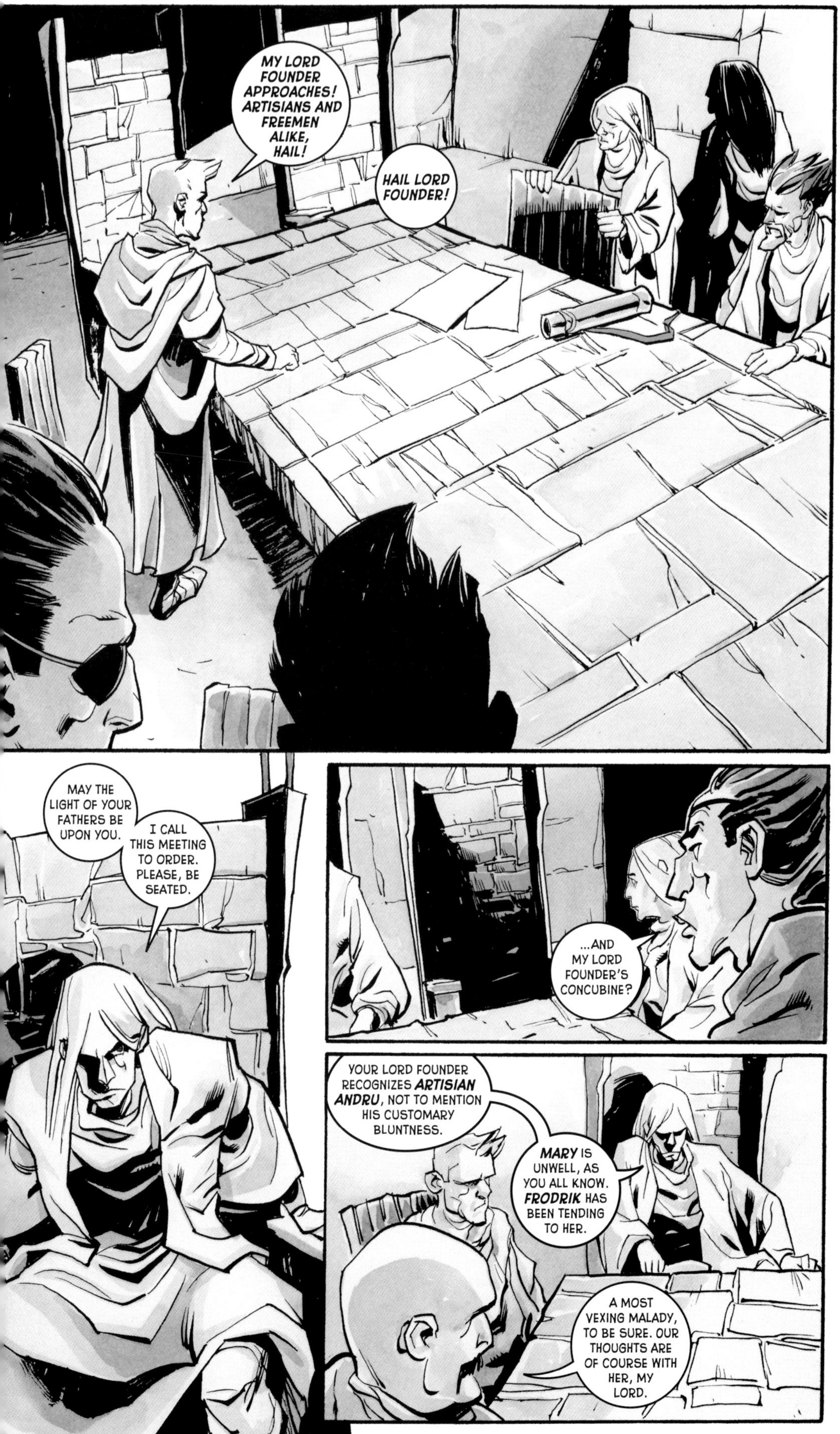

MY LORD FOUNDER APPROACHES! ARTISIANS AND FREEMEN ALIKE, HAIL!
HAIL LORD FOUNDER!
MAY THE LIGHT OF YOUR FATHERS BE UPON YOU.
I CALL THIS MEETING TO ORDER. PLEASE, BE SEATED.
...AND MY LORD FOUNDER'S CONCUBINE?
YOUR LORD FOUNDER RECOGNIZES ARTISIAN ANDRU, NOT TO MENTION HIS CUSTOMARY BLUNTNESS.
MARY IS UNWELL, AS YOU ALL KNOW. FRODRIK HAS BEEN TENDING TO HER.
A MOST VEXING MALADY, TO BE SURE. OUR THOUGHTS ARE OF COURSE WITH HER, MY LORD.

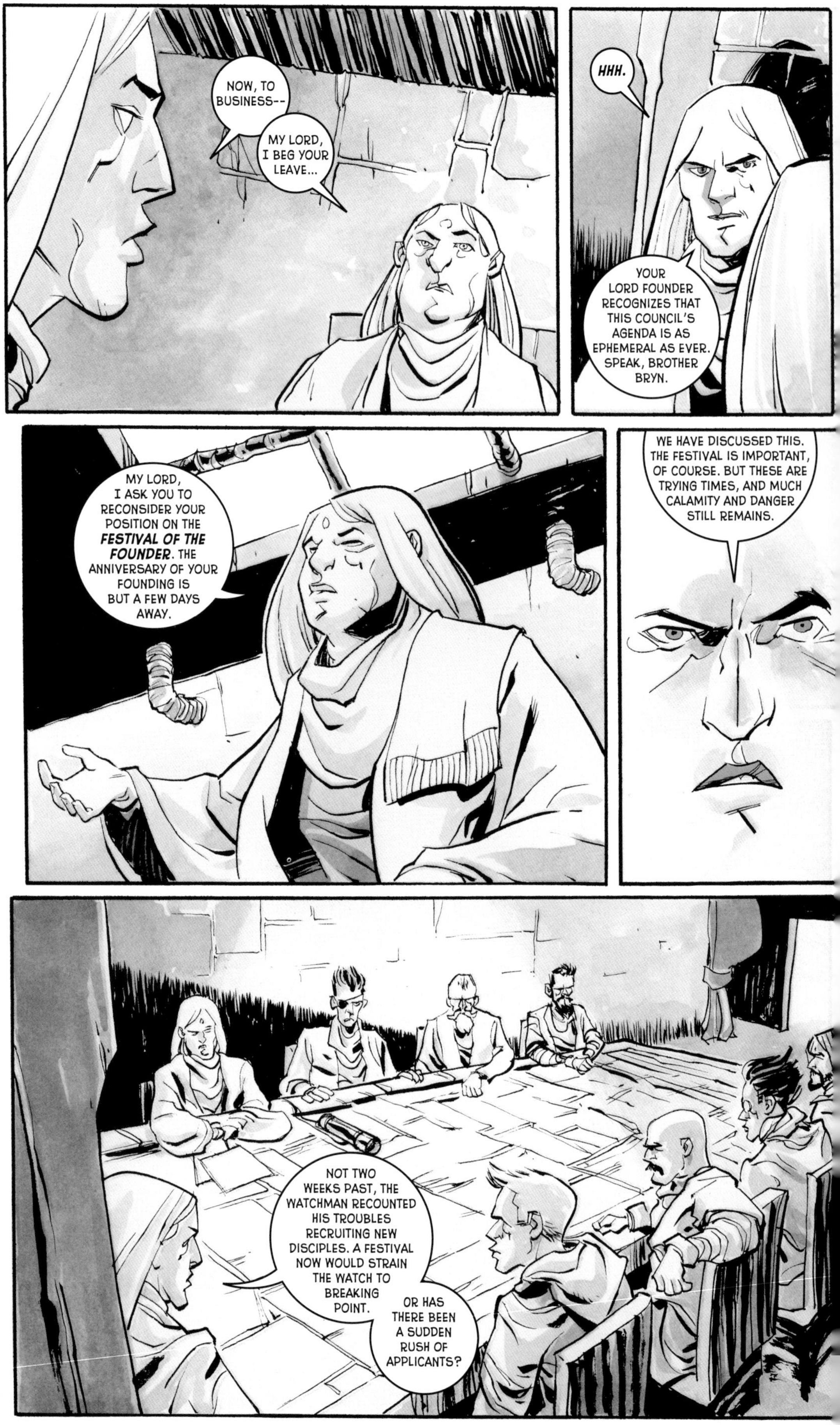
NOW, TO BUSINESS--
MY LORD, I BEG YOUR LEAVE...
HHH.
YOUR LORD FOUNDER RECOGNIZES THAT THIS COUNCIL'S AGENDA IS AS EPHEMERAL AS EVER. SPEAK, BROTHER BRYN.
MY LORD, I ASK YOU TO RECONSIDER YOUR POSITION ON THE ***FESTIVAL OF THE FOUNDER***. THE ANNIVERSARY OF YOUR FOUNDING IS BUT A FEW DAYS AWAY.
WE HAVE DISCUSSED THIS. THE FESTIVAL IS IMPORTANT, OF COURSE. BUT THESE ARE TRYING TIMES, AND MUCH CALAMITY AND DANGER STILL REMAINS.
NOT TWO WEEKS PAST, THE WATCHMAN RECOUNTED HIS TROUBLES RECRUITING NEW DISCIPLES. A FESTIVAL NOW WOULD STRAIN THE WATCH TO BREAKING POINT.
OR HAS THERE BEEN A SUDDEN RUSH OF APPLICANTS?

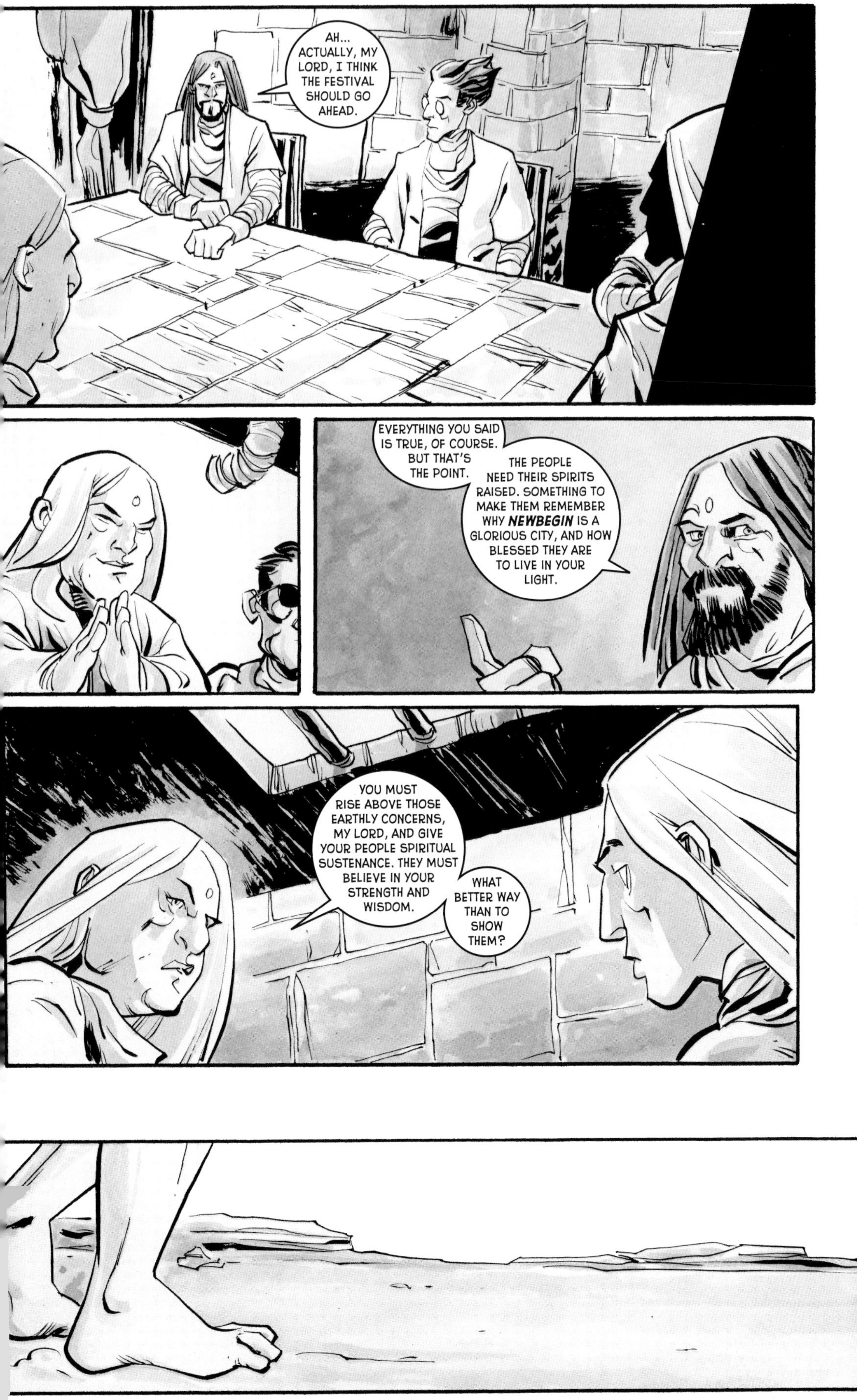
AH... ACTUALLY, MY LORD, I THINK THE FESTIVAL SHOULD GO AHEAD.
EVERYTHING YOU SAID IS TRUE, OF COURSE. BUT THAT'S THE POINT.
THE PEOPLE NEED THEIR SPIRITS RAISED. SOMETHING TO MAKE THEM REMEMBER WHY NEWBEGIN IS A GLORIOUS CITY, AND HOW BLESSED THEY ARE TO LIVE IN YOUR LIGHT.
YOU MUST RISE ABOVE THOSE EARTHLY CONCERNS, MY LORD, AND GIVE YOUR PEOPLE SPIRITUAL SUSTENANCE. THEY MUST BELIEVE IN YOUR STRENGTH AND WISDOM.
WHAT BETTER WAY THAN TO SHOW THEM?

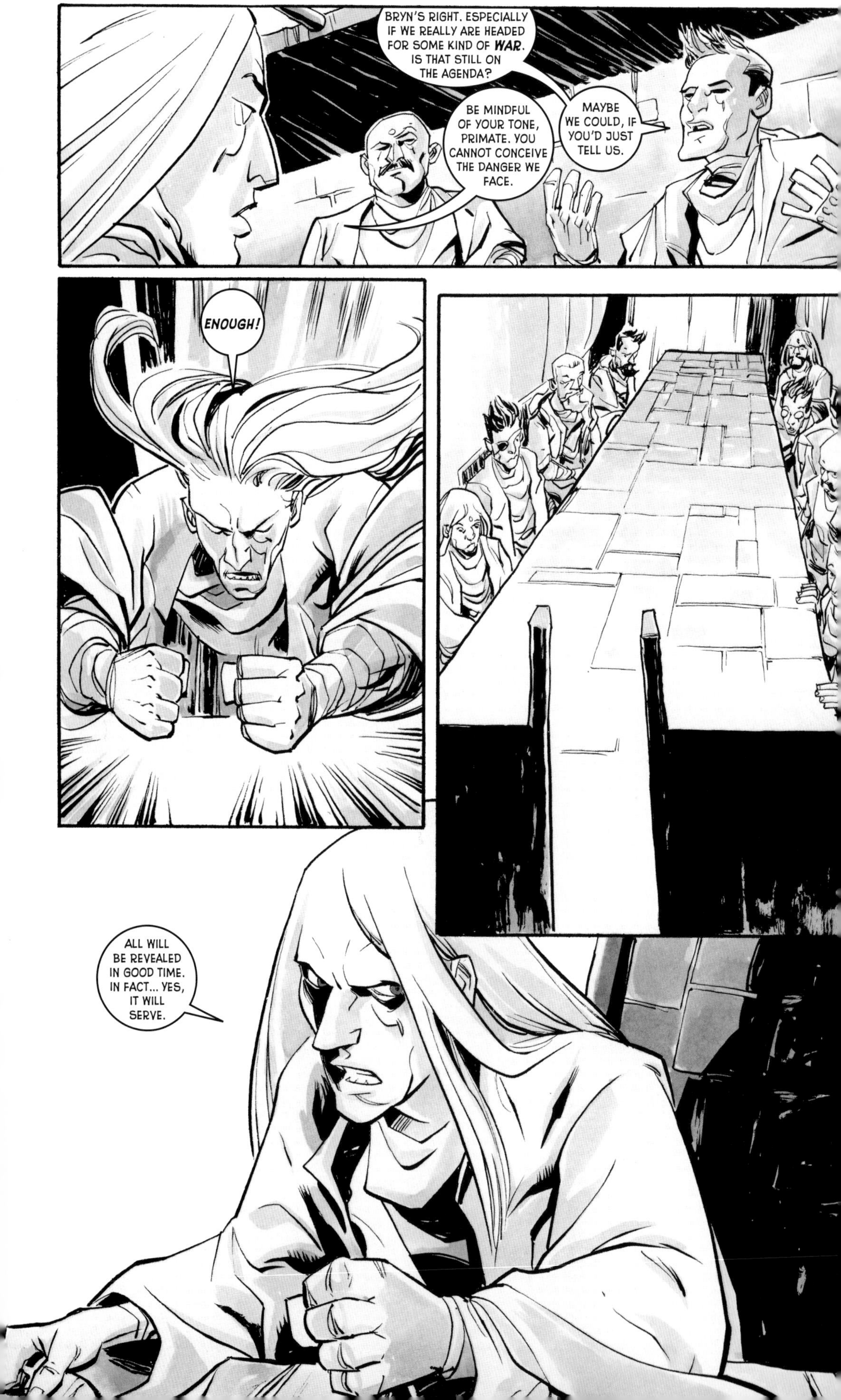
BRYN'S RIGHT. ESPECIALLY IF WE REALLY ARE HEADED FOR SOME KIND OF **WAR**. IS THAT STILL ON THE AGENDA?
BE MINDFUL OF YOUR TONE, PRIMATE. YOU CANNOT CONCEIVE THE DANGER WE FACE.
MAYBE WE COULD, IF YOU'D JUST TELL US.
ENOUGH!
ALL WILL BE REVEALED IN GOOD TIME. IN FACT... YES, IT WILL SERVE.

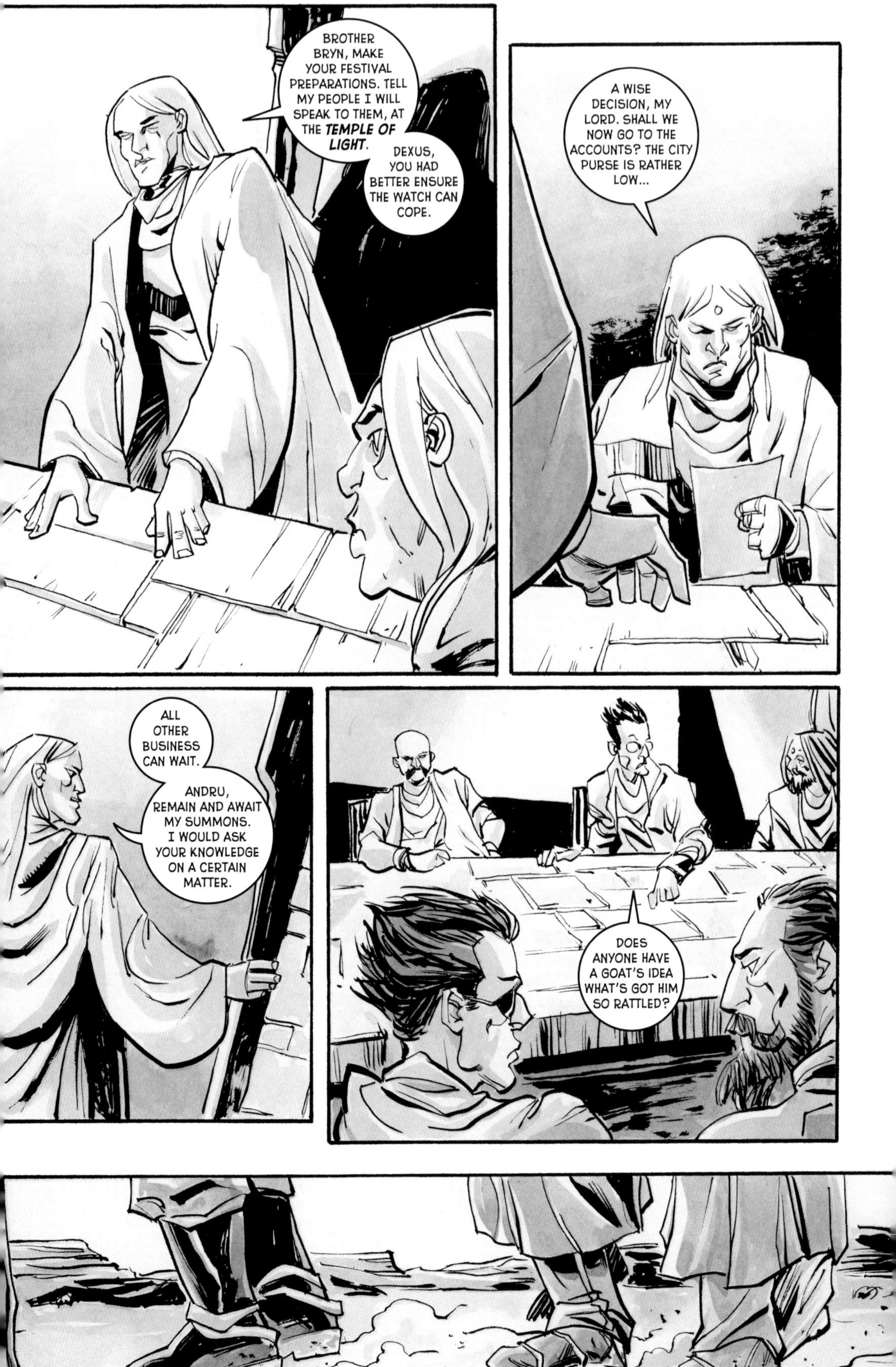
BROTHER BRYN, MAKE YOUR FESTIVAL PREPARATIONS. TELL MY PEOPLE I WILL SPEAK TO THEM, AT THE ***TEMPLE OF LIGHT***.
DEXUS, YOU HAD BETTER ENSURE THE WATCH CAN COPE.
A WISE DECISION, MY LORD. SHALL WE NOW GO TO THE ACCOUNTS? THE CITY PURSE IS RATHER LOW...
ALL OTHER BUSINESS CAN WAIT.
ANDRU, REMAIN AND AWAIT MY SUMMONS. I WOULD ASK YOUR KNOWLEDGE ON A CERTAIN MATTER.
DOES ANYONE HAVE A GOAT'S IDEA WHAT'S GOT HIM SO RATTLED?

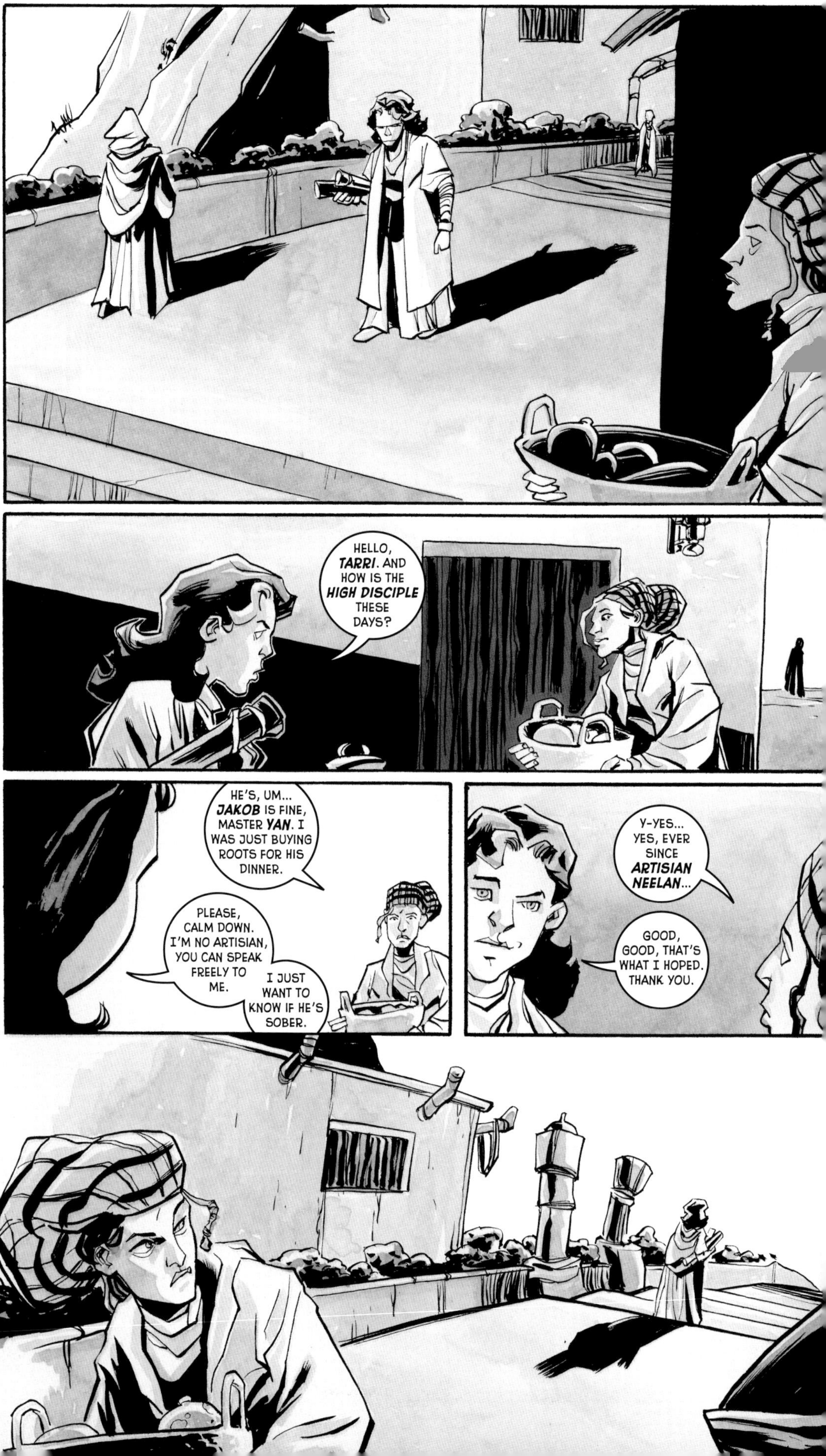
HELLO, TARRI. AND HOW IS THE HIGH DISCIPLE THESE DAYS?
HE'S, UM... JAKOB IS FINE, MASTER YAN. I WAS JUST BUYING ROOTS FOR HIS DINNER.
PLEASE, CALM DOWN. I'M NO ARTISIAN, YOU CAN SPEAK FREELY TO ME.
I JUST WANT TO KNOW IF HE'S SOBER.
Y-YES... YES, EVER SINCE ARTISIAN NEELAN...
GOOD, GOOD, THAT'S WHAT I HOPED. THANK YOU.

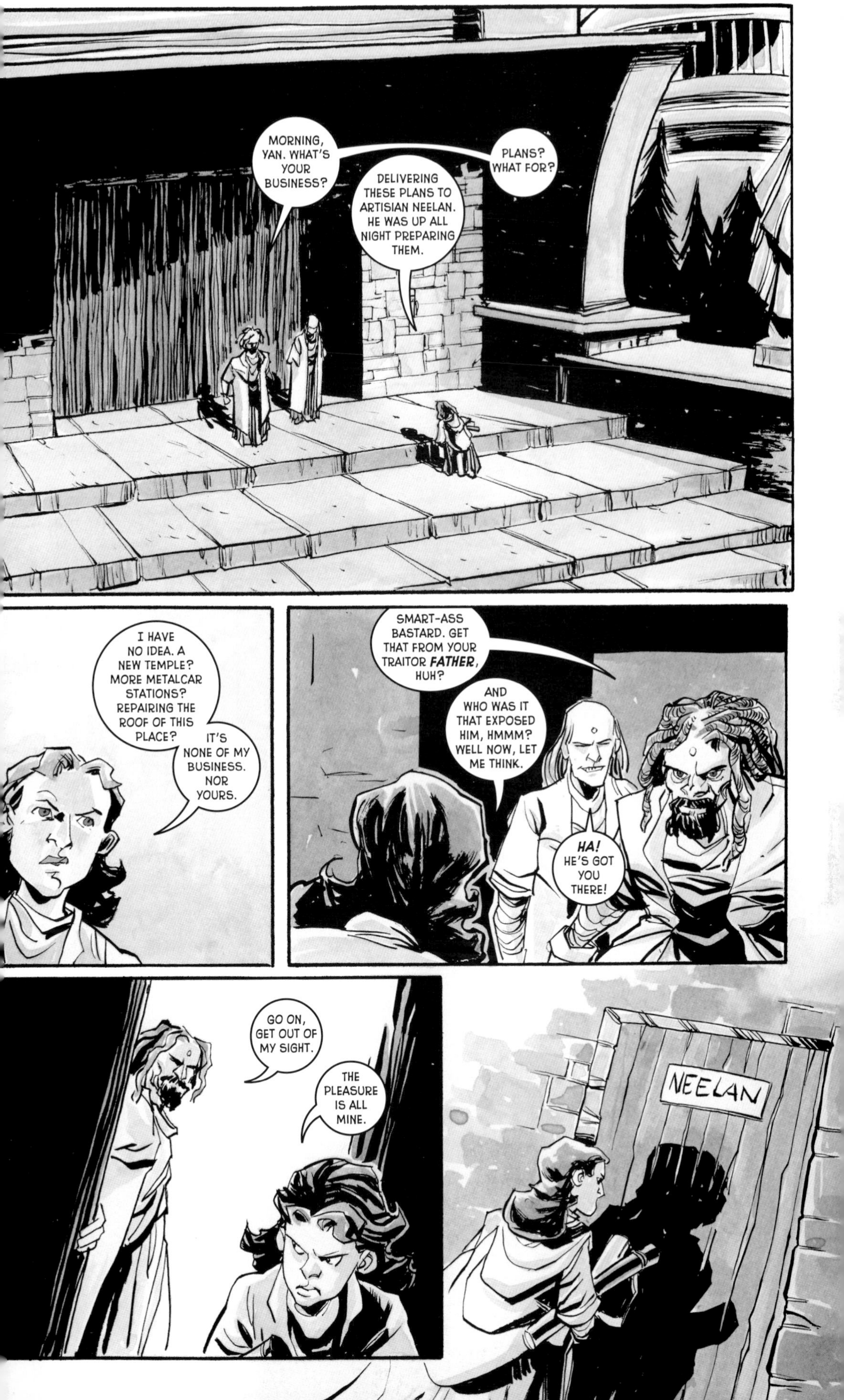
MORNING, YAN. WHAT'S YOUR BUSINESS?
DELIVERING THESE PLANS TO ARTISIAN NEELAN. HE WAS UP ALL NIGHT PREPARING THEM.
PLANS? WHAT FOR?
I HAVE NO IDEA. A NEW TEMPLE? MORE METALCAR STATIONS? REPAIRING THE ROOF OF THIS PLACE?
IT'S NONE OF MY BUSINESS. NOR YOURS.
SMART-ASS BASTARD. GET THAT FROM YOUR TRAITOR **FATHER**, HUH?
AND WHO WAS IT THAT EXPOSED HIM, HMMM? WELL NOW, LET ME THINK.
HA! HE'S GOT YOU THERE!
GO ON, GET OUT OF MY SIGHT.
THE PLEASURE IS ALL MINE.
NEELAN

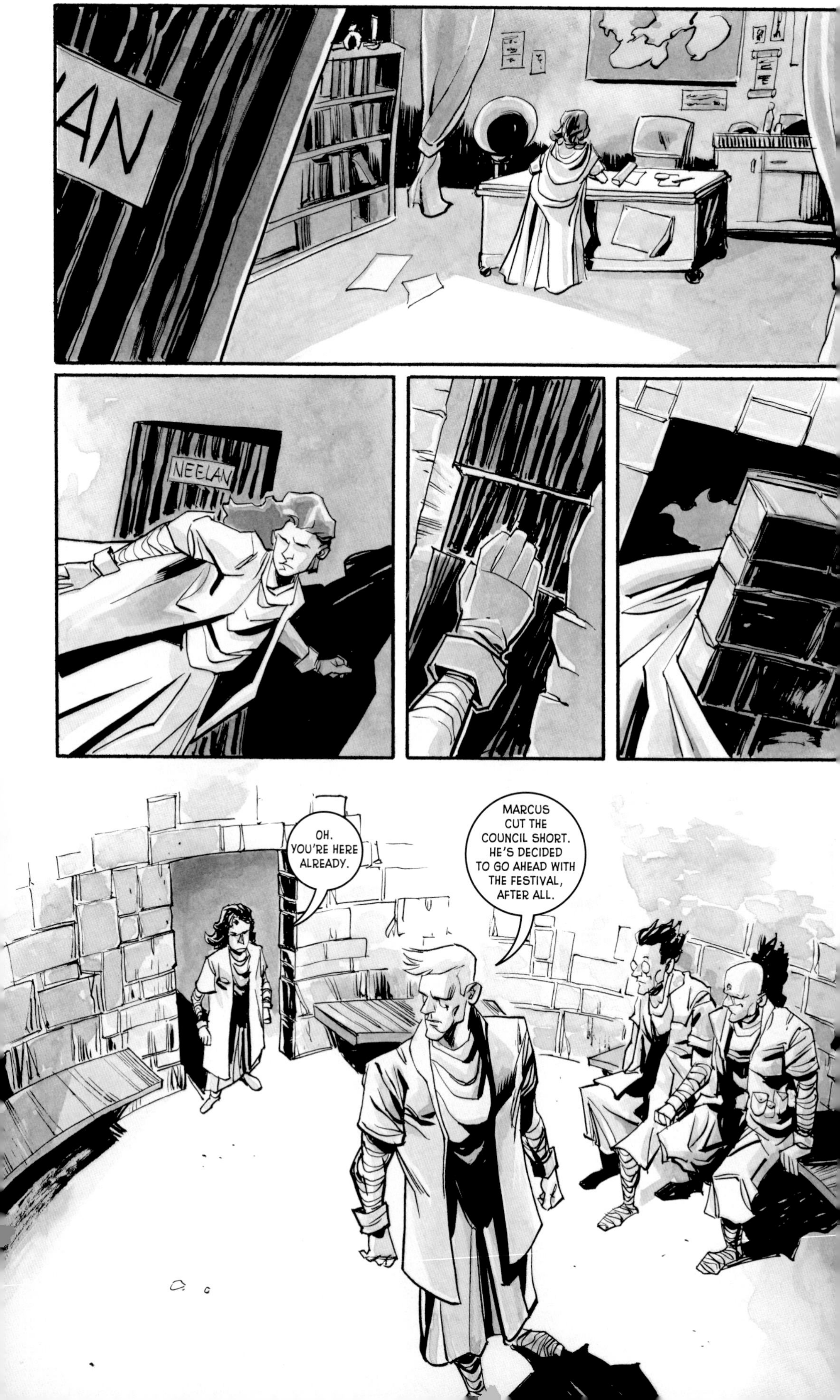
IAN
NEELAN
OH. YOU'RE HERE ALREADY.
MARCUS CUT THE COUNCIL SHORT. HE'S DECIDED TO GO AHEAD WITH THE FESTIVAL, AFTER ALL.

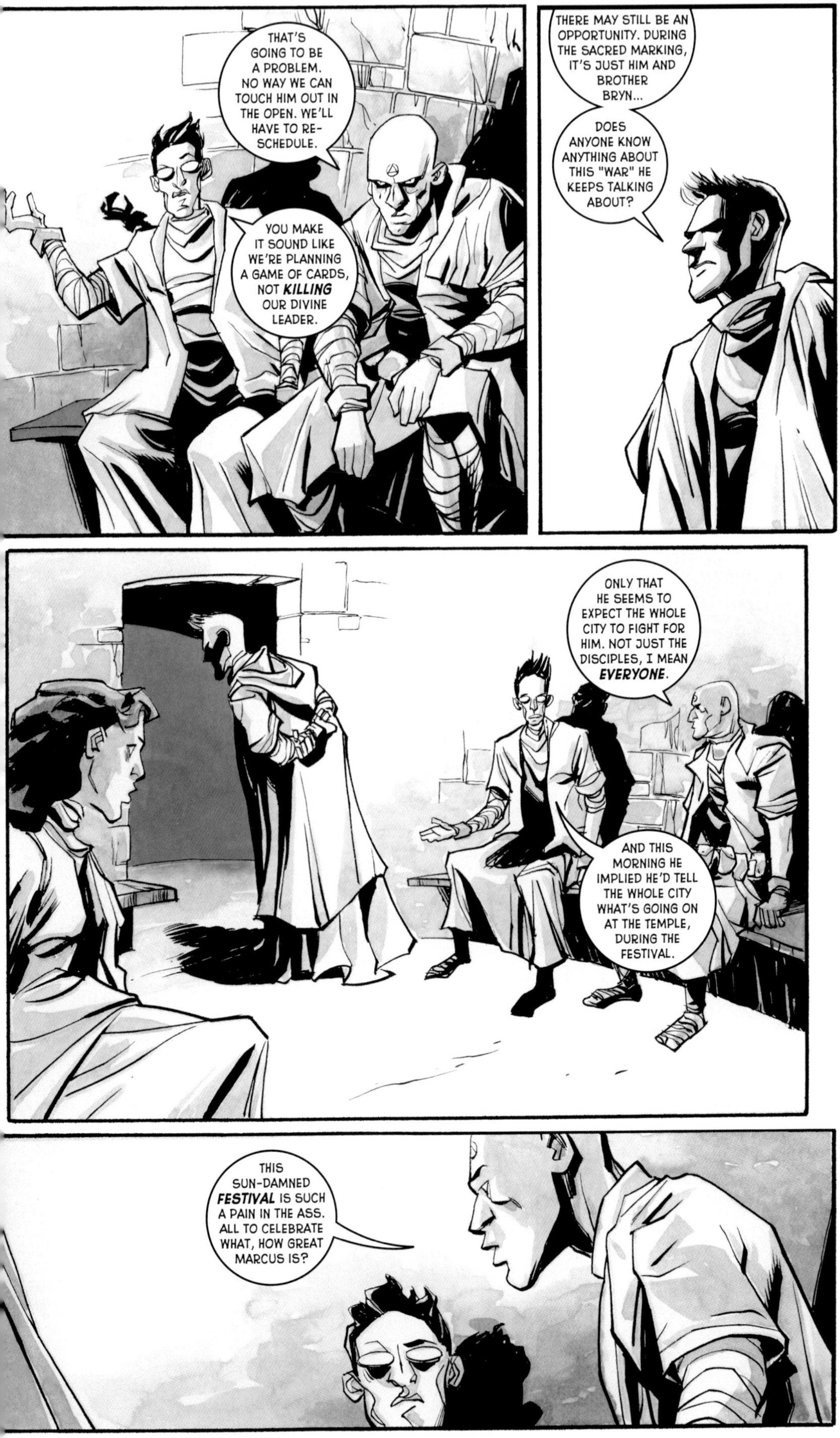
THAT'S GOING TO BE A PROBLEM. NO WAY WE CAN TOUCH HIM OUT IN THE OPEN. WE'LL HAVE TO RE-SCHEDULE.
YOU MAKE IT SOUND LIKE WE'RE PLANNING A GAME OF CARDS, NOT **KILLING** OUR DIVINE LEADER.
THERE MAY STILL BE AN OPPORTUNITY. DURING THE SACRED MARKING, IT'S JUST HIM AND BROTHER BRYN...
DOES ANYONE KNOW ANYTHING ABOUT THIS "WAR" HE KEEPS TALKING ABOUT?
ONLY THAT HE SEEMS TO EXPECT THE WHOLE CITY TO FIGHT FOR HIM. NOT JUST THE DISCIPLES, I MEAN **EVERYONE**.
AND THIS MORNING HE IMPLIED HE'D TELL THE WHOLE CITY WHAT'S GOING ON AT THE TEMPLE, DURING THE FESTIVAL.
THIS SUN-DAMNED **FESTIVAL** IS SUCH A PAIN IN THE ASS. ALL TO CELEBRATE WHAT, HOW GREAT MARCUS IS?

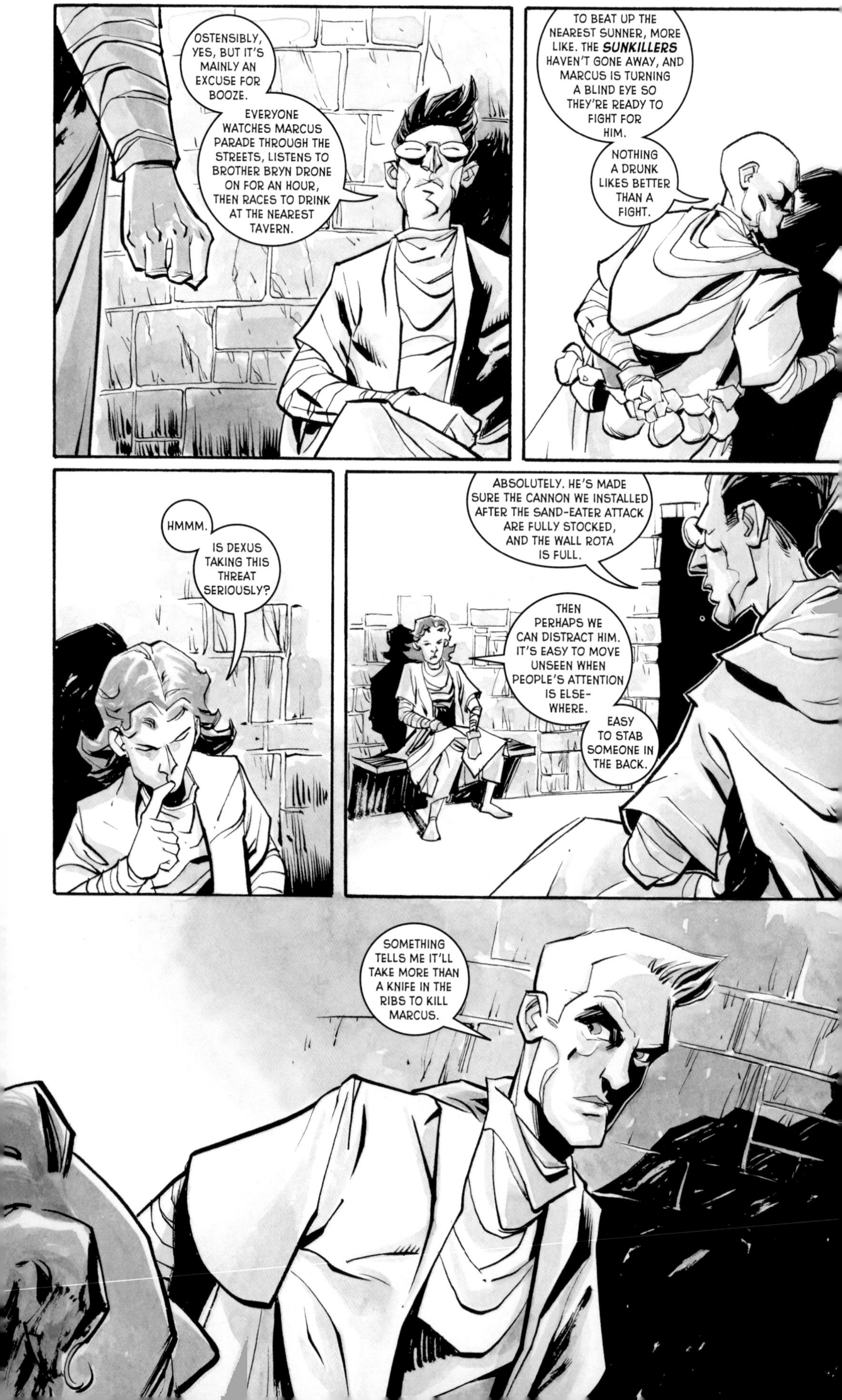
OSTENSIBLY, YES, BUT IT'S MAINLY AN EXCUSE FOR BOOZE.
EVERYONE WATCHES MARCUS PARADE THROUGH THE STREETS, LISTENS TO BROTHER BRYN DRONE ON FOR AN HOUR, THEN RACES TO DRINK AT THE NEAREST TAVERN.
TO BEAT UP THE NEAREST SUNNER, MORE LIKE. THE SUNKILLERS HAVEN'T GONE AWAY, AND MARCUS IS TURNING A BLIND EYE SO THEY'RE READY TO FIGHT FOR HIM.
NOTHING A DRUNK LIKES BETTER THAN A FIGHT.
HMMM.
IS DEXUS TAKING THIS THREAT SERIOUSLY?
ABSOLUTELY. HE'S MADE SURE THE CANNON WE INSTALLED AFTER THE SAND-EATER ATTACK ARE FULLY STOCKED, AND THE WALL ROTA IS FULL.
THEN PERHAPS WE CAN DISTRACT HIM. IT'S EASY TO MOVE UNSEEN WHEN PEOPLE'S ATTENTION IS ELSE-WHERE.
EASY TO STAB SOMEONE IN THE BACK.
SOMETHING TELLS ME IT'LL TAKE MORE THAN A KNIFE IN THE RIBS TO KILL MARCUS.

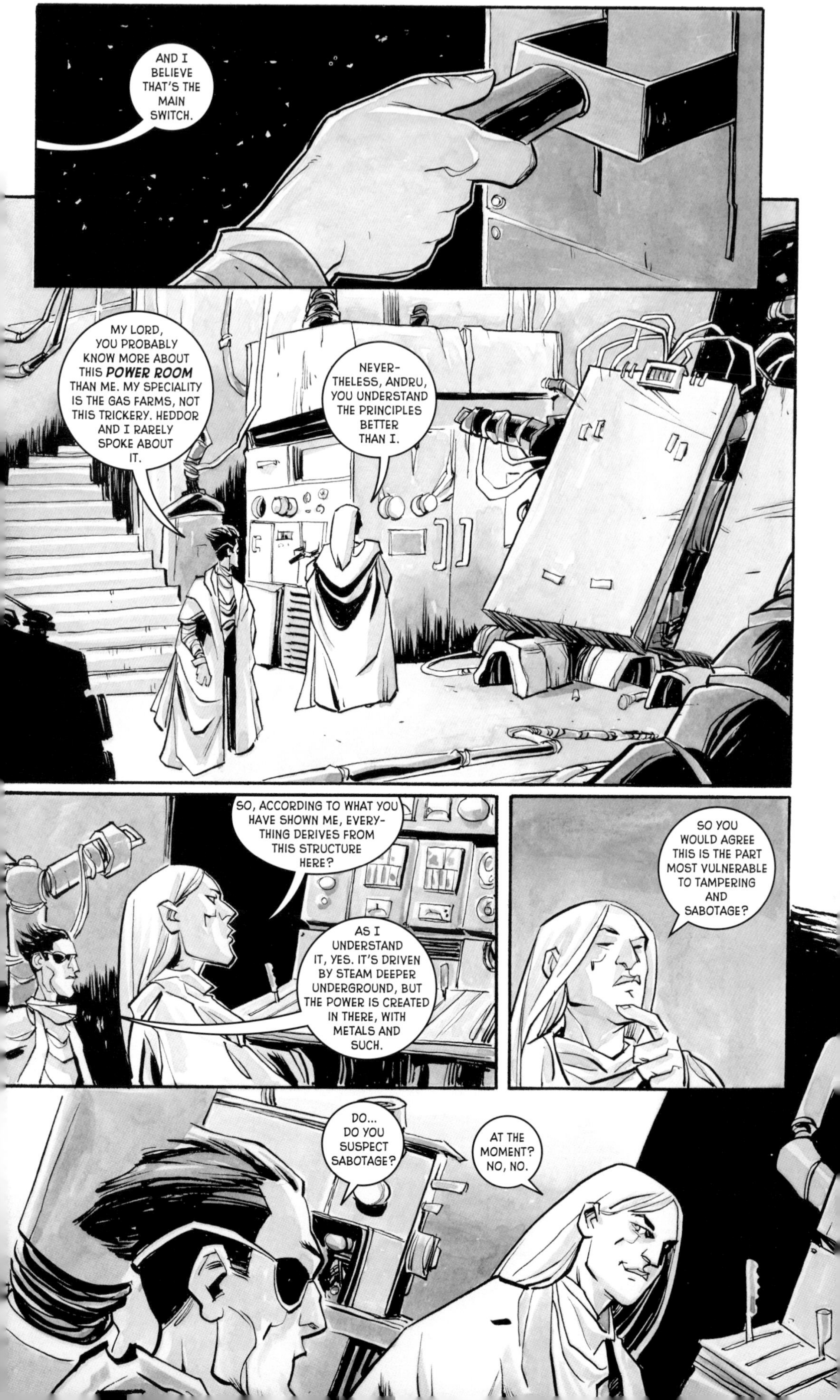
AND I BELIEVE THAT'S THE MAIN SWITCH.
MY LORD, YOU PROBABLY KNOW MORE ABOUT THIS **POWER ROOM** THAN ME. MY SPECIALITY IS THE GAS FARMS, NOT THIS TRICKERY. HEDDOR AND I RARELY SPOKE ABOUT IT.
NEVER-THELESS, ANDRU, YOU UNDERSTAND THE PRINCIPLES BETTER THAN I.
SO, ACCORDING TO WHAT YOU HAVE SHOWN ME, EVERY-THING DERIVES FROM THIS STRUCTURE HERE?
AS I UNDERSTAND IT, YES. IT'S DRIVEN BY STEAM DEEPER UNDERGROUND, BUT THE POWER IS CREATED IN THERE, WITH METALS AND SUCH.
SO YOU WOULD AGREE THIS IS THE PART MOST VULNERABLE TO TAMPERING AND SABOTAGE?
DO... DO YOU SUSPECT SABOTAGE?
AT THE MOMENT? NO, NO.

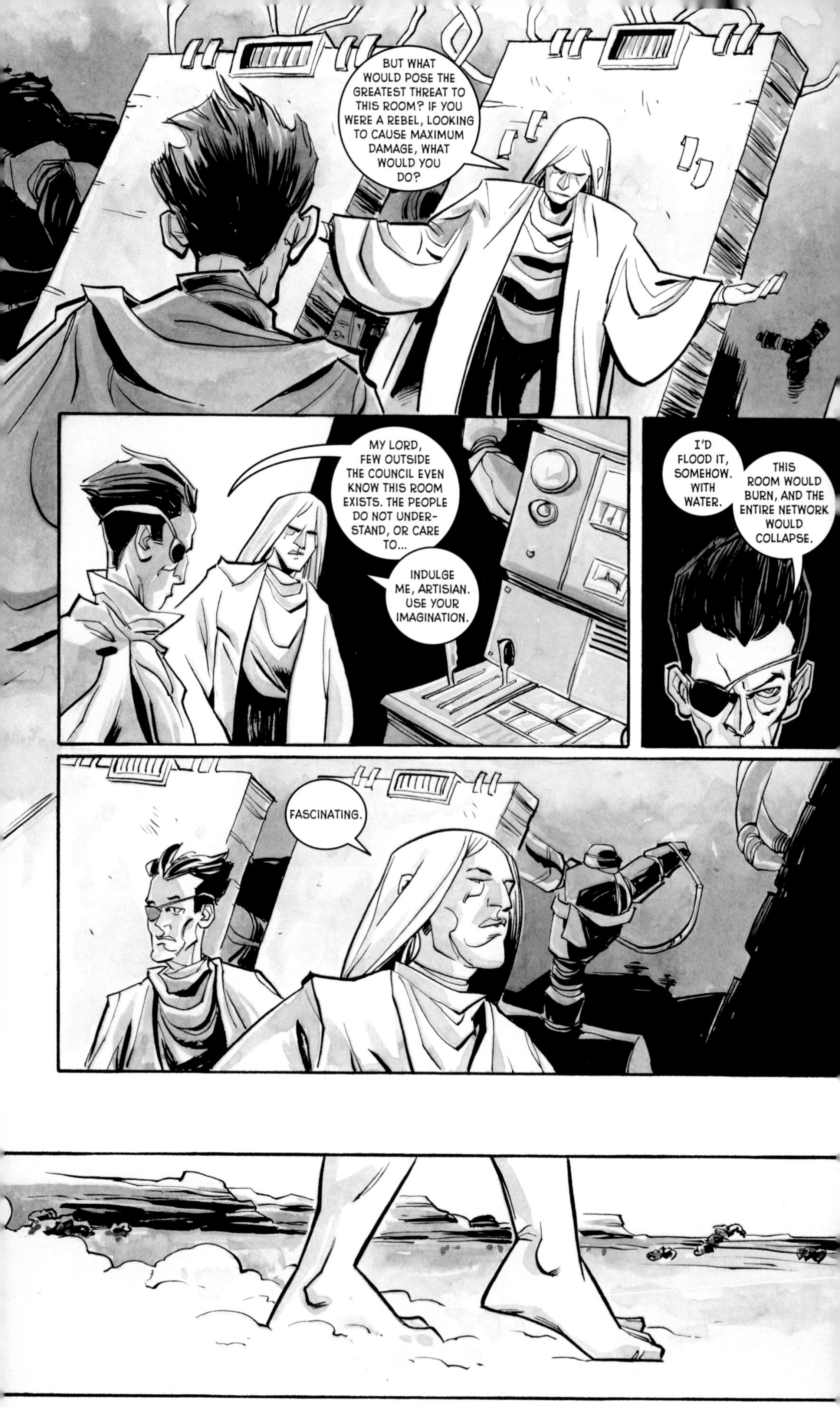
BUT WHAT WOULD POSE THE GREATEST THREAT TO THIS ROOM? IF YOU WERE A REBEL, LOOKING TO CAUSE MAXIMUM DAMAGE, WHAT WOULD YOU DO?
MY LORD, FEW OUTSIDE THE COUNCIL EVEN KNOW THIS ROOM EXISTS. THE PEOPLE DO NOT UNDER-STAND, OR CARE TO...
INDULGE ME, ARTISIAN. USE YOUR IMAGINATION.
I'D FLOOD IT, SOMEHOW. WITH WATER.
THIS ROOM WOULD BURN, AND THE ENTIRE NETWORK WOULD COLLAPSE.
FASCINATING.

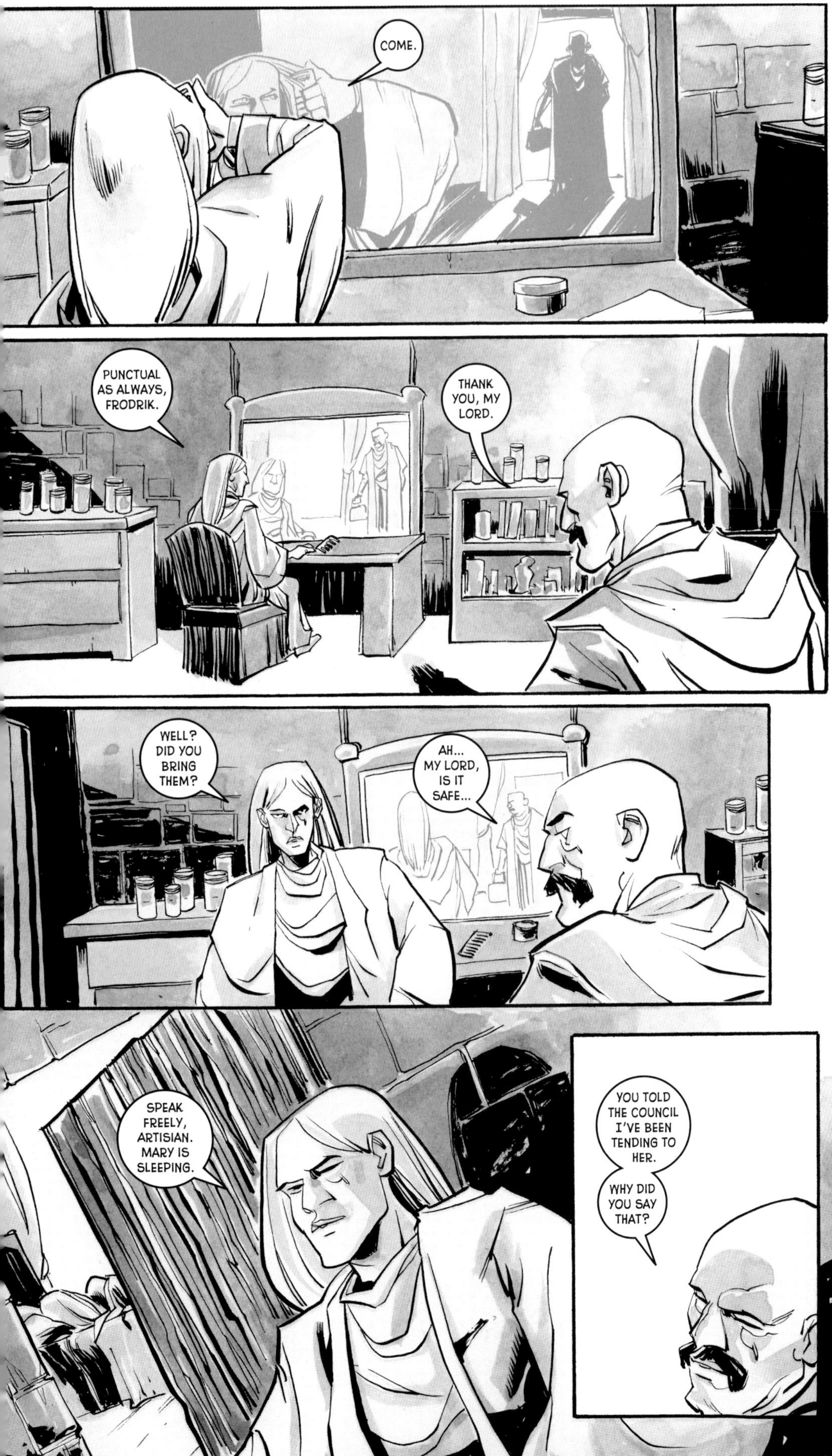
COME.
PUNCTUAL AS ALWAYS, FRODRIK.
THANK YOU, MY LORD.
WELL? DID YOU BRING THEM?
AH... MY LORD, IS IT SAFE...
SPEAK FREELY, ARTISIAN. MARY IS SLEEPING.
YOU TOLD THE COUNCIL I'VE BEEN TENDING TO HER.
WHY DID YOU SAY THAT?

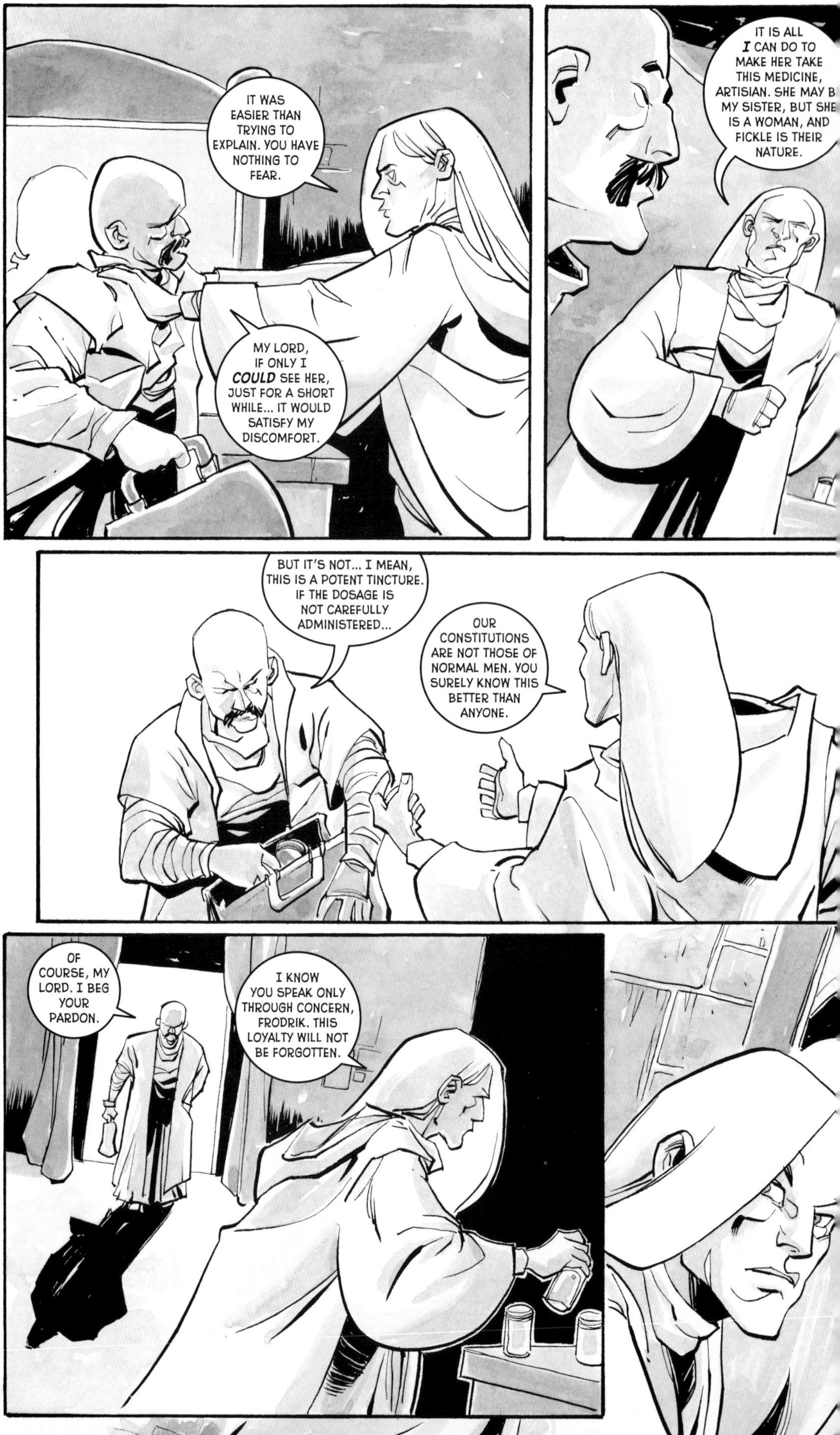
IT WAS EASIER THAN TRYING TO EXPLAIN. YOU HAVE NOTHING TO FEAR.
MY LORD, IF ONLY I **COULD** SEE HER, JUST FOR A SHORT WHILE... IT WOULD SATISFY MY DISCOMFORT.
IT IS ALL **I** CAN DO TO MAKE HER TAKE THIS MEDICINE, ARTISIAN. SHE MAY B MY SISTER, BUT SHE IS A WOMAN, AND FICKLE IS THEIR NATURE.
BUT IT'S NOT... I MEAN, THIS IS A POTENT TINCTURE. IF THE DOSAGE IS NOT CAREFULLY ADMINISTERED...
OUR CONSTITUTIONS ARE NOT THOSE OF NORMAL MEN. YOU SURELY KNOW THIS BETTER THAN ANYONE.
OF COURSE, MY LORD. I BEG YOUR PARDON.
I KNOW YOU SPEAK ONLY THROUGH CONCERN, FRODRIK. THIS LOYALTY WILL NOT BE FORGOTTEN.

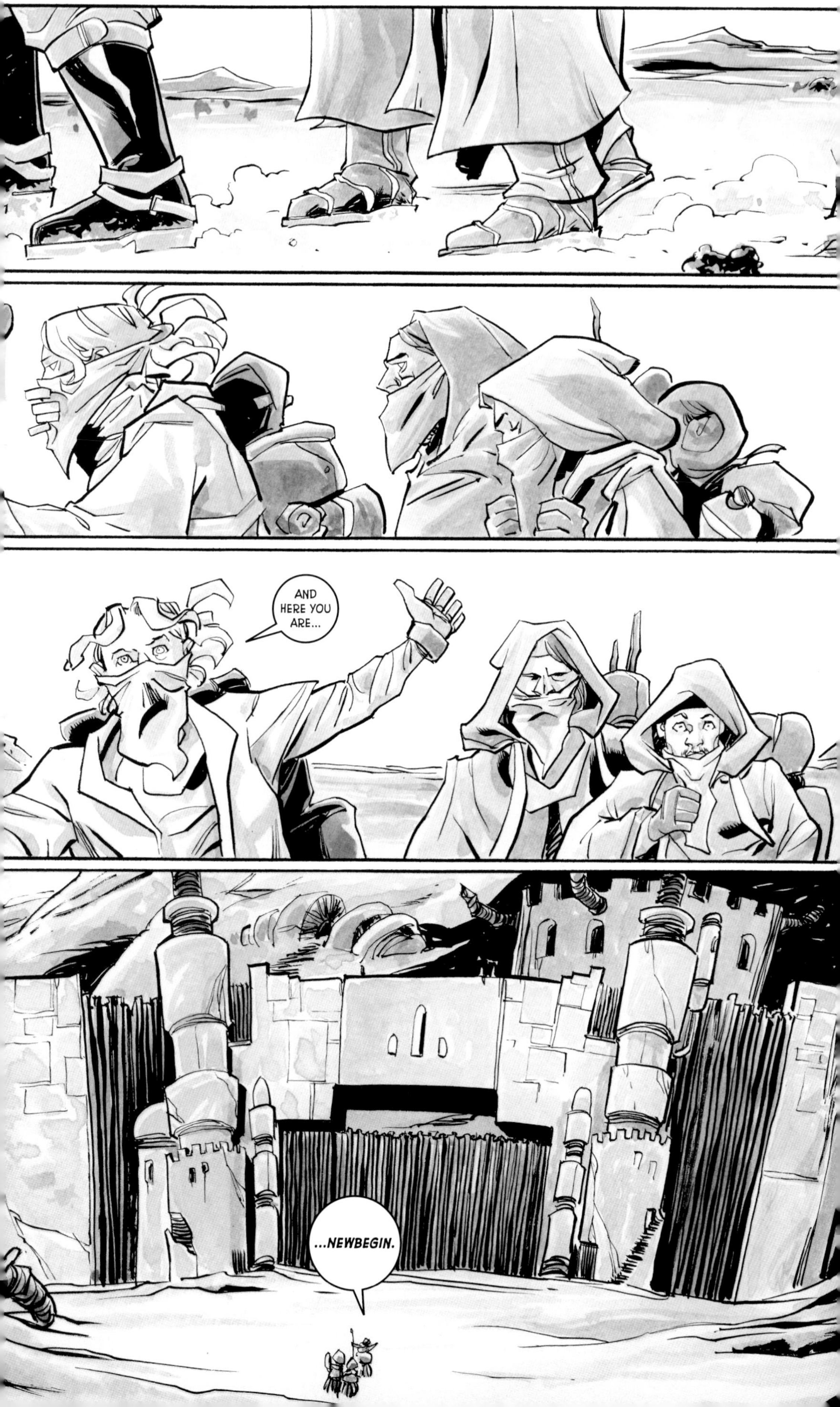
AND HERE YOU ARE...
...NEWBEGIN.

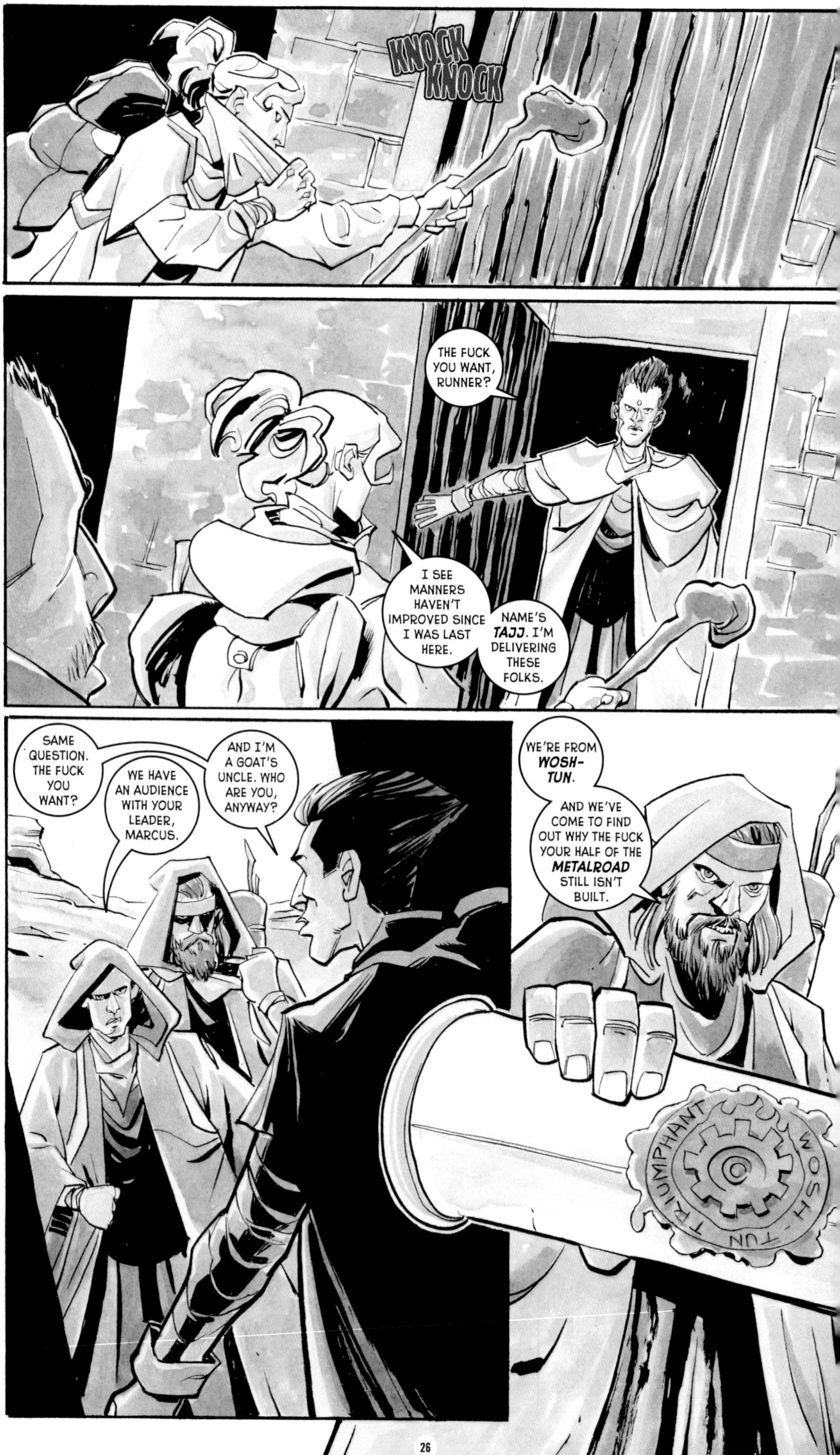
KNOCK KNOCK
THE FUCK YOU WANT, RUNNER?
I SEE MANNERS HAVEN'T IMPROVED SINCE I WAS LAST HERE.
NAME'S TAJJ. I'M DELIVERING THESE FOLKS.
SAME QUESTION. THE FUCK YOU WANT?
WE HAVE AN AUDIENCE WITH YOUR LEADER, MARCUS.
AND I'M A GOAT'S UNCLE. WHO ARE YOU, ANYWAY?
WE'RE FROM WOSH-TUN.
AND WE'VE COME TO FIND OUT WHY THE FUCK YOUR HALF OF THE METALROAD STILL ISN'T BUILT.
TRIUMPHANT WOSH-TUN

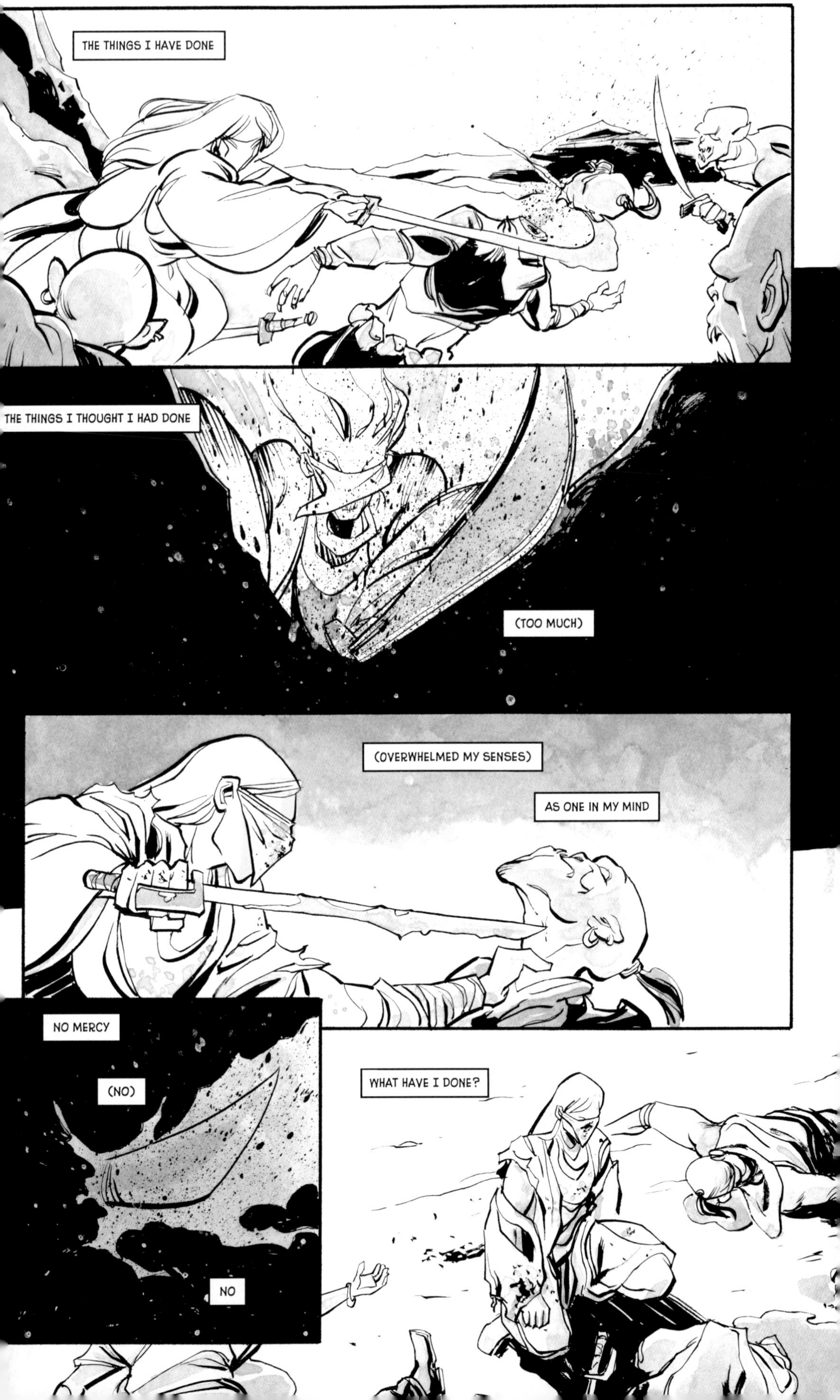
THE THINGS I HAVE DONE
THE THINGS I THOUGHT I HAD DONE
(TOO MUCH)
(OVERWHELMED MY SENSES)
AS ONE IN MY MIND
NO MERCY
(NO)
NO
WHAT HAVE I DONE?

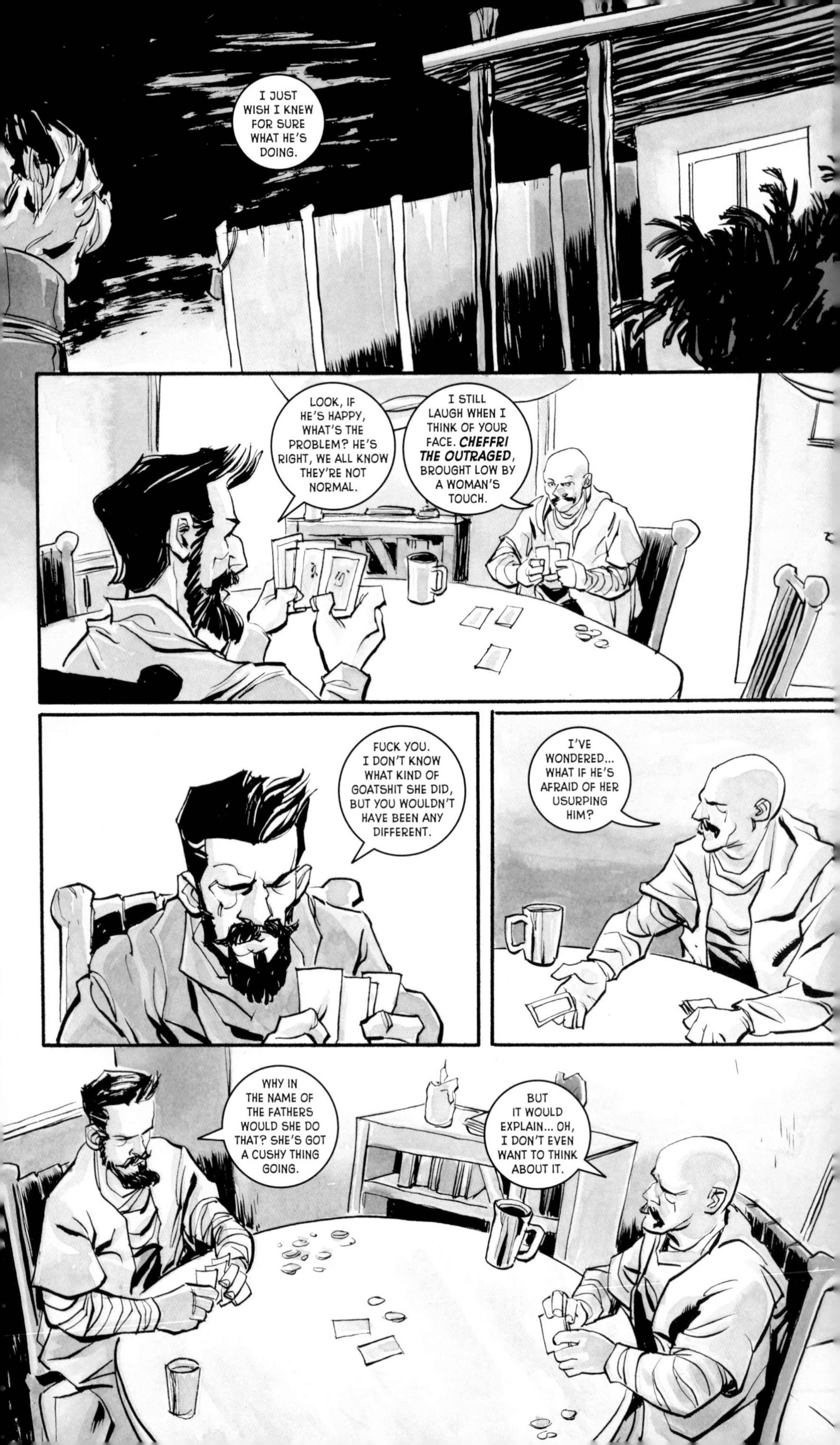
I JUST WISH I KNEW FOR SURE WHAT HE'S DOING.
LOOK, IF HE'S HAPPY, WHAT'S THE PROBLEM? HE'S RIGHT, WE ALL KNOW THEY'RE NOT NORMAL.
I STILL LAUGH WHEN I THINK OF YOUR FACE. ***CHEFFRI THE OUTRAGED***, BROUGHT LOW BY A WOMAN'S TOUCH.
FUCK YOU. I DON'T KNOW WHAT KIND OF GOATSHIT SHE DID, BUT YOU WOULDN'T HAVE BEEN ANY DIFFERENT.
I'VE WONDERED... WHAT IF HE'S AFRAID OF HER USURPING HIM?
WHY IN THE NAME OF THE FATHERS WOULD SHE DO THAT? SHE'S GOT A CUSHY THING GOING.
BUT IT WOULD EXPLAIN... OH, I DON'T EVEN WANT TO THINK ABOUT IT.

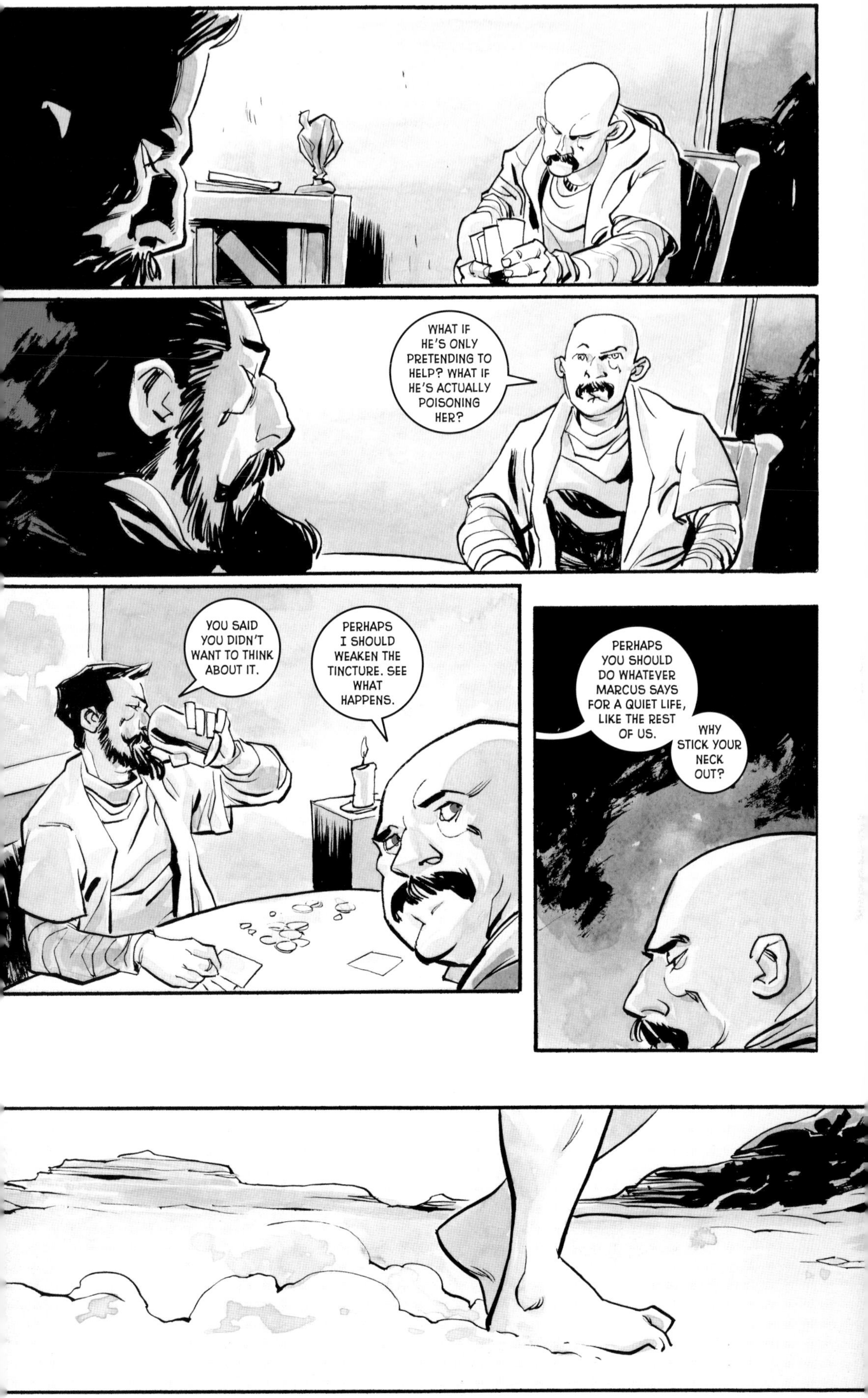
WHAT IF HE'S ONLY PRETENDING TO HELP? WHAT IF HE'S ACTUALLY POISONING HER?
YOU SAID YOU DIDN'T WANT TO THINK ABOUT IT.
PERHAPS I SHOULD WEAKEN THE TINCTURE. SEE WHAT HAPPENS.
PERHAPS YOU SHOULD DO WHATEVER MARCUS SAYS FOR A QUIET LIFE, LIKE THE REST OF US.
WHY STICK YOUR NECK OUT?

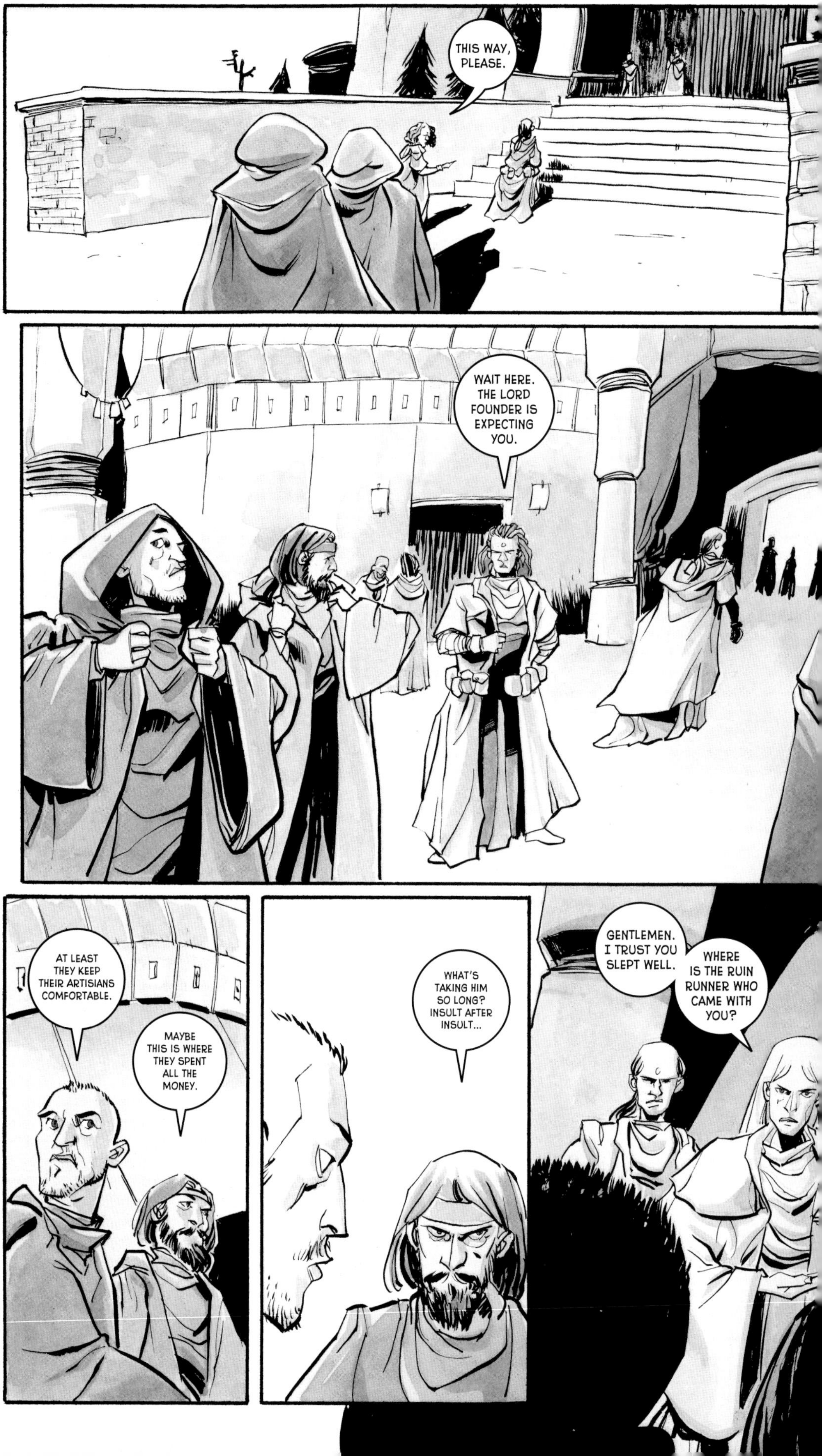
THIS WAY, PLEASE.
WAIT HERE. THE LORD FOUNDER IS EXPECTING YOU.
AT LEAST THEY KEEP THEIR ARTISIANS COMFORTABLE.
MAYBE THIS IS WHERE THEY SPENT ALL THE MONEY.
WHAT'S TAKING HIM SO LONG? INSULT AFTER INSULT...
GENTLEMEN. I TRUST YOU SLEPT WELL.
WHERE IS THE RUIN RUNNER WHO CAME WITH YOU?

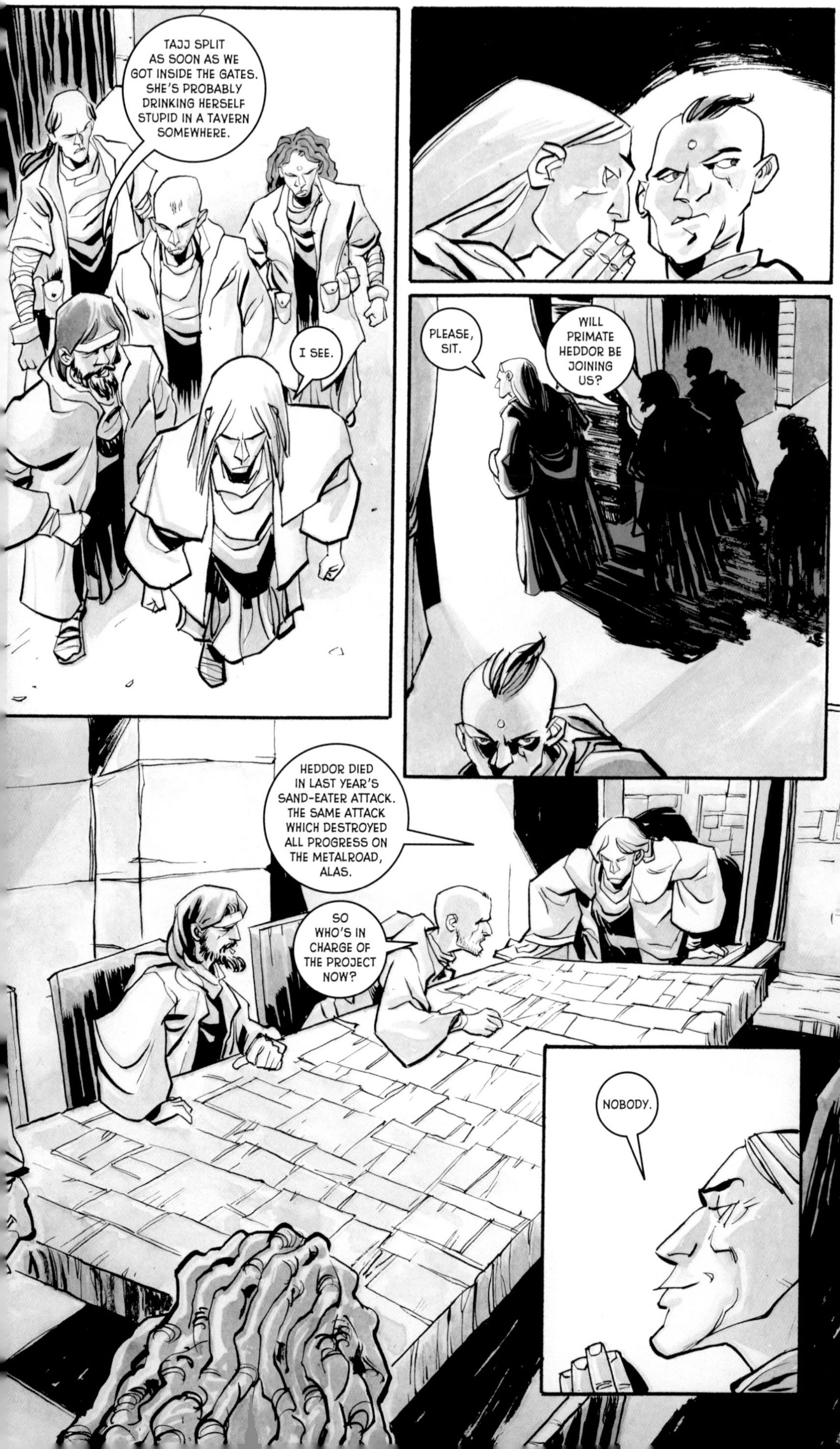
TAJJ SPLIT AS SOON AS WE GOT INSIDE THE GATES. SHE'S PROBABLY DRINKING HERSELF STUPID IN A TAVERN SOMEWHERE.
I SEE.
PLEASE, SIT.
WILL PRIMATE HEDDOR BE JOINING US?
HEDDOR DIED IN LAST YEAR'S SAND-EATER ATTACK. THE SAME ATTACK WHICH DESTROYED ALL PROGRESS ON THE METALROAD, ALAS.
SO WHO'S IN CHARGE OF THE PROJECT NOW?
NOBODY.

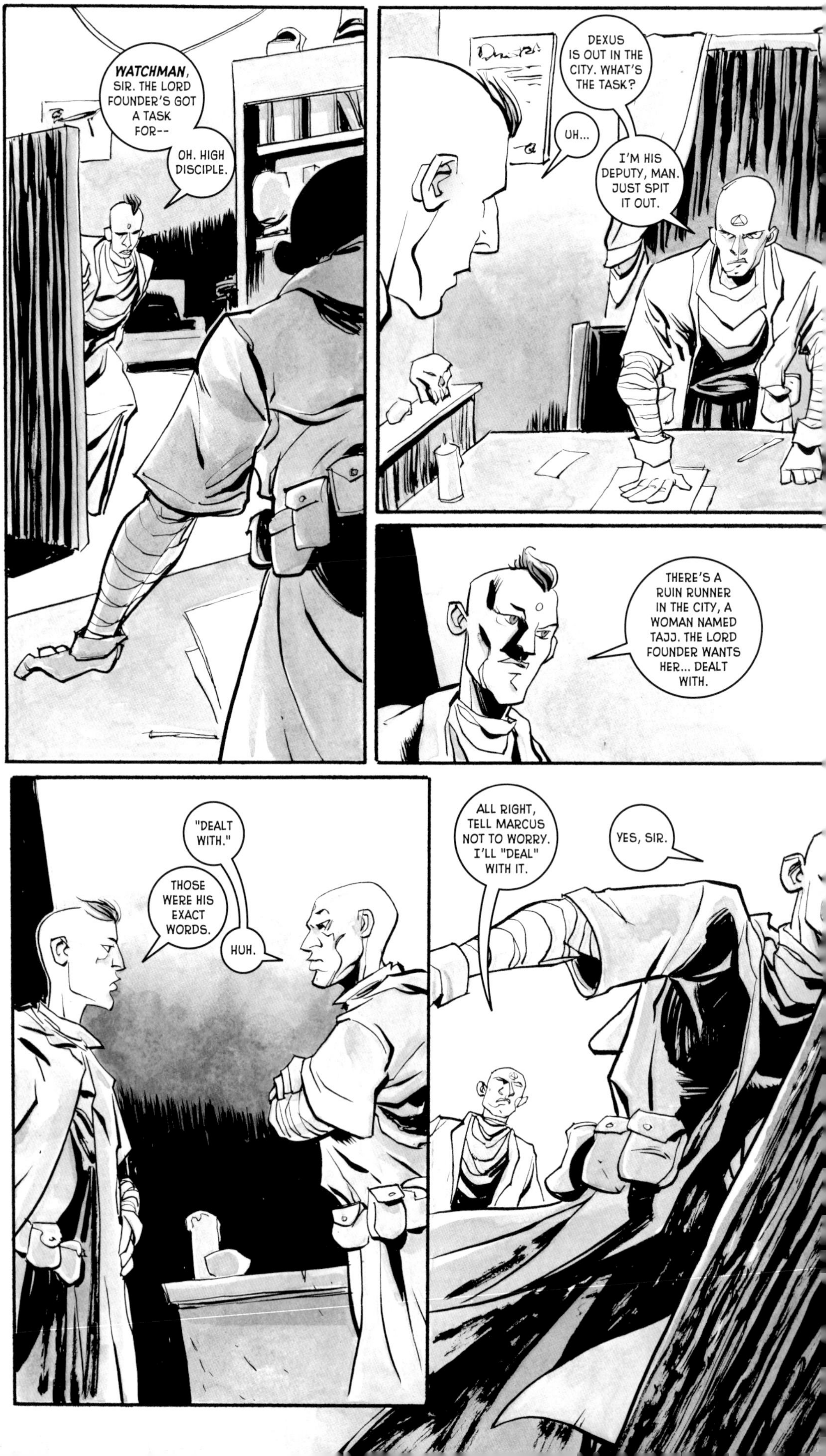
WATCHMAN, SIR. THE LORD FOUNDER'S GOT A TASK FOR--
OH. HIGH DISCIPLE.
DEXUS IS OUT IN THE CITY. WHAT'S THE TASK?
UH...
I'M HIS DEPUTY, MAN. JUST SPIT IT OUT.
THERE'S A RUIN RUNNER IN THE CITY, A WOMAN NAMED TAJJ. THE LORD FOUNDER WANTS HER... DEALT WITH.
"DEALT WITH."
THOSE WERE HIS EXACT WORDS.
HUH.
ALL RIGHT, TELL MARCUS NOT TO WORRY. I'LL "DEAL" WITH IT.
YES, SIR.

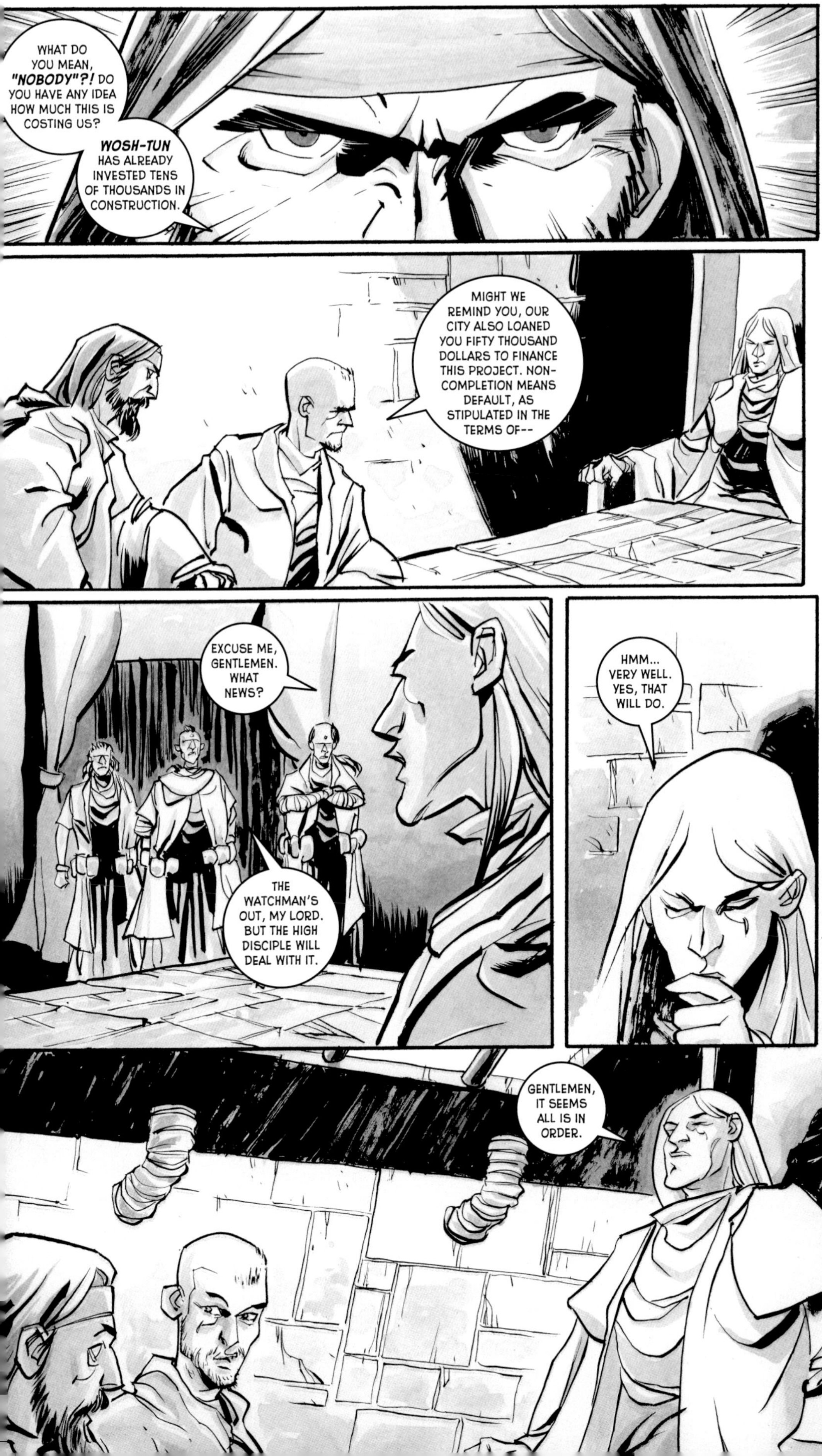
WHAT DO YOU MEAN, "NOBODY"?! DO YOU HAVE ANY IDEA HOW MUCH THIS IS COSTING US?
WOSH-TUN HAS ALREADY INVESTED TENS OF THOUSANDS IN CONSTRUCTION.
MIGHT WE REMIND YOU, OUR CITY ALSO LOANED YOU FIFTY THOUSAND DOLLARS TO FINANCE THIS PROJECT. NON-COMPLETION MEANS DEFAULT, AS STIPULATED IN THE TERMS OF--
EXCUSE ME, GENTLEMEN. WHAT NEWS?
THE WATCHMAN'S OUT, MY LORD. BUT THE HIGH DISCIPLE WILL DEAL WITH IT.
HMM... VERY WELL. YES, THAT WILL DO.
GENTLEMEN, IT SEEMS ALL IS IN ORDER.

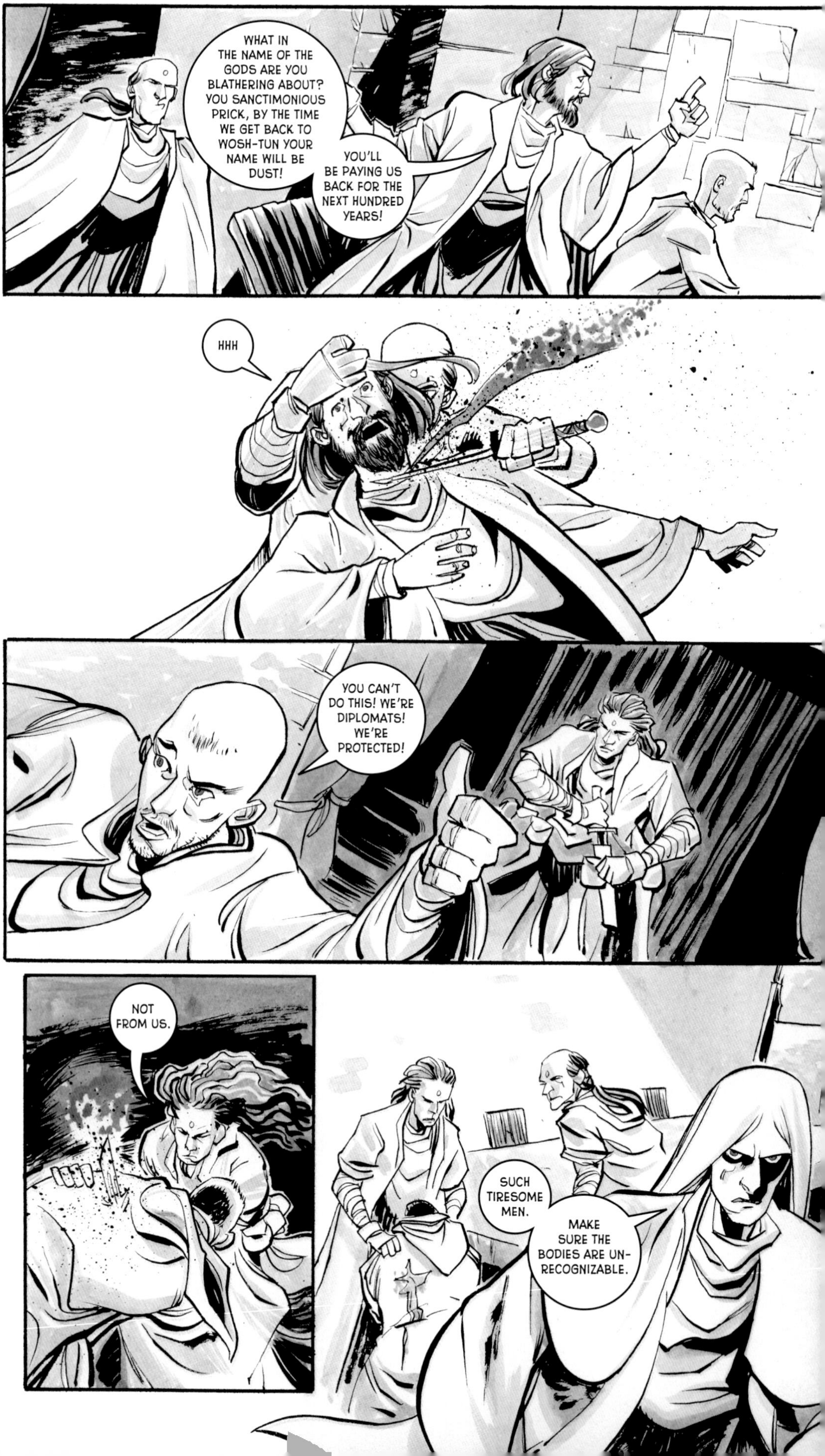
WHAT IN THE NAME OF THE GODS ARE YOU BLATHERING ABOUT? YOU SANCTIMONIOUS PRICK, BY THE TIME WE GET BACK TO WOSH-TUN YOUR NAME WILL BE DUST!
YOU'LL BE PAYING US BACK FOR THE NEXT HUNDRED YEARS!
HHH
YOU CAN'T DO THIS! WE'RE DIPLOMATS! WE'RE PROTECTED!
NOT FROM US.
SUCH TIRESOME MEN.
MAKE SURE THE BODIES ARE UN-RECOGNIZABLE.

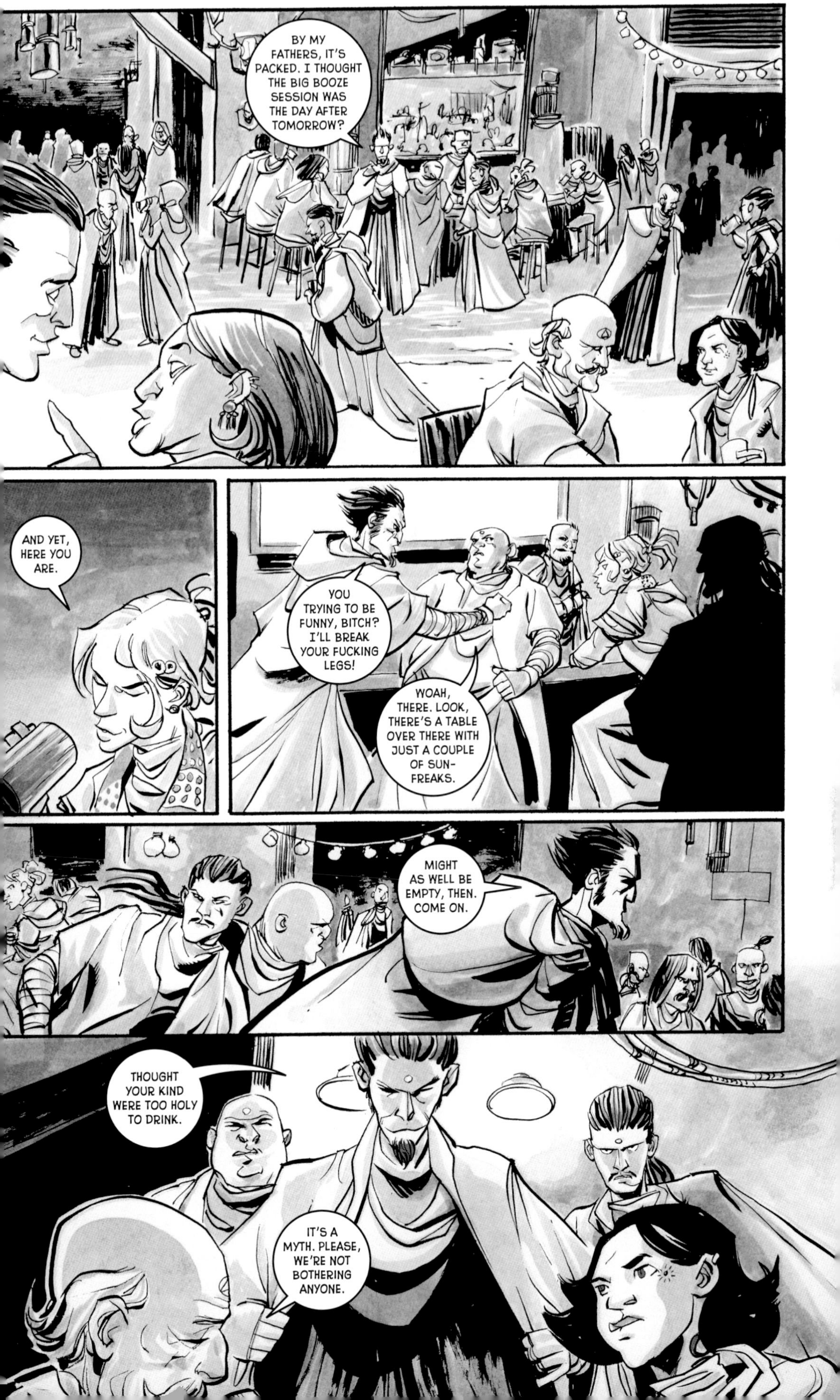
BY MY FATHERS, IT'S PACKED. I THOUGHT THE BIG BOOZE SESSION WAS THE DAY AFTER TOMORROW?
AND YET, HERE YOU ARE.
YOU TRYING TO BE FUNNY, BITCH? I'LL BREAK YOUR FUCKING LEGS!
WOAH, THERE. LOOK, THERE'S A TABLE OVER THERE WITH JUST A COUPLE OF SUN-FREAKS.
MIGHT AS WELL BE EMPTY, THEN. COME ON.
THOUGHT YOUR KIND WERE TOO HOLY TO DRINK.
IT'S A MYTH. PLEASE, WE'RE NOT BOTHERING ANYONE.

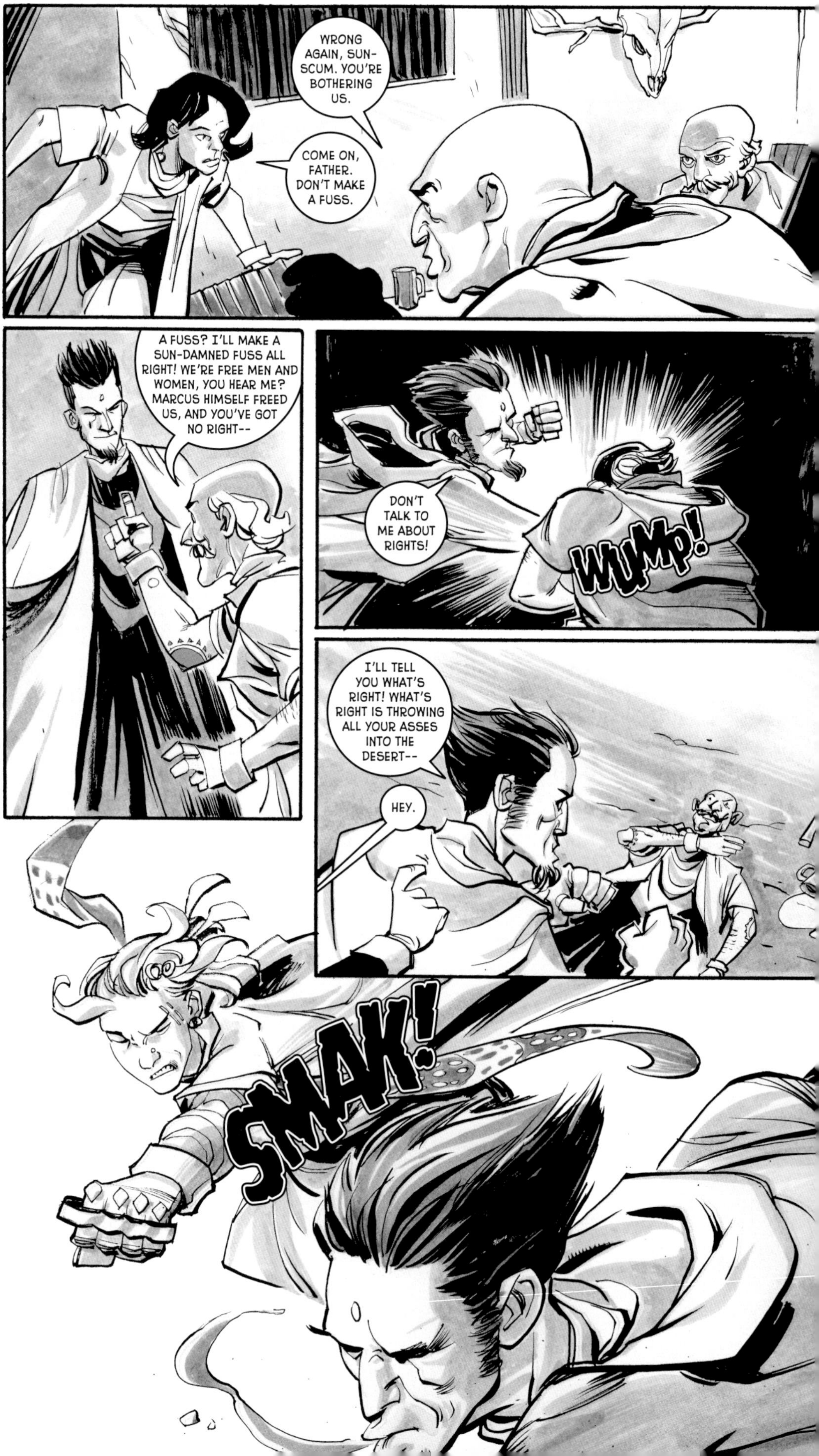
WRONG AGAIN, SUN-SCUM. YOU'RE BOTHERING US.
COME ON, FATHER. DON'T MAKE A FUSS.
A FUSS? I'LL MAKE A SUN-DAMNED FUSS ALL RIGHT! WE'RE FREE MEN AND WOMEN, YOU HEAR ME? MARCUS HIMSELF FREED US, AND YOU'VE GOT NO RIGHT--
DON'T TALK TO ME ABOUT RIGHTS!
WUMP!
I'LL TELL YOU WHAT'S RIGHT! WHAT'S RIGHT IS THROWING ALL YOUR ASSES INTO THE DESERT--
HEY.
SMAK!

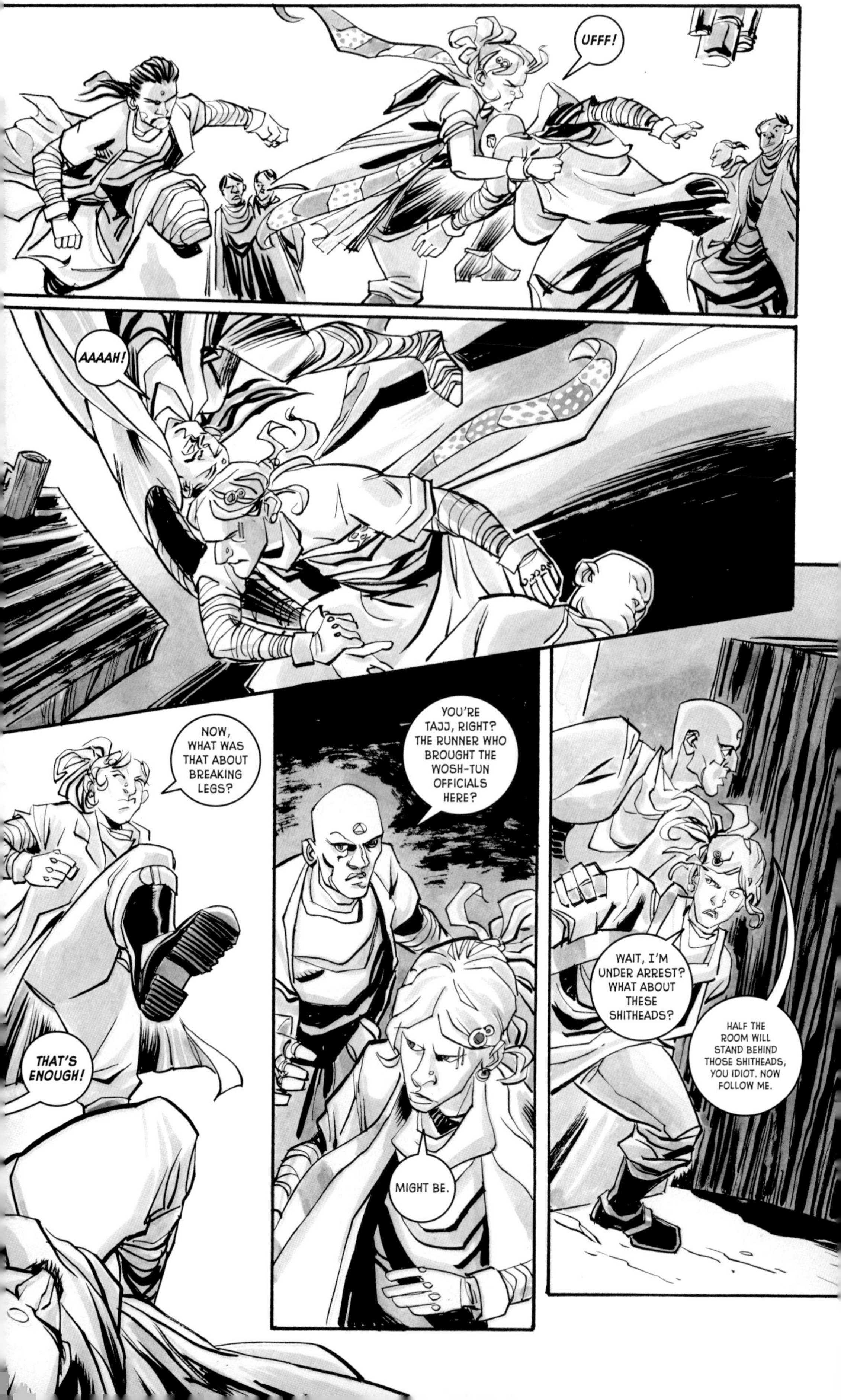

UFFF!
AAAAH!
NOW, WHAT WAS THAT ABOUT BREAKING LEGS?
THAT'S ENOUGH!
YOU'RE TAJJ, RIGHT? THE RUNNER WHO BROUGHT THE WOSH-TUN OFFICIALS HERE?
MIGHT BE.
WAIT, I'M UNDER ARREST? WHAT ABOUT THESE SHITHEADS?
HALF THE ROOM WILL STAND BEHIND THOSE SHITHEADS, YOU IDIOT. NOW FOLLOW ME.

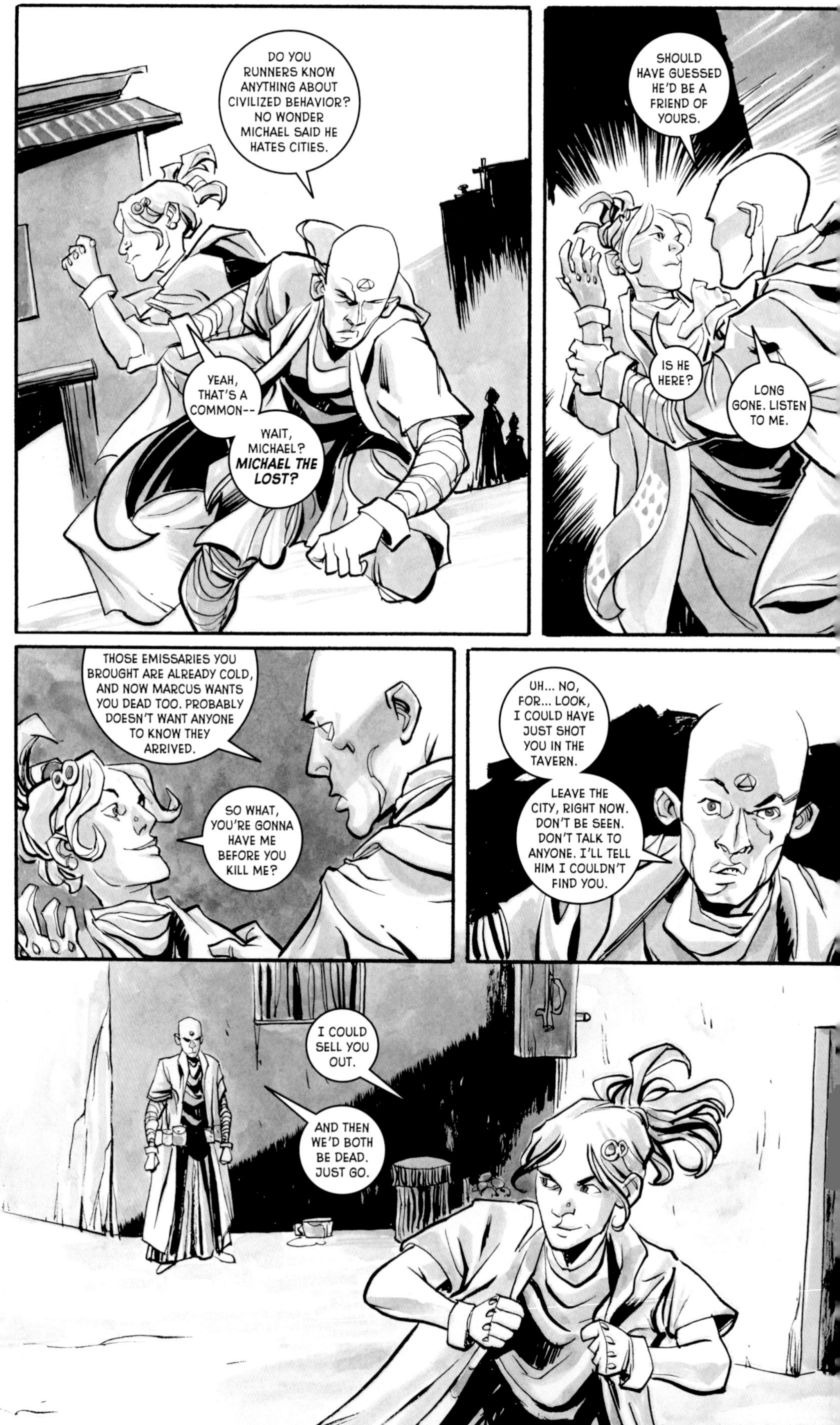
DO YOU RUNNERS KNOW ANYTHING ABOUT CIVILIZED BEHAVIOR? NO WONDER MICHAEL SAID HE HATES CITIES.
YEAH, THAT'S A COMMON--
WAIT, MICHAEL? *MICHAEL THE LOST?*
SHOULD HAVE GUESSED HE'D BE A FRIEND OF YOURS.
IS HE HERE?
LONG GONE. LISTEN TO ME.
THOSE EMISSARIES YOU BROUGHT ARE ALREADY COLD, AND NOW MARCUS WANTS YOU DEAD TOO. PROBABLY DOESN'T WANT ANYONE TO KNOW THEY ARRIVED.
SO WHAT, YOU'RE GONNA HAVE ME BEFORE YOU KILL ME?
UH... NO, FOR... LOOK, I COULD HAVE JUST SHOT YOU IN THE TAVERN.
LEAVE THE CITY, RIGHT NOW. DON'T BE SEEN. DON'T TALK TO ANYONE. I'LL TELL HIM I COULDN'T FIND YOU.
I COULD SELL YOU OUT.
AND THEN WE'D BOTH BE DEAD. JUST GO.

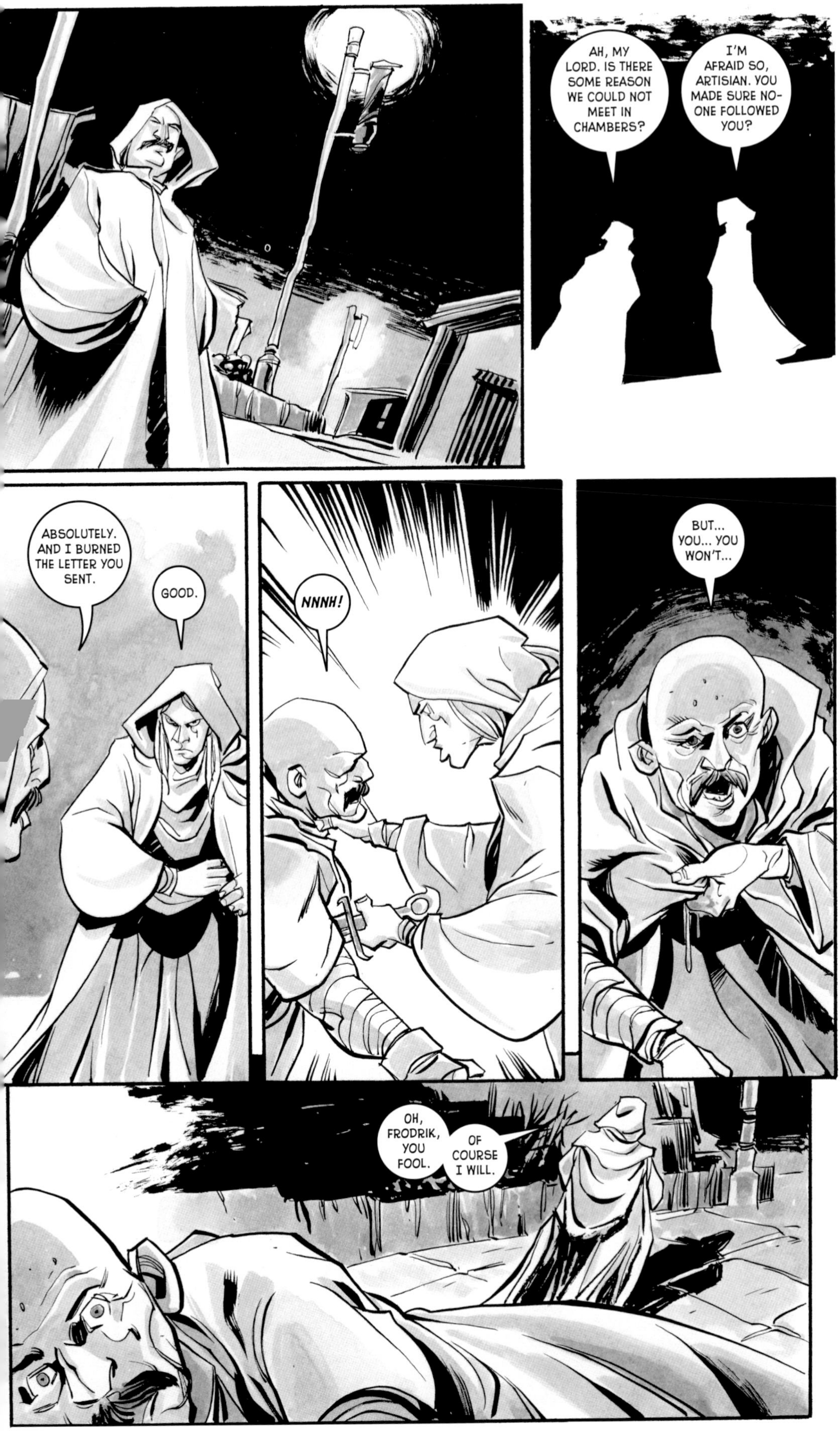
AH, MY LORD. IS THERE SOME REASON WE COULD NOT MEET IN CHAMBERS?
I'M AFRAID SO, ARTISIAN. YOU MADE SURE NO-ONE FOLLOWED YOU?
ABSOLUTELY. AND I BURNED THE LETTER YOU SENT.
GOOD.
NNNH!
BUT... YOU... YOU WON'T...
OH, FRODRIK, YOU FOOL.
OF COURSE I WILL.

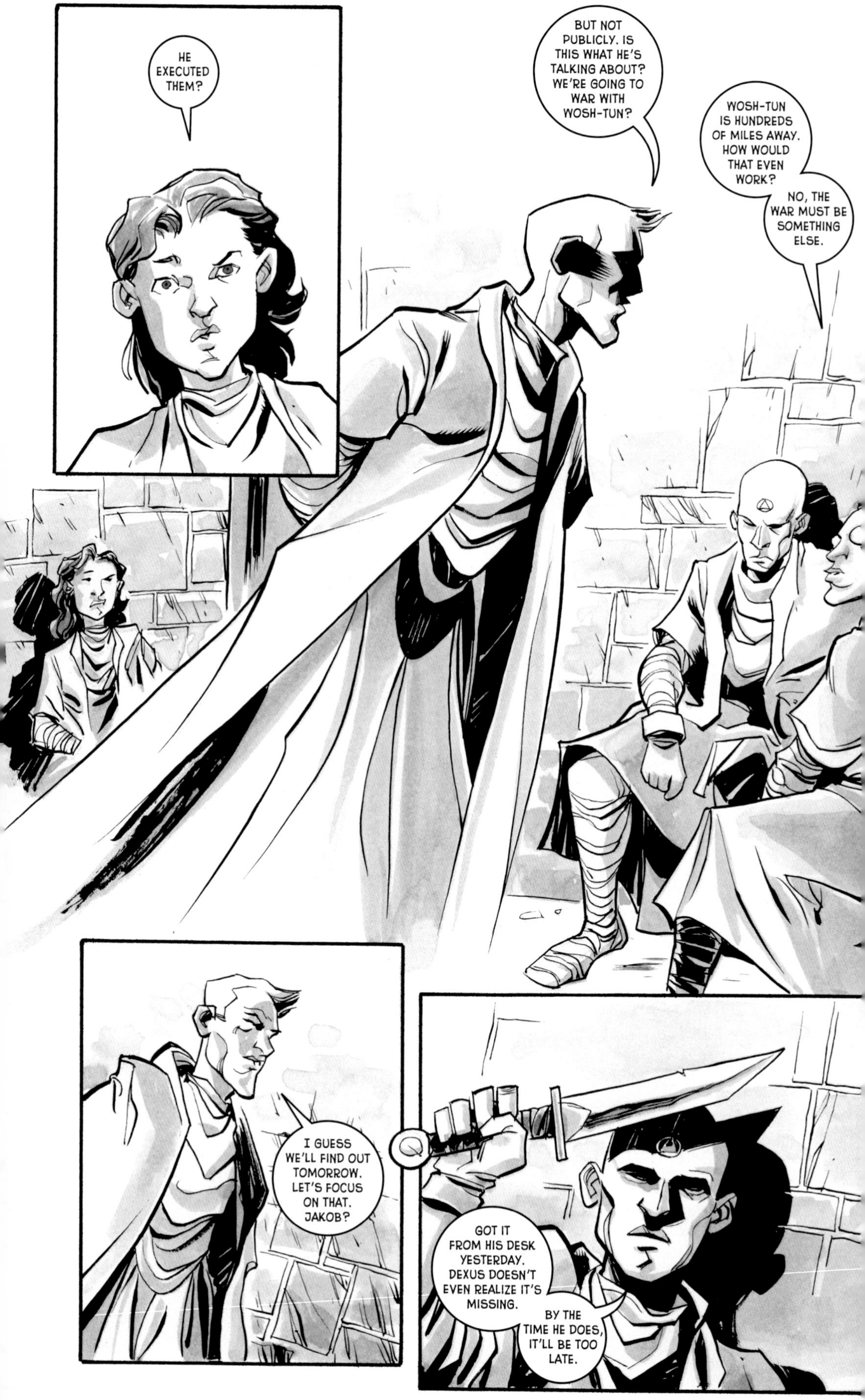
HE EXECUTED THEM?
BUT NOT PUBLICLY. IS THIS WHAT HE'S TALKING ABOUT? WE'RE GOING TO WAR WITH WOSH-TUN?
WOSH-TUN IS HUNDREDS OF MILES AWAY. HOW WOULD THAT EVEN WORK?
NO, THE WAR MUST BE SOMETHING ELSE.
I GUESS WE'LL FIND OUT TOMORROW. LET'S FOCUS ON THAT. JAKOB?
GOT IT FROM HIS DESK YESTERDAY. DEXUS DOESN'T EVEN REALIZE IT'S MISSING.
BY THE TIME HE DOES, IT'LL BE TOO LATE.

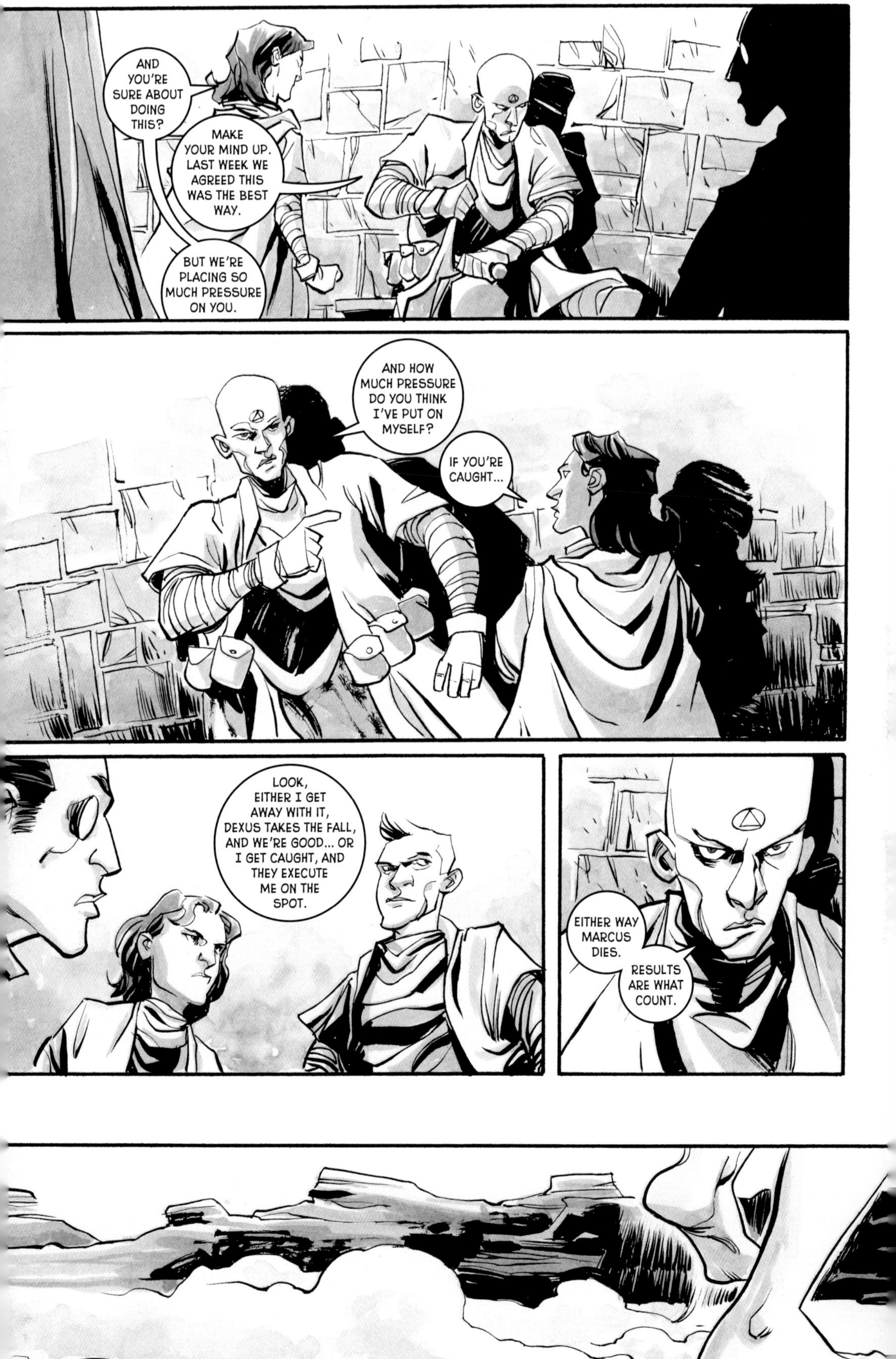
AND YOU'RE SURE ABOUT DOING THIS?
MAKE YOUR MIND UP. LAST WEEK WE AGREED THIS WAS THE BEST WAY.
BUT WE'RE PLACING SO MUCH PRESSURE ON YOU.
AND HOW MUCH PRESSURE DO YOU THINK I'VE PUT ON MYSELF?
IF YOU'RE CAUGHT...
LOOK, EITHER I GET AWAY WITH IT, DEXUS TAKES THE FALL, AND WE'RE GOOD... OR I GET CAUGHT, AND THEY EXECUTE ME ON THE SPOT.
EITHER WAY MARCUS DIES.
RESULTS ARE WHAT COUNT.

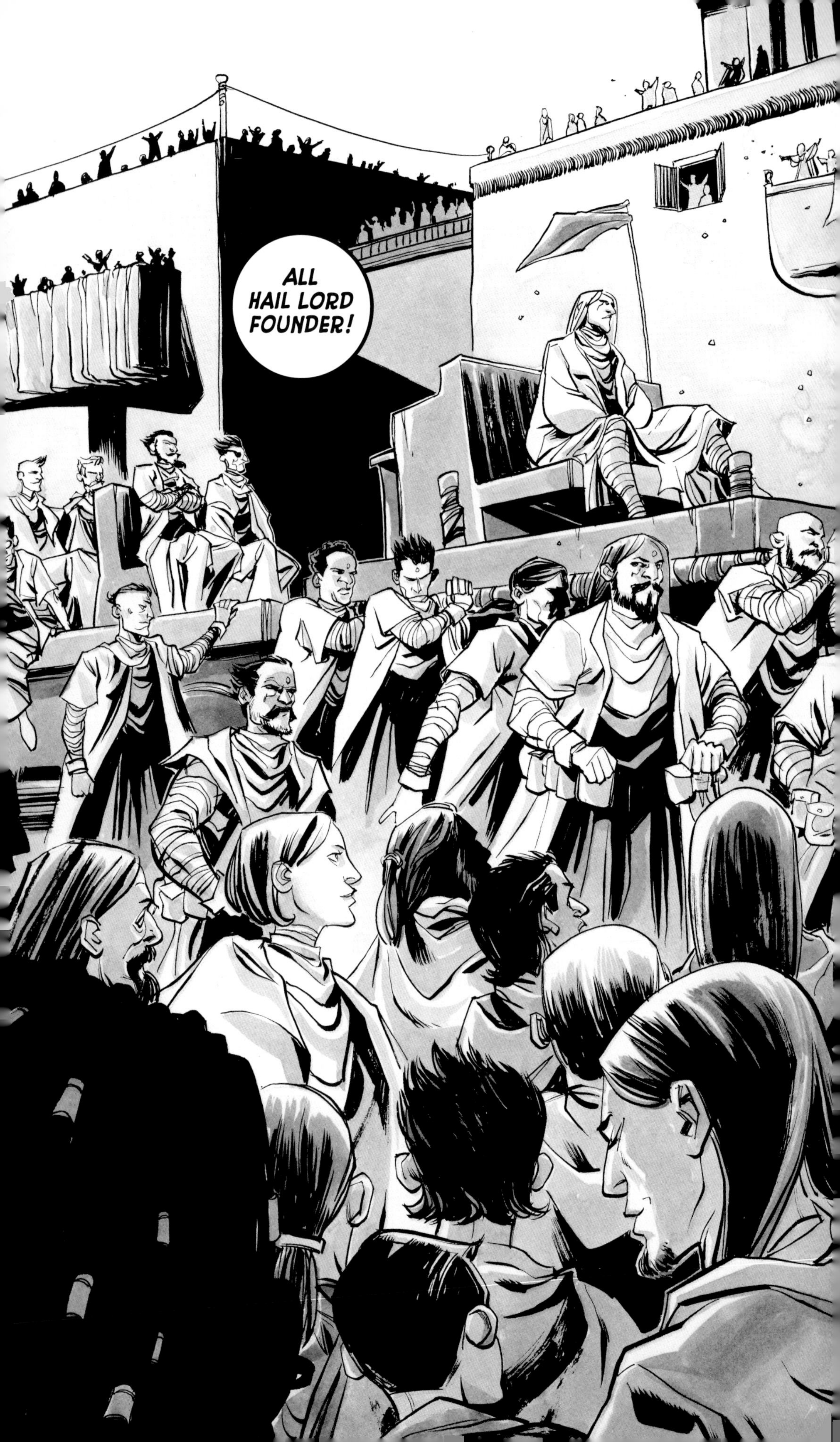
ALL HAIL LORD FOUNDER!

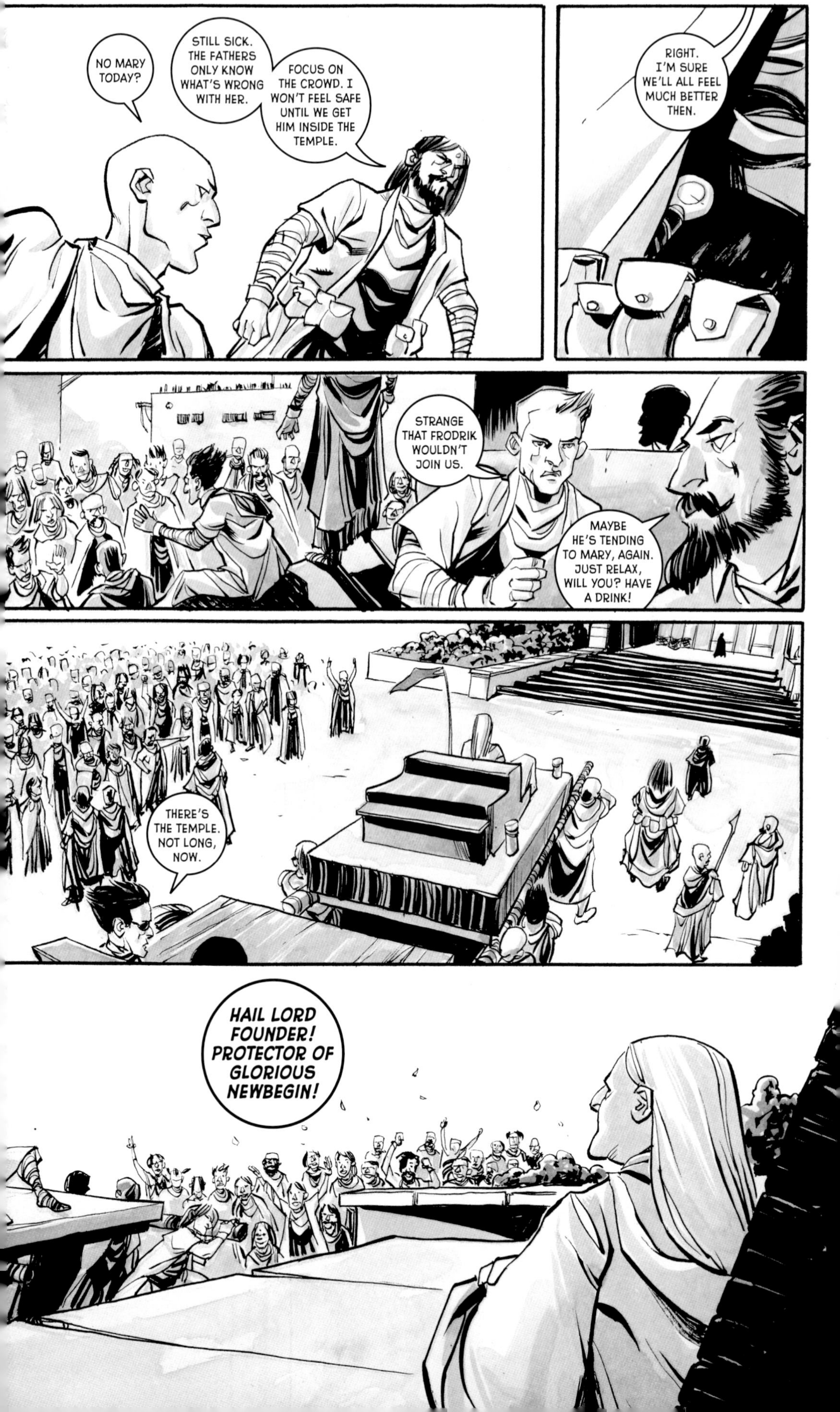
NO MARY TODAY?
STILL SICK. THE FATHERS ONLY KNOW WHAT'S WRONG WITH HER.
FOCUS ON THE CROWD. I WON'T FEEL SAFE UNTIL WE GET HIM INSIDE THE TEMPLE.
RIGHT. I'M SURE WE'LL ALL FEEL MUCH BETTER THEN.
STRANGE THAT FRODRIK WOULDN'T JOIN US.
MAYBE HE'S TENDING TO MARY, AGAIN. JUST RELAX, WILL YOU? HAVE A DRINK!
THERE'S THE TEMPLE. NOT LONG, NOW.
HAIL LORD FOUNDER! PROTECTOR OF GLORIOUS NEWBEGIN!

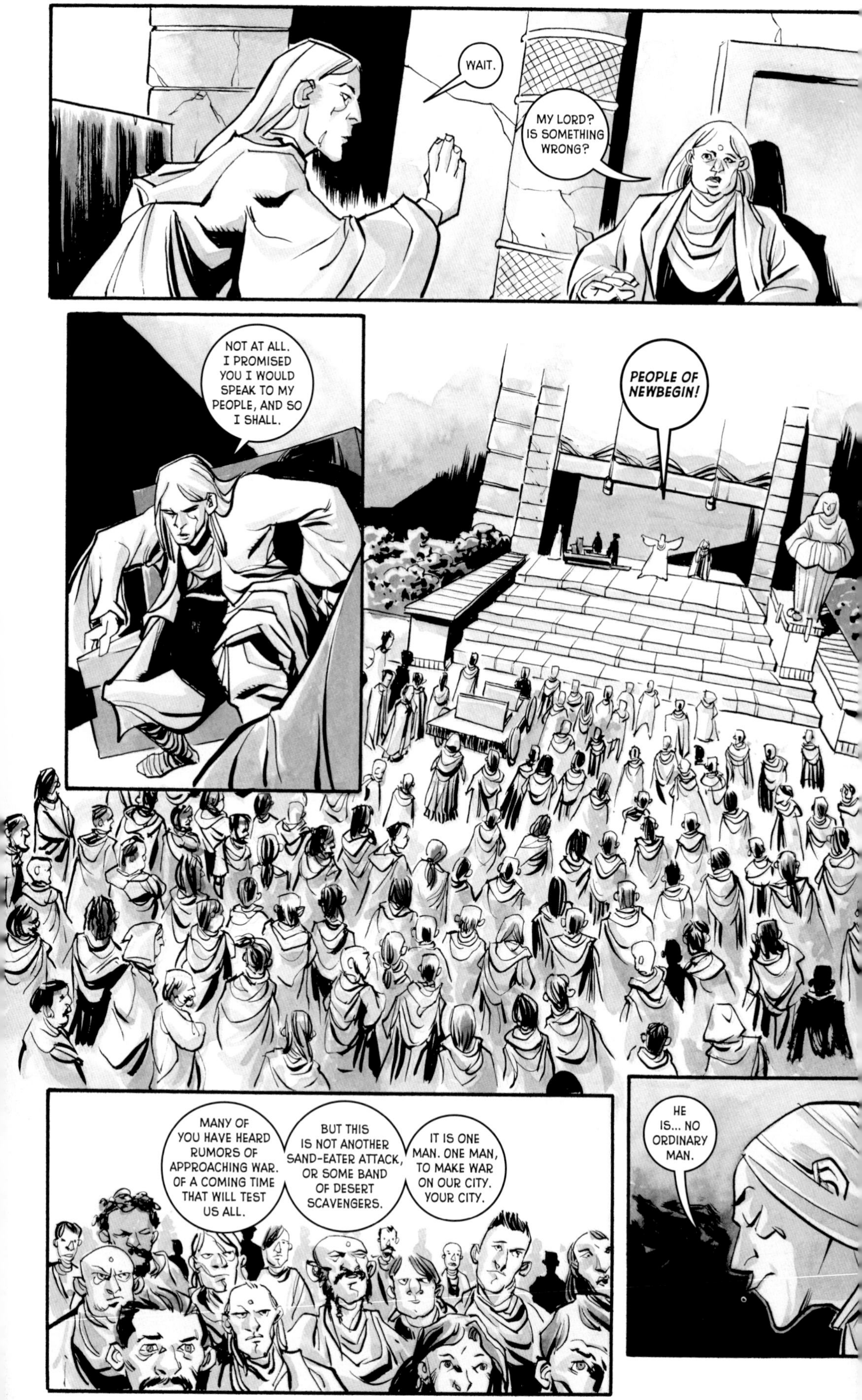
WAIT.
MY LORD? IS SOMETHING WRONG?
NOT AT ALL. I PROMISED YOU I WOULD SPEAK TO MY PEOPLE, AND SO I SHALL.
PEOPLE OF NEWBEGIN!
MANY OF YOU HAVE HEARD RUMORS OF APPROACHING WAR. OF A COMING TIME THAT WILL TEST US ALL.
BUT THIS IS NOT ANOTHER SAND-EATER ATTACK, OR SOME BAND OF DESERT SCAVENGERS.
IT IS ONE MAN. ONE MAN, TO MAKE WAR ON OUR CITY. YOUR CITY.
HE IS... NO ORDINARY MAN.

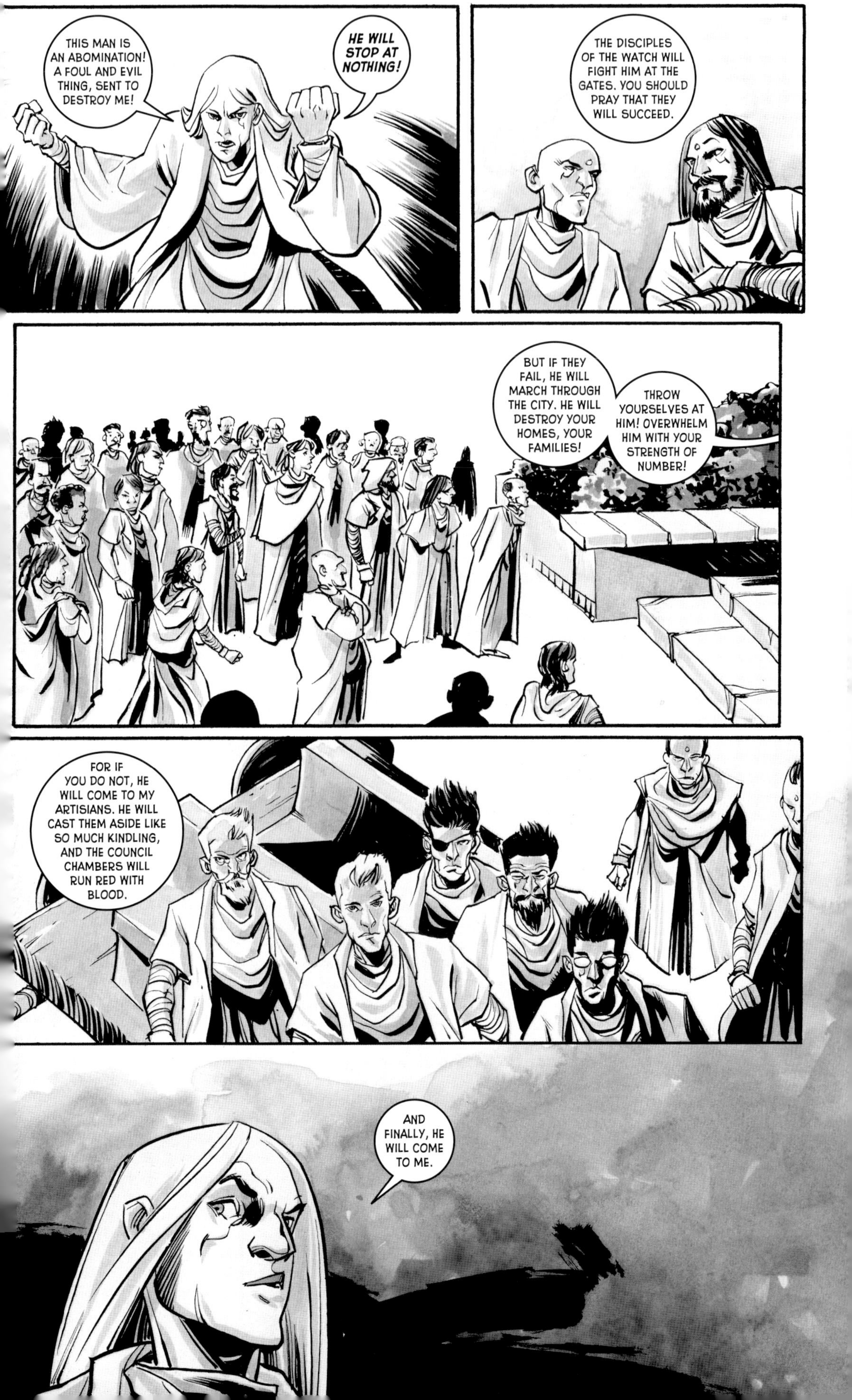
THIS MAN IS AN ABOMINATION! A FOUL AND EVIL THING, SENT TO DESTROY ME!
HE WILL STOP AT NOTHING!
THE DISCIPLES OF THE WATCH WILL FIGHT HIM AT THE GATES. YOU SHOULD PRAY THAT THEY WILL SUCCEED.
BUT IF THEY FAIL, HE WILL MARCH THROUGH THE CITY. HE WILL DESTROY YOUR HOMES, YOUR FAMILIES!
THROW YOURSELVES AT HIM! OVERWHELM HIM WITH YOUR STRENGTH OF NUMBER!
FOR IF YOU DO NOT, HE WILL COME TO MY ARTISIANS. HE WILL CAST THEM ASIDE LIKE SO MUCH KINDLING, AND THE COUNCIL CHAMBERS WILL RUN RED WITH BLOOD.
AND FINALLY, HE WILL COME TO ME.

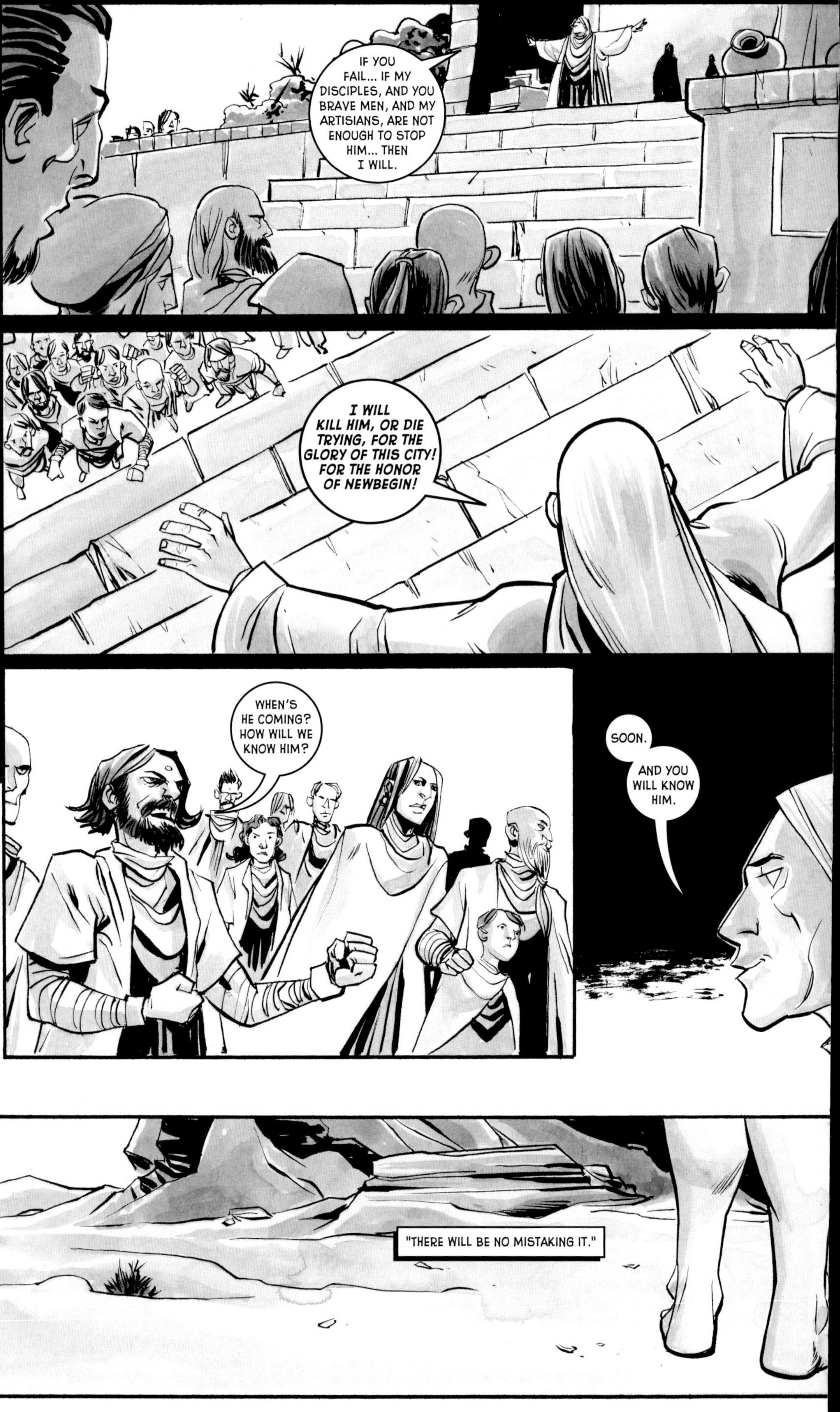
IF YOU FAIL... IF MY DISCIPLES, AND YOU BRAVE MEN, AND MY ARTISIANS, ARE NOT ENOUGH TO STOP HIM... THEN I WILL.
I WILL KILL HIM, OR DIE TRYING, FOR THE GLORY OF THIS CITY! FOR THE HONOR OF NEWBEGIN!
WHEN'S HE COMING? HOW WILL WE KNOW HIM?
SOON.
AND YOU WILL KNOW HIM.
"THERE WILL BE NO MISTAKING IT."

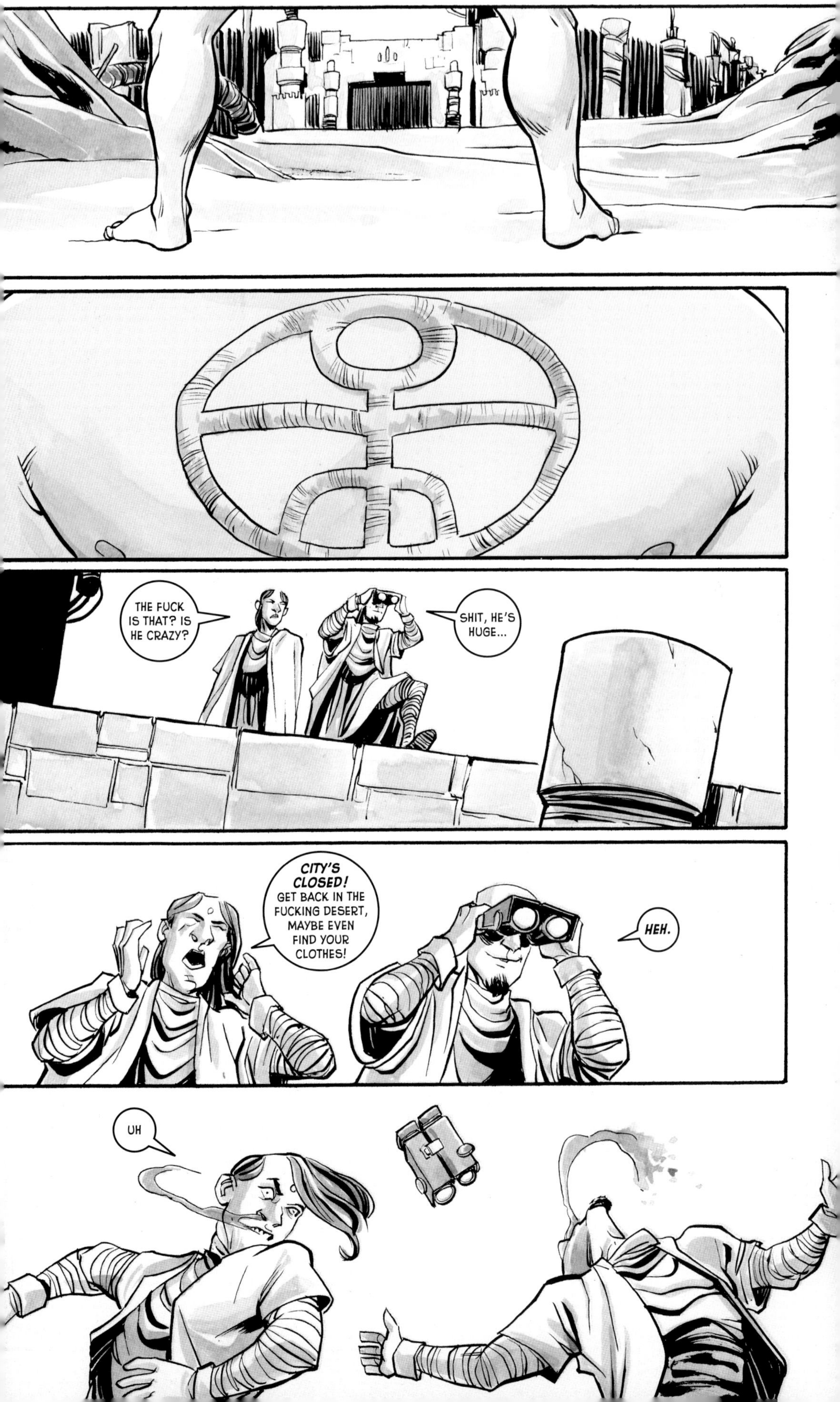
THE FUCK IS THAT? IS HE CRAZY?
SHIT, HE'S HUGE...
CITY'S CLOSED! GET BACK IN THE FUCKING DESERT, MAYBE EVEN FIND YOUR CLOTHES!
HEH.
UH

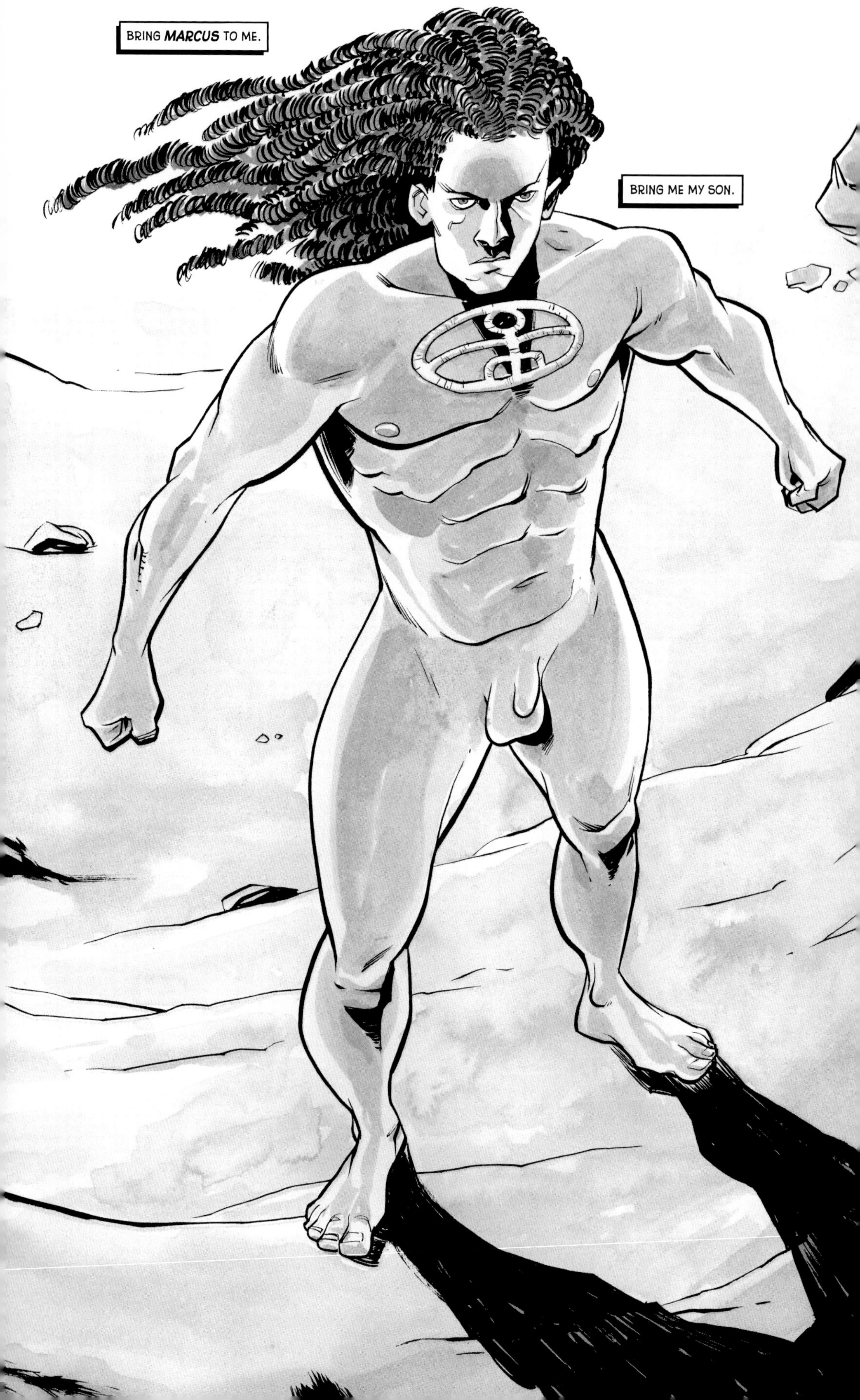
BRING *MARCUS* TO ME.
BRING ME MY SON.

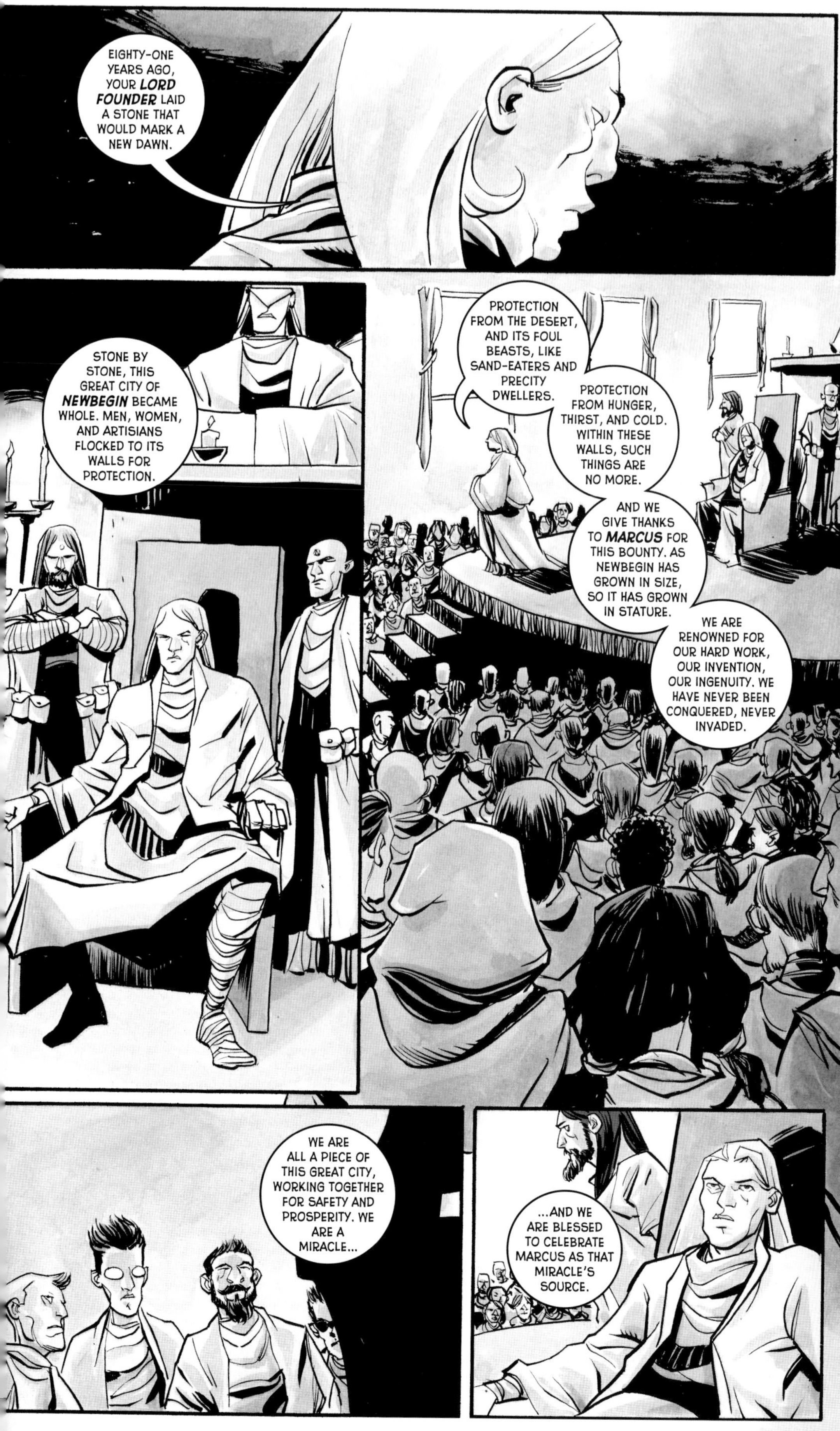
EIGHTY-ONE YEARS AGO, YOUR LORD FOUNDER LAID A STONE THAT WOULD MARK A NEW DAWN.
STONE BY STONE, THIS GREAT CITY OF NEWBEGIN BECAME WHOLE. MEN, WOMEN, AND ARTISIANS FLOCKED TO ITS WALLS FOR PROTECTION.
PROTECTION FROM THE DESERT, AND ITS FOUL BEASTS, LIKE SAND-EATERS AND PRECITY DWELLERS.
PROTECTION FROM HUNGER, THIRST, AND COLD. WITHIN THESE WALLS, SUCH THINGS ARE NO MORE.
AND WE GIVE THANKS TO MARCUS FOR THIS BOUNTY. AS NEWBEGIN HAS GROWN IN SIZE, SO IT HAS GROWN IN STATURE.
WE ARE RENOWNED FOR OUR HARD WORK, OUR INVENTION, OUR INGENUITY. WE HAVE NEVER BEEN CONQUERED, NEVER INVADED.
WE ARE ALL A PIECE OF THIS GREAT CITY, WORKING TOGETHER FOR SAFETY AND PROSPERITY. WE ARE A MIRACLE...
...AND WE ARE BLESSED TO CELEBRATE MARCUS AS THAT MIRACLE'S SOURCE.

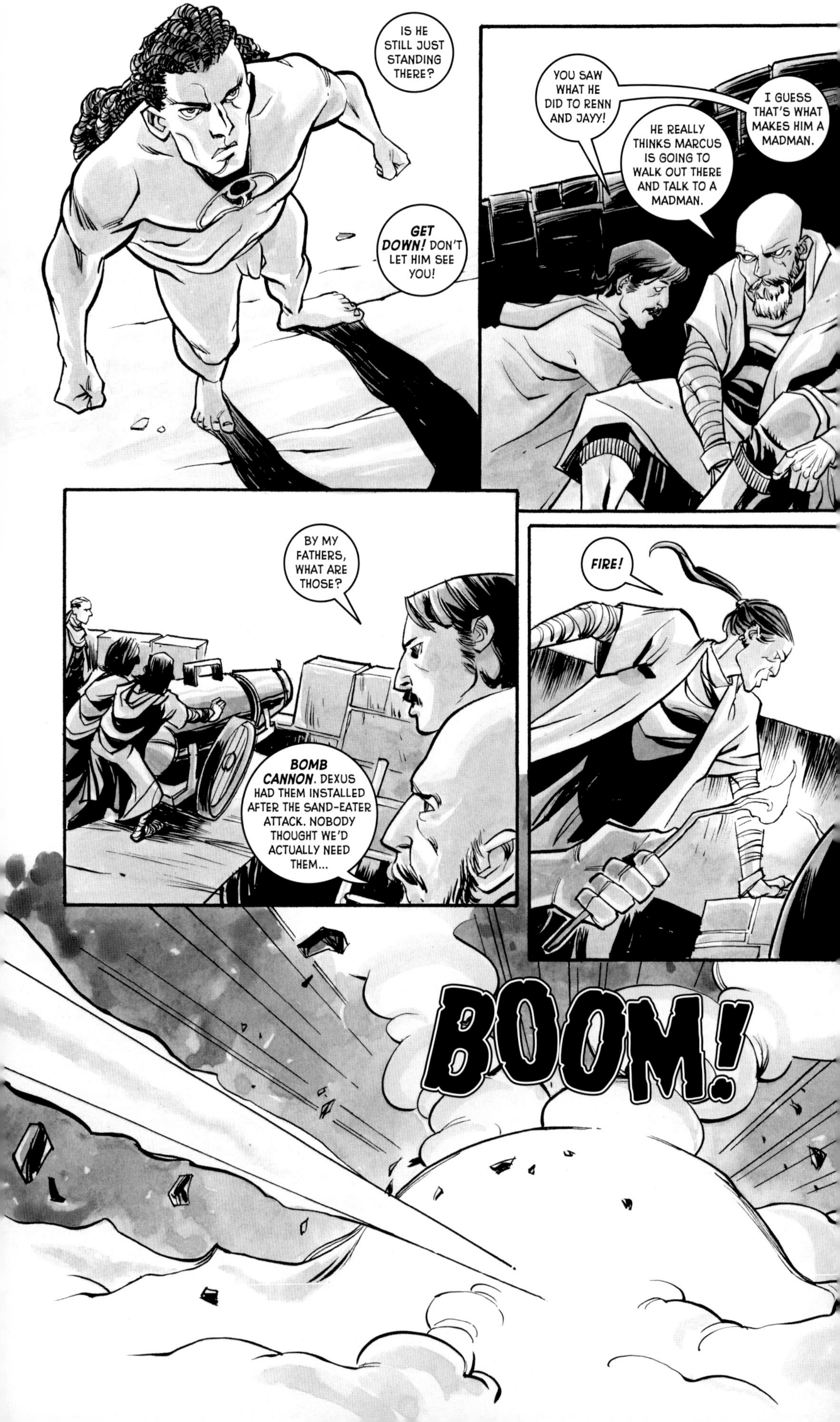
IS HE STILL JUST STANDING THERE?
GET DOWN! DON'T LET HIM SEE YOU!
YOU SAW WHAT HE DID TO RENN AND JAYY!
HE REALLY THINKS MARCUS IS GOING TO WALK OUT THERE AND TALK TO A MADMAN.
I GUESS THAT'S WHAT MAKES HIM A MADMAN.
BY MY FATHERS, WHAT ARE THOSE?
BOMB CANNON. DEXUS HAD THEM INSTALLED AFTER THE SAND-EATER ATTACK. NOBODY THOUGHT WE'D ACTUALLY NEED THEM...
FIRE!
BOOM!

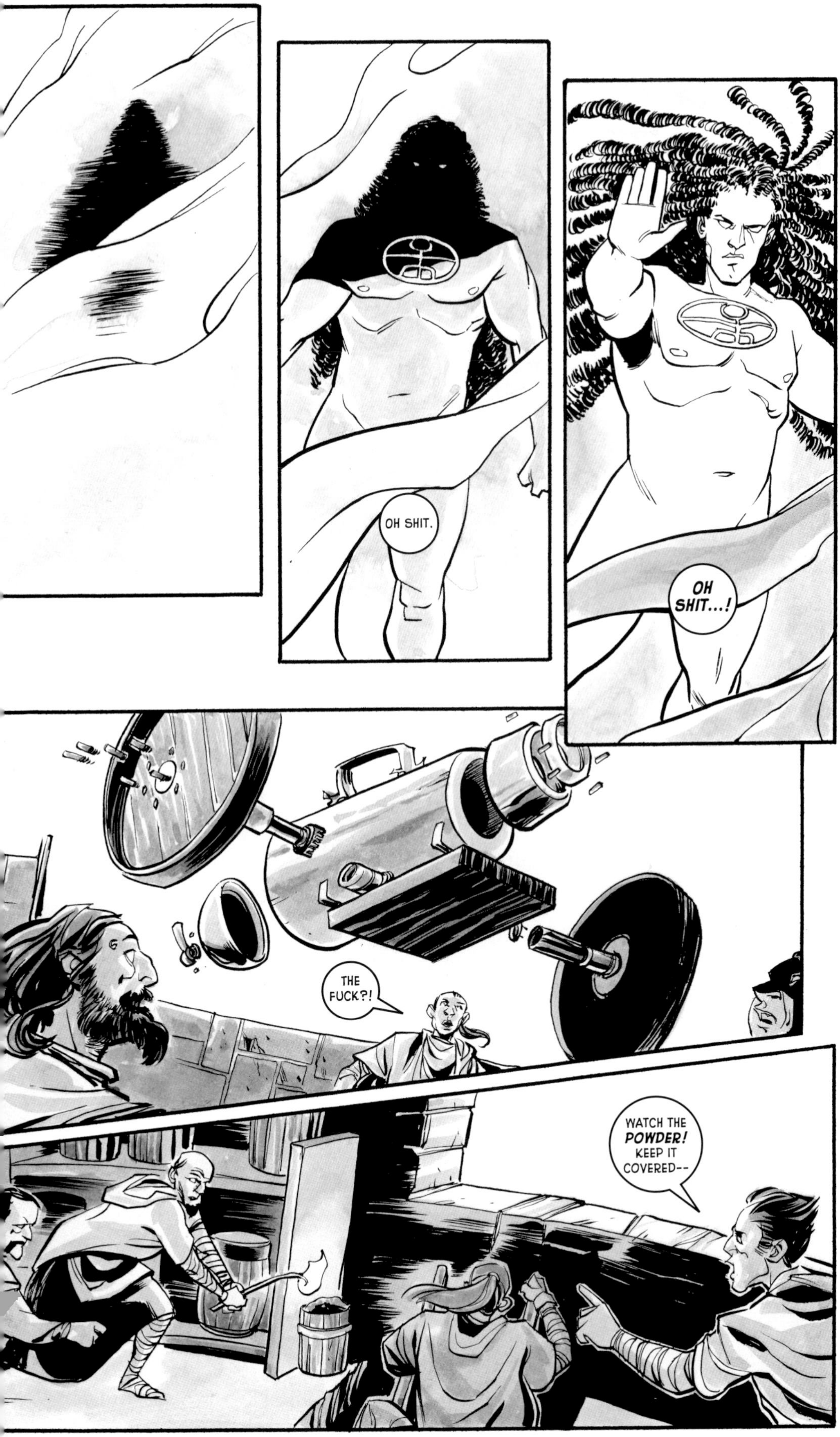
OH SHIT.
OH SHIT...!
THE FUCK?!
WATCH THE POWDER! KEEP IT COVERED--

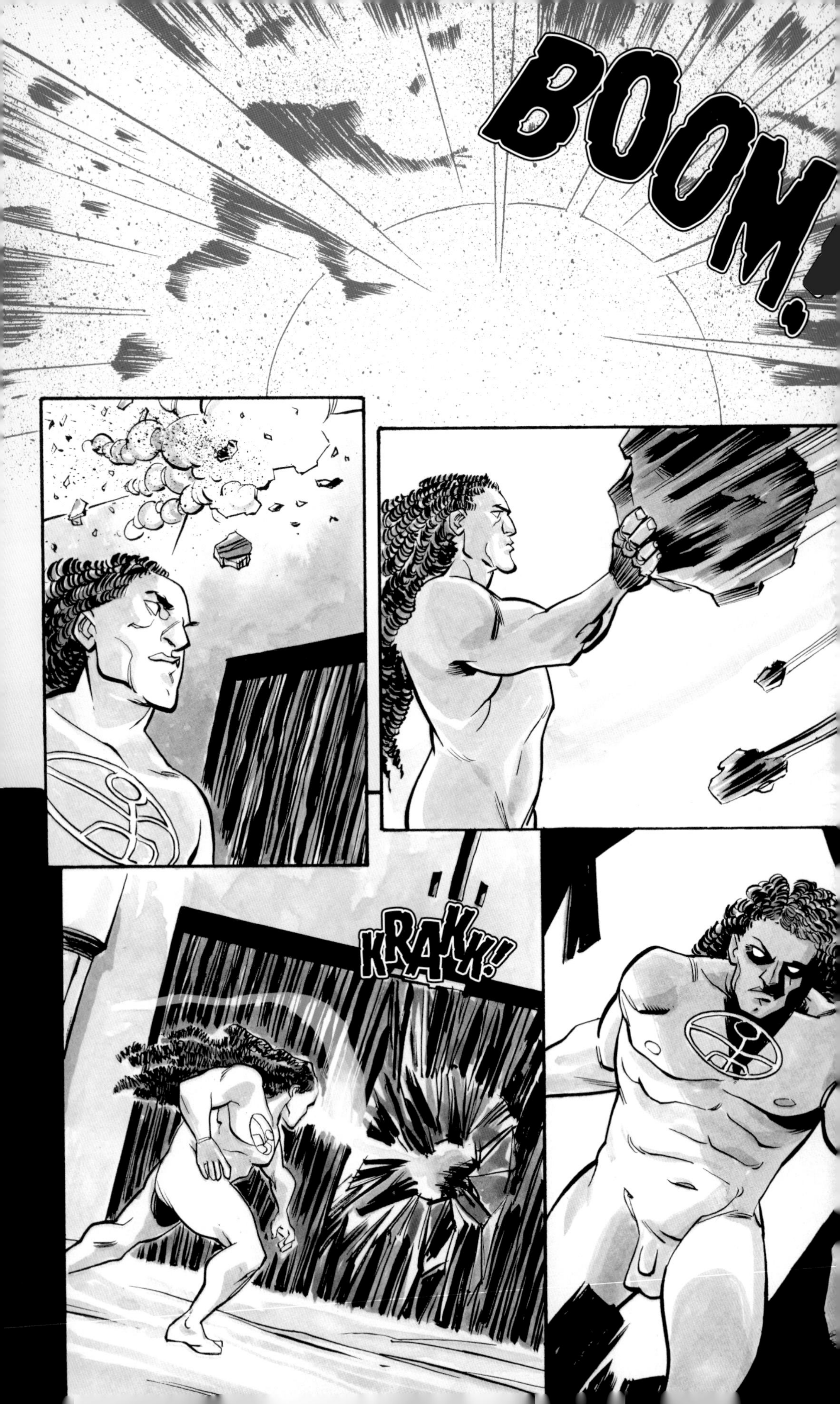
BOOM!
KRAKK!

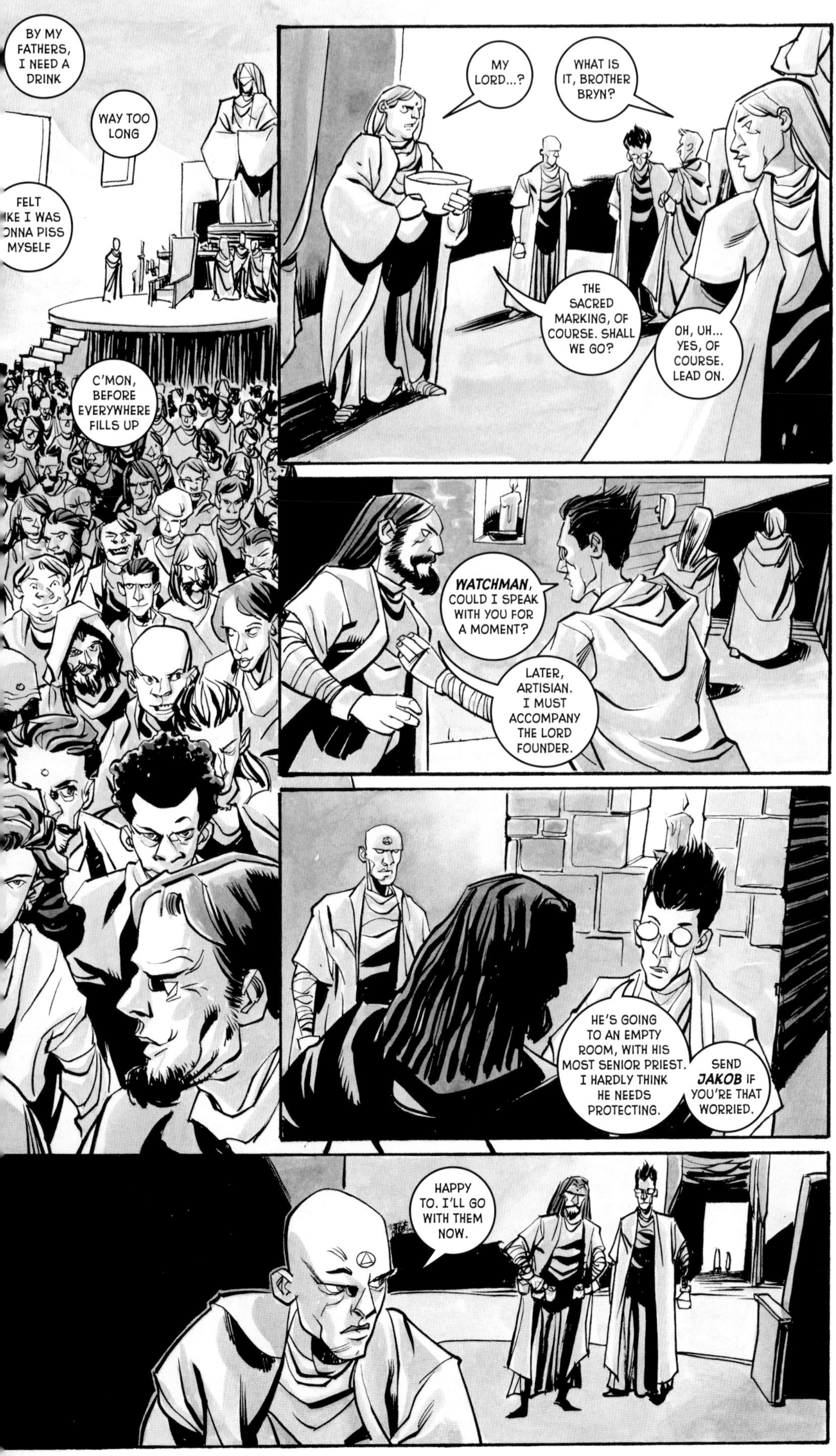
BY MY FATHERS, I NEED A DRINK
WAY TOO LONG
FELT KE I WAS ONNA PISS MYSELF
C'MON, BEFORE EVERYWHERE FILLS UP
MY LORD...?
WHAT IS IT, BROTHER BRYN?
THE SACRED MARKING, OF COURSE. SHALL WE GO?
OH, UH... YES, OF COURSE. LEAD ON.
WATCHMAN, COULD I SPEAK WITH YOU FOR A MOMENT?
LATER, ARTISIAN. I MUST ACCOMPANY THE LORD FOUNDER.
HE'S GOING TO AN EMPTY ROOM, WITH HIS MOST SENIOR PRIEST. I HARDLY THINK HE NEEDS PROTECTING.
SEND JAKOB IF YOU'RE THAT WORRIED.
HAPPY TO. I'LL GO WITH THEM NOW.

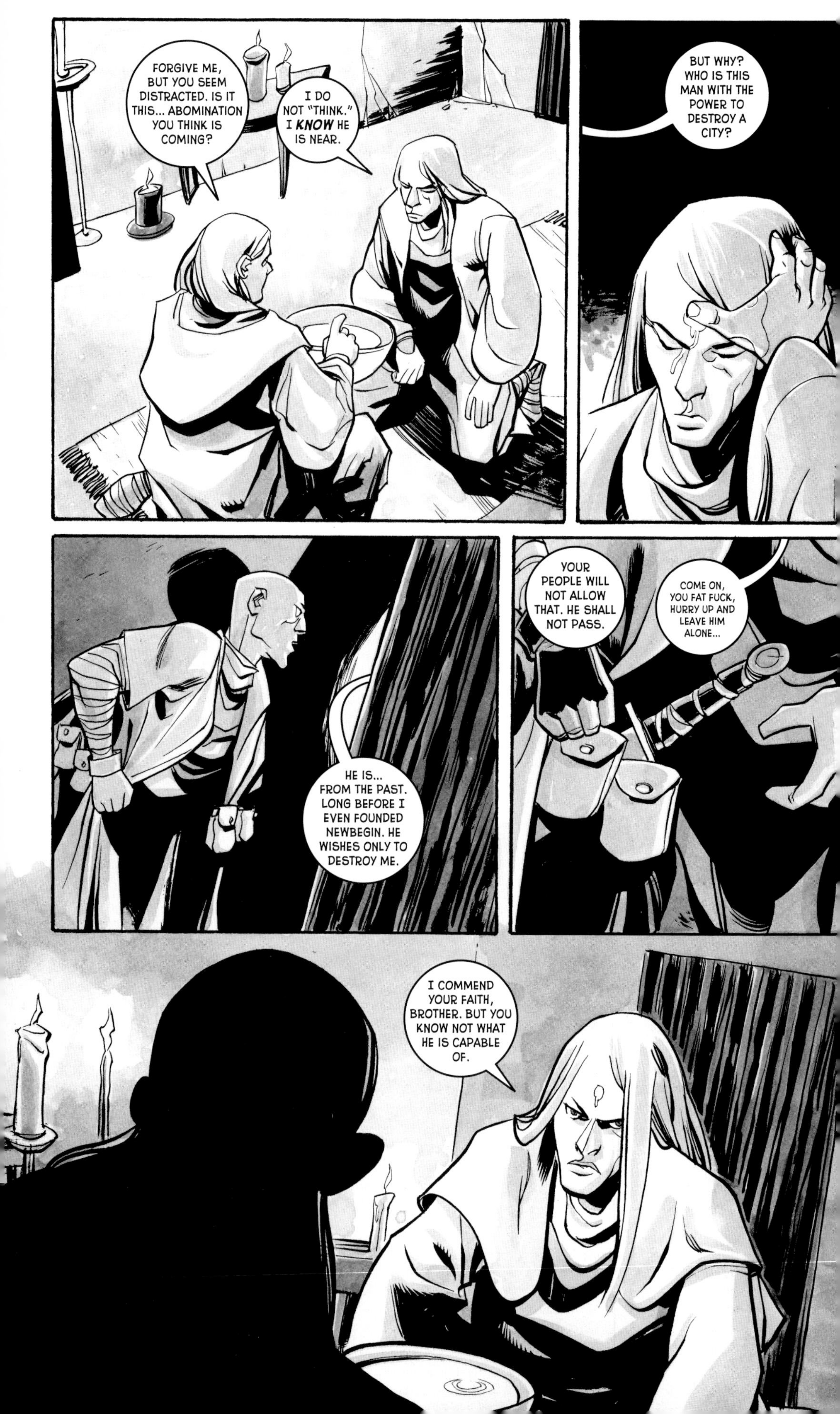

FORGIVE ME, BUT YOU SEEM DISTRACTED. IS IT THIS... ABOMINATION YOU THINK IS COMING?
I DO NOT "THINK." I **KNOW** HE IS NEAR.
BUT WHY? WHO IS THIS MAN WITH THE POWER TO DESTROY A CITY?
HE IS... FROM THE PAST. LONG BEFORE I EVEN FOUNDED NEWBEGIN. HE WISHES ONLY TO DESTROY ME.
YOUR PEOPLE WILL NOT ALLOW THAT. HE SHALL NOT PASS.
COME ON, YOU FAT FUCK, HURRY UP AND LEAVE HIM ALONE...
I COMMEND YOUR FAITH, BROTHER. BUT YOU KNOW NOT WHAT HE IS CAPABLE OF.

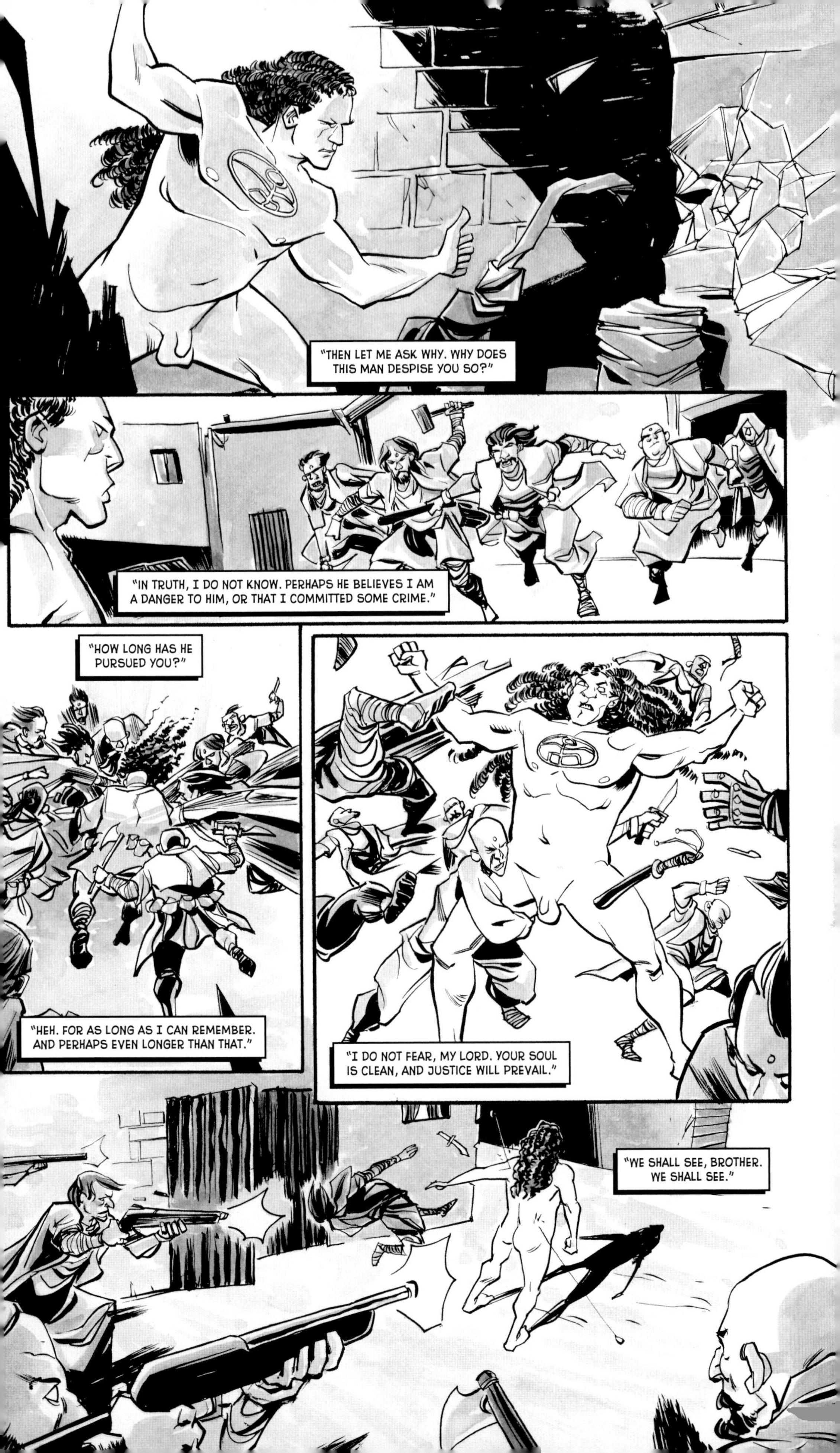
"THEN LET ME ASK WHY. WHY DOES THIS MAN DESPISE YOU SO?"
"IN TRUTH, I DO NOT KNOW. PERHAPS HE BELIEVES I AM A DANGER TO HIM, OR THAT I COMMITTED SOME CRIME."
"HOW LONG HAS HE PURSUED YOU?"
"HEH. FOR AS LONG AS I CAN REMEMBER. AND PERHAPS EVEN LONGER THAN THAT."
"I DO NOT FEAR, MY LORD. YOUR SOUL IS CLEAN, AND JUSTICE WILL PREVAIL."
"WE SHALL SEE, BROTHER. WE SHALL SEE."

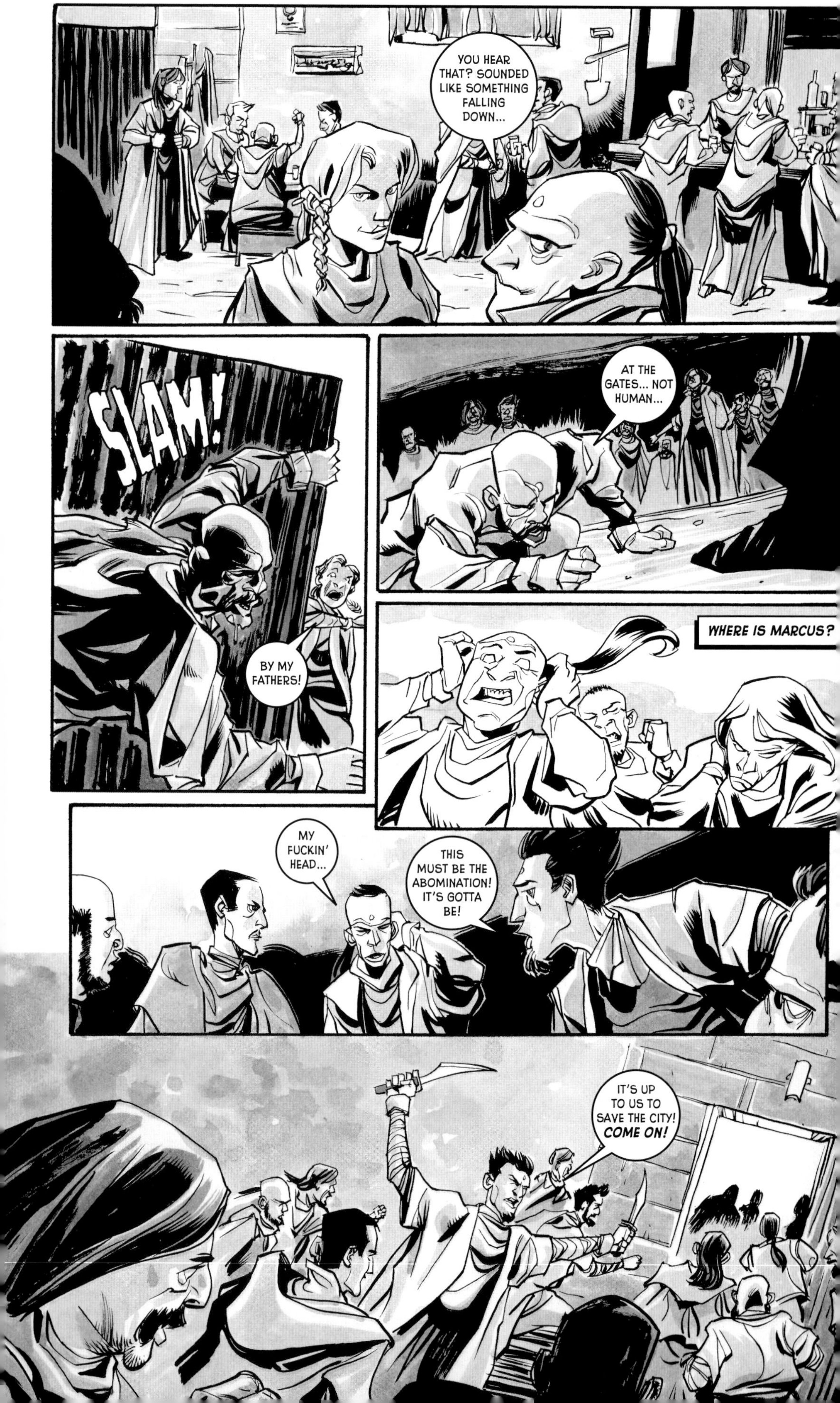
YOU HEAR THAT? SOUNDED LIKE SOMETHING FALLING DOWN...
SLAM!
BY MY FATHERS!
AT THE GATES... NOT HUMAN...
WHERE IS MARCUS?
MY FUCKIN' HEAD...
THIS MUST BE THE ABOMINATION! IT'S GOTTA BE!
IT'S UP TO US TO SAVE THE CITY! COME ON!

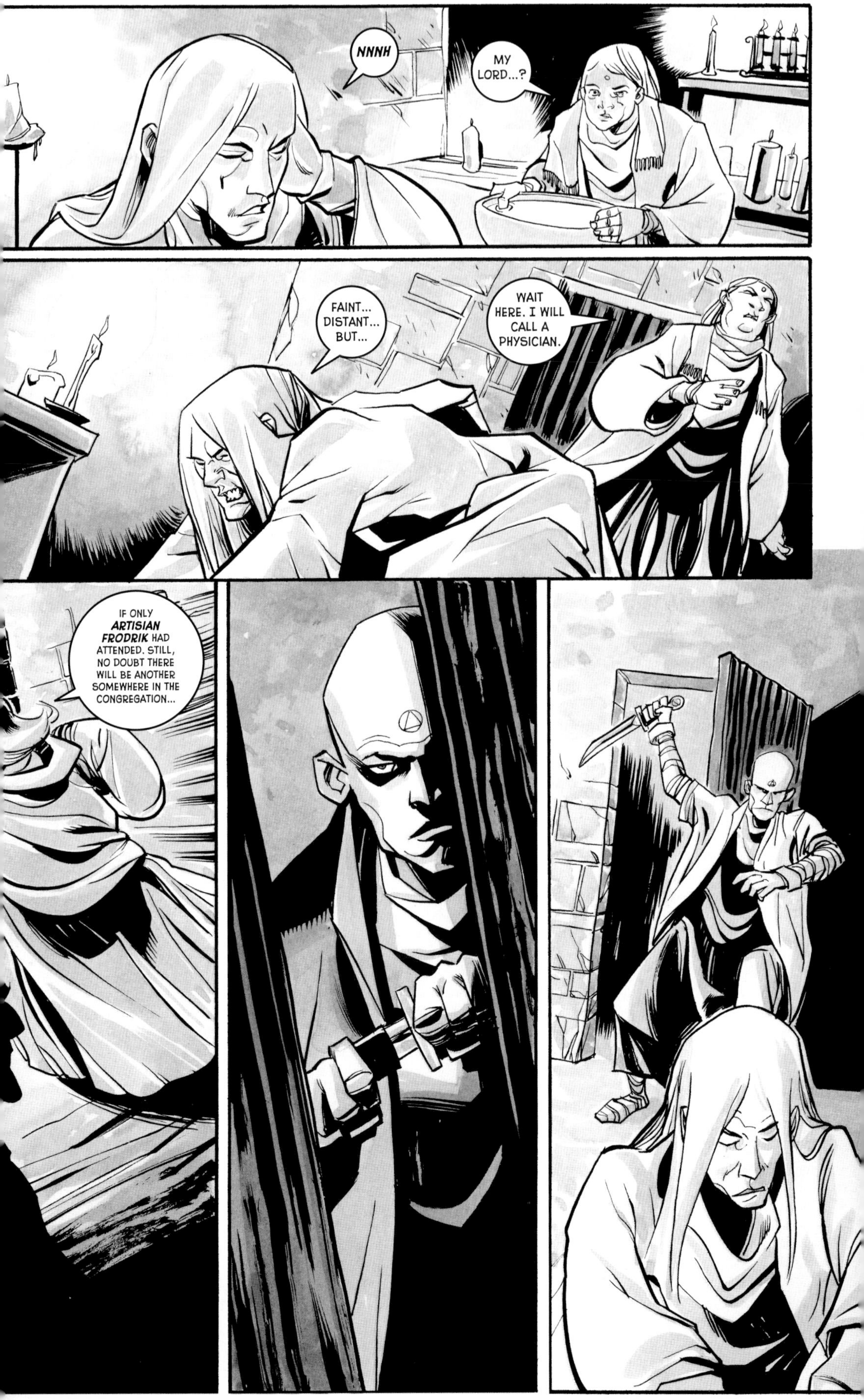
NNNH
MY LORD...?
FAINT... DISTANT... BUT...
WAIT HERE. I WILL CALL A PHYSICIAN.
IF ONLY ARTISIAN FRODRIK HAD ATTENDED. STILL, NO DOUBT THERE WILL BE ANOTHER SOMEWHERE IN THE CONGREGATION...

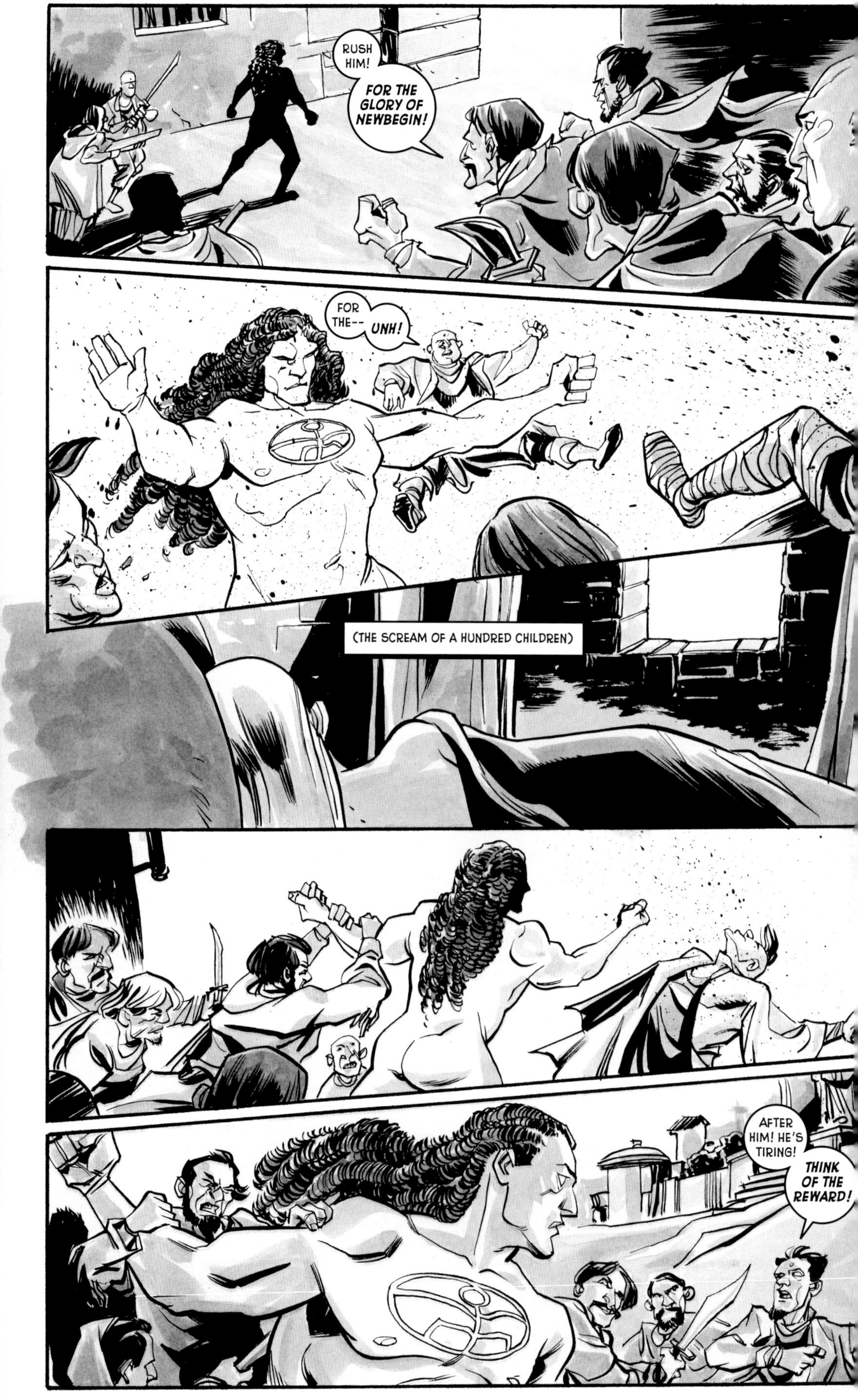
RUSH HIM!
FOR THE GLORY OF NEWBEGIN!
FOR THE--
UNH!
(THE SCREAM OF A HUNDRED CHILDREN)
AFTER HIM! HE'S TIRING!
THINK OF THE REWARD!

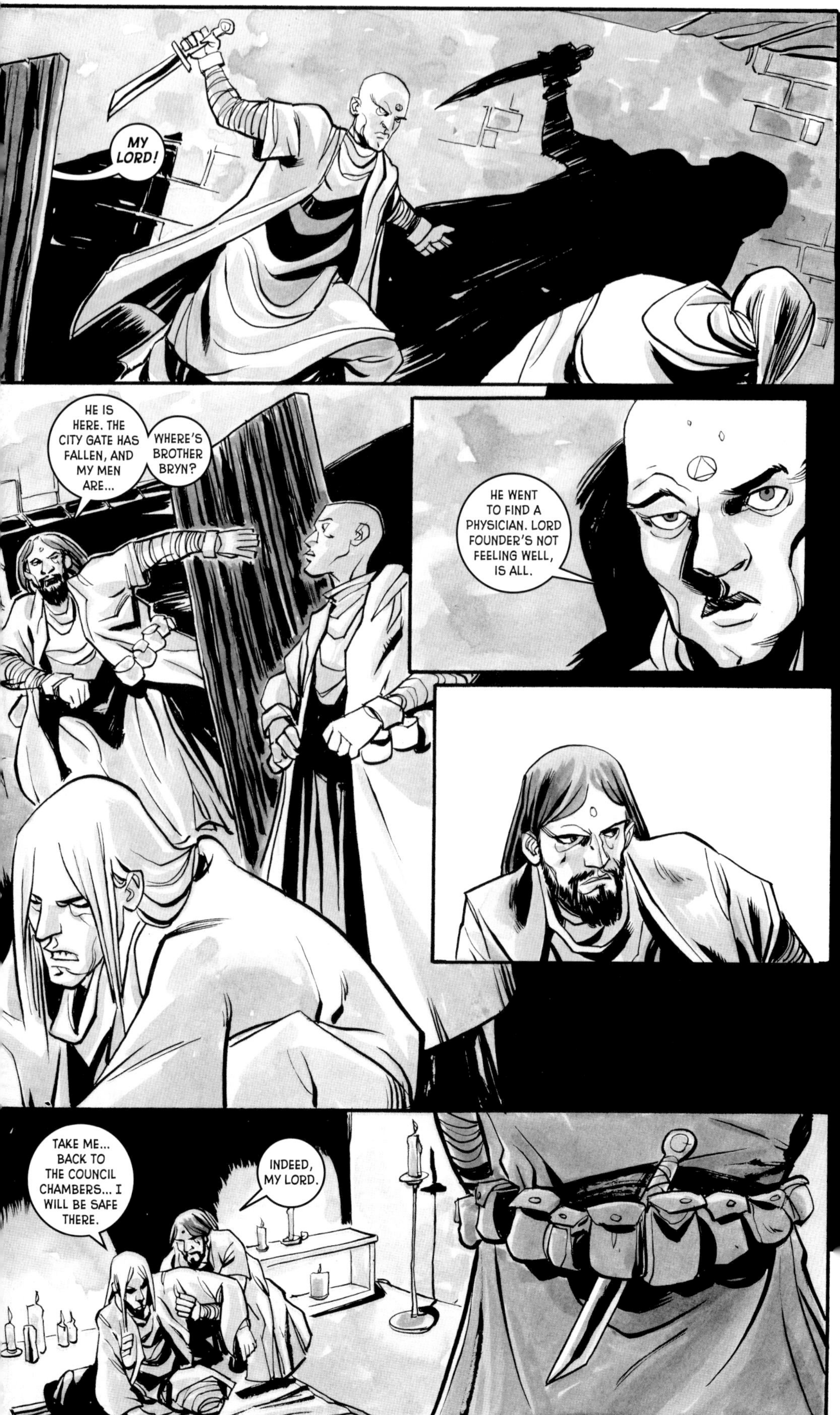
MY LORD!
HE IS HERE. THE CITY GATE HAS FALLEN, AND MY MEN ARE...
WHERE'S BROTHER BRYN?
HE WENT TO FIND A PHYSICIAN. LORD FOUNDER'S NOT FEELING WELL, IS ALL.
TAKE ME... BACK TO THE COUNCIL CHAMBERS... I WILL BE SAFE THERE.
INDEED, MY LORD.

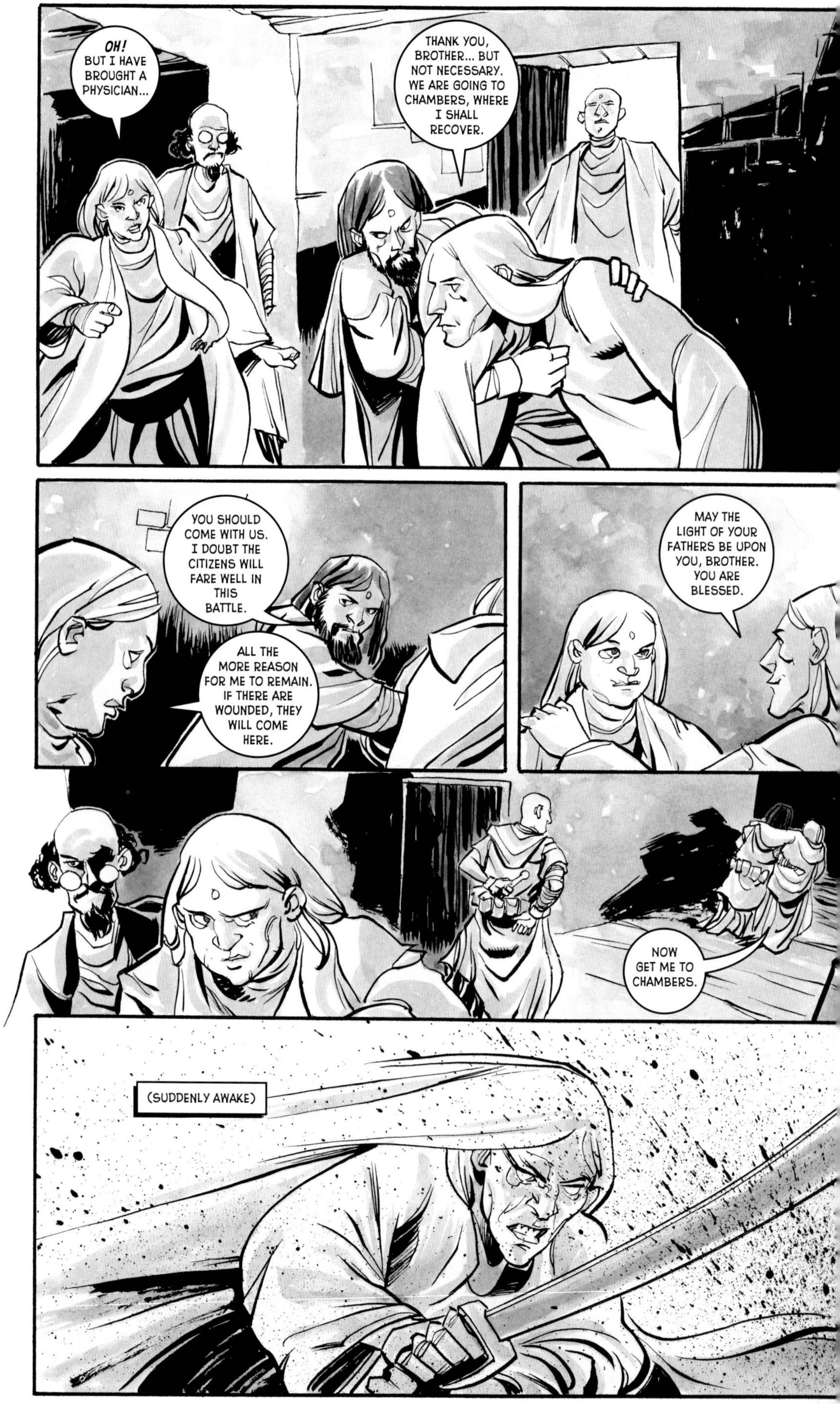
OH! BUT I HAVE BROUGHT A PHYSICIAN...
THANK YOU, BROTHER... BUT NOT NECESSARY. WE ARE GOING TO CHAMBERS, WHERE I SHALL RECOVER.
YOU SHOULD COME WITH US. I DOUBT THE CITIZENS WILL FARE WELL IN THIS BATTLE.
ALL THE MORE REASON FOR ME TO REMAIN. IF THERE ARE WOUNDED, THEY WILL COME HERE.
MAY THE LIGHT OF YOUR FATHERS BE UPON YOU, BROTHER. YOU ARE BLESSED.
NOW GET ME TO CHAMBERS.
(SUDDENLY AWAKE)

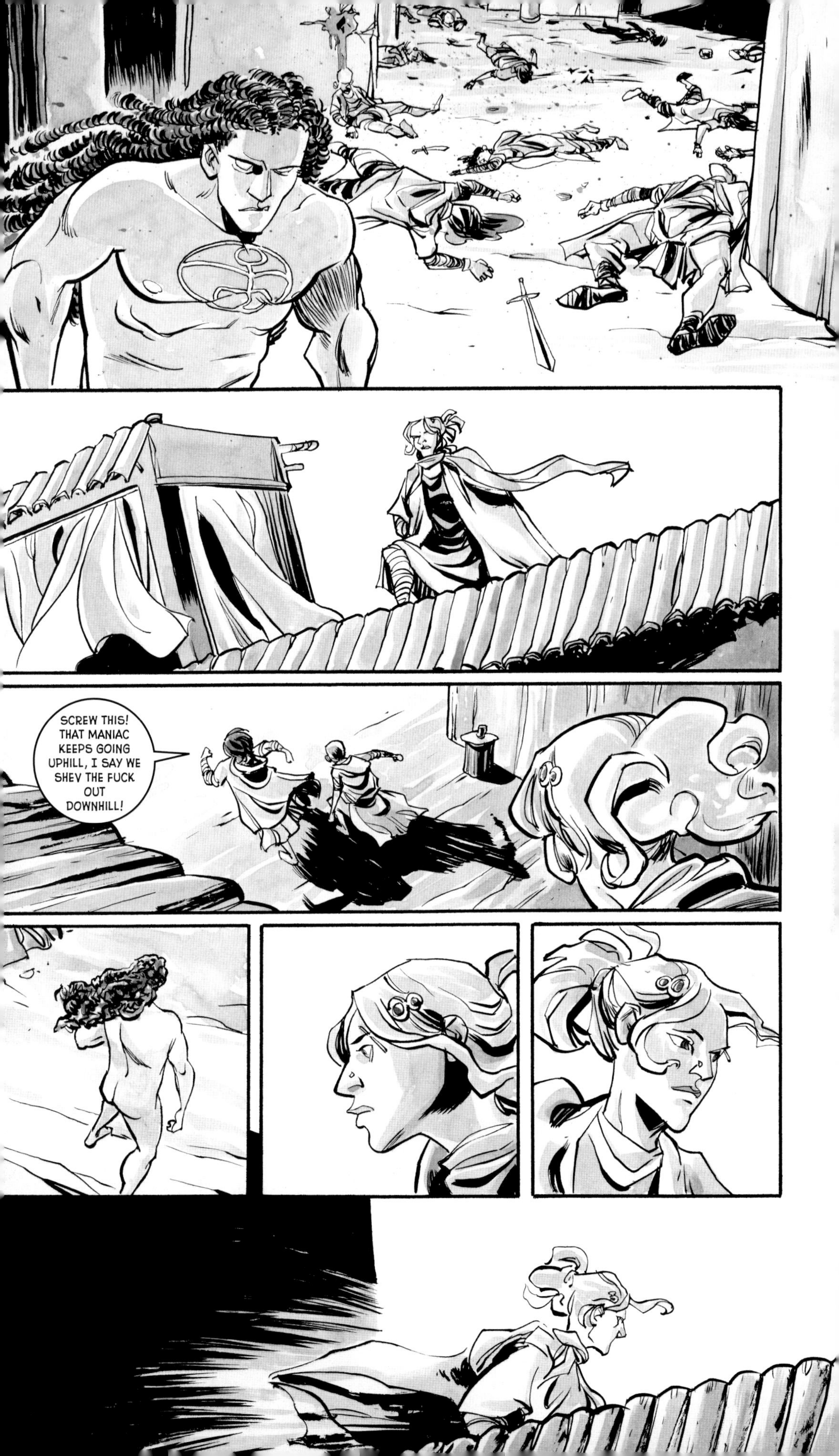
SCREW THIS! THAT MANIAC KEEPS GOING UPHILL, I SAY WE SHEV THE FUCK OUT DOWNHILL!

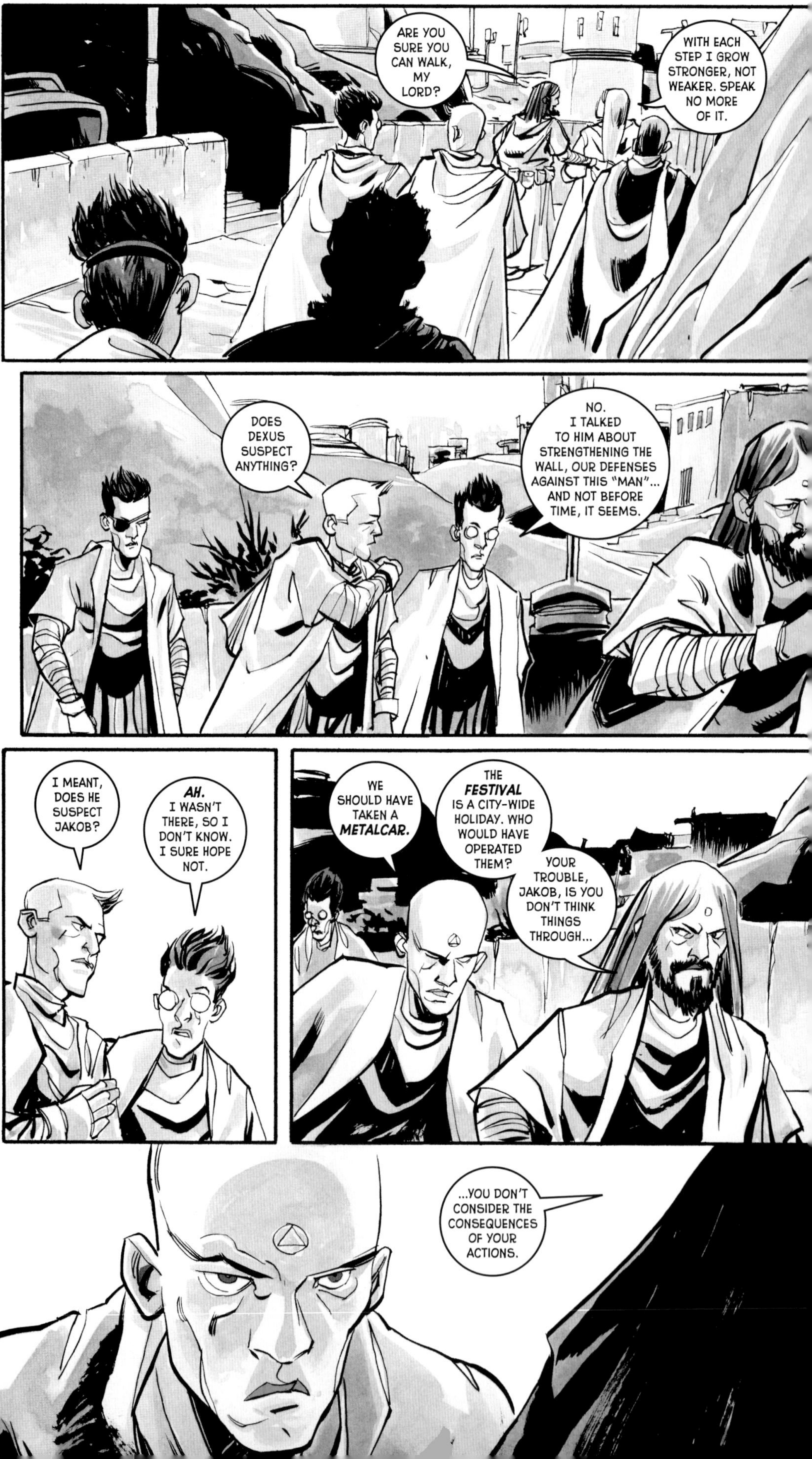
ARE YOU SURE YOU CAN WALK, MY LORD?
WITH EACH STEP I GROW STRONGER, NOT WEAKER. SPEAK NO MORE OF IT.
DOES DEXUS SUSPECT ANYTHING?
NO. I TALKED TO HIM ABOUT STRENGTHENING THE WALL, OUR DEFENSES AGAINST THIS "MAN"... AND NOT BEFORE TIME, IT SEEMS.
I MEANT, DOES HE SUSPECT JAKOB?
AH. I WASN'T THERE, SO I DON'T KNOW. I SURE HOPE NOT.
WE SHOULD HAVE TAKEN A METALCAR.
THE FESTIVAL IS A CITY-WIDE HOLIDAY. WHO WOULD HAVE OPERATED THEM?
YOUR TROUBLE, JAKOB, IS YOU DON'T THINK THINGS THROUGH...
...YOU DON'T CONSIDER THE CONSEQUENCES OF YOUR ACTIONS.

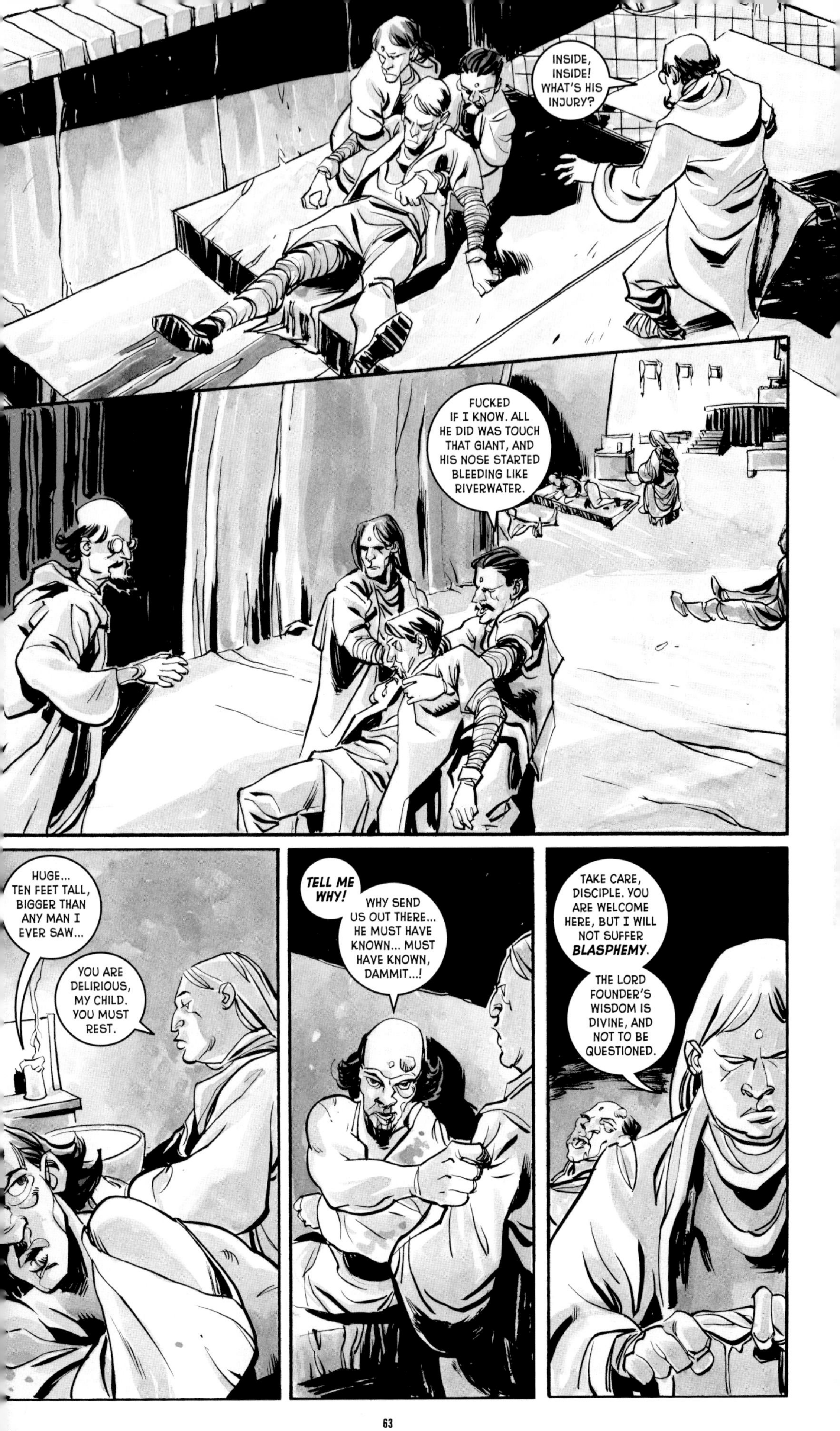
INSIDE, INSIDE! WHAT'S HIS INJURY?
FUCKED IF I KNOW. ALL HE DID WAS TOUCH THAT GIANT, AND HIS NOSE STARTED BLEEDING LIKE RIVERWATER.
HUGE... TEN FEET TALL, BIGGER THAN ANY MAN I EVER SAW...
YOU ARE DELIRIOUS, MY CHILD. YOU MUST REST.
TELL ME WHY!
WHY SEND US OUT THERE... HE MUST HAVE KNOWN... MUST HAVE KNOWN, DAMMIT...!
TAKE CARE, DISCIPLE. YOU ARE WELCOME HERE, BUT I WILL NOT SUFFER BLASPHEMY.
THE LORD FOUNDER'S WISDOM IS DIVINE, AND NOT TO BE QUESTIONED.

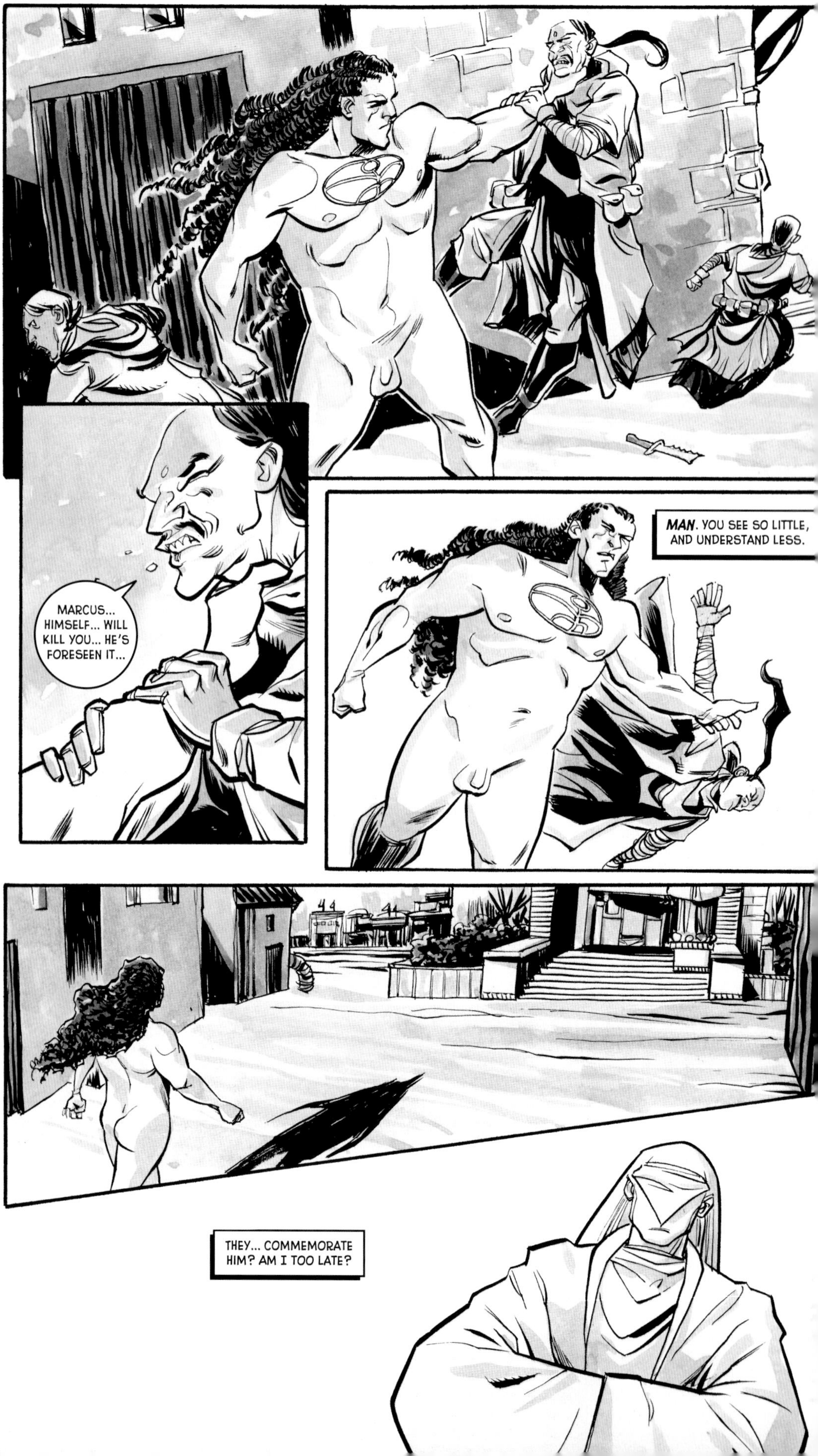
MARCUS... HIMSELF... WILL KILL YOU... HE'S FORESEEN IT...
MAN. YOU SEE SO LITTLE, AND UNDERSTAND LESS.
THEY... COMMEMORATE HIM? AM I TOO LATE?

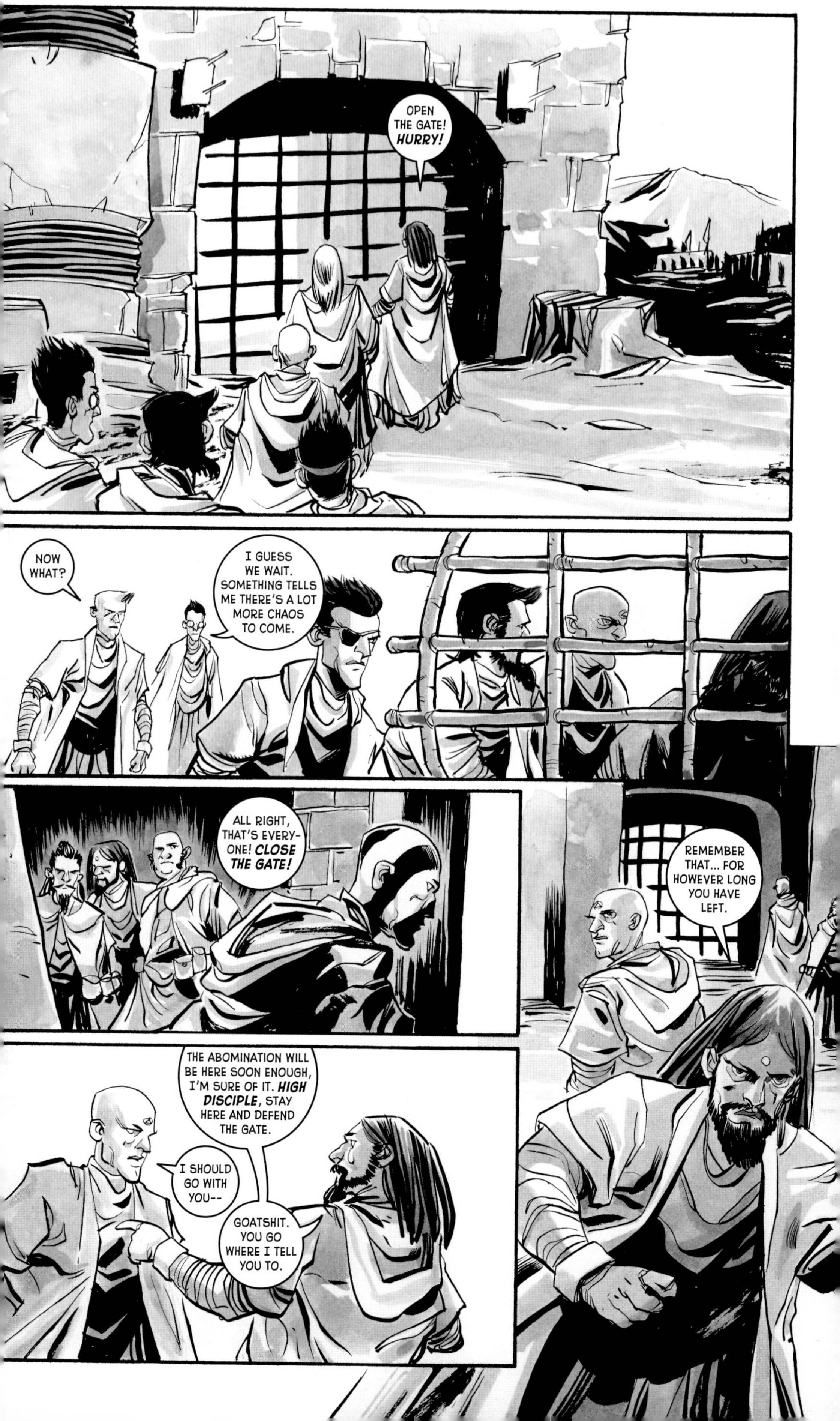
OPEN THE GATE! HURRY!
NOW WHAT?
I GUESS WE WAIT. SOMETHING TELLS ME THERE'S A LOT MORE CHAOS TO COME.
ALL RIGHT, THAT'S EVERY-ONE! CLOSE THE GATE!
REMEMBER THAT... FOR HOWEVER LONG YOU HAVE LEFT.
THE ABOMINATION WILL BE HERE SOON ENOUGH, I'M SURE OF IT. HIGH DISCIPLE, STAY HERE AND DEFEND THE GATE.
I SHOULD GO WITH YOU--
GOATSHIT. YOU GO WHERE I TELL YOU TO.

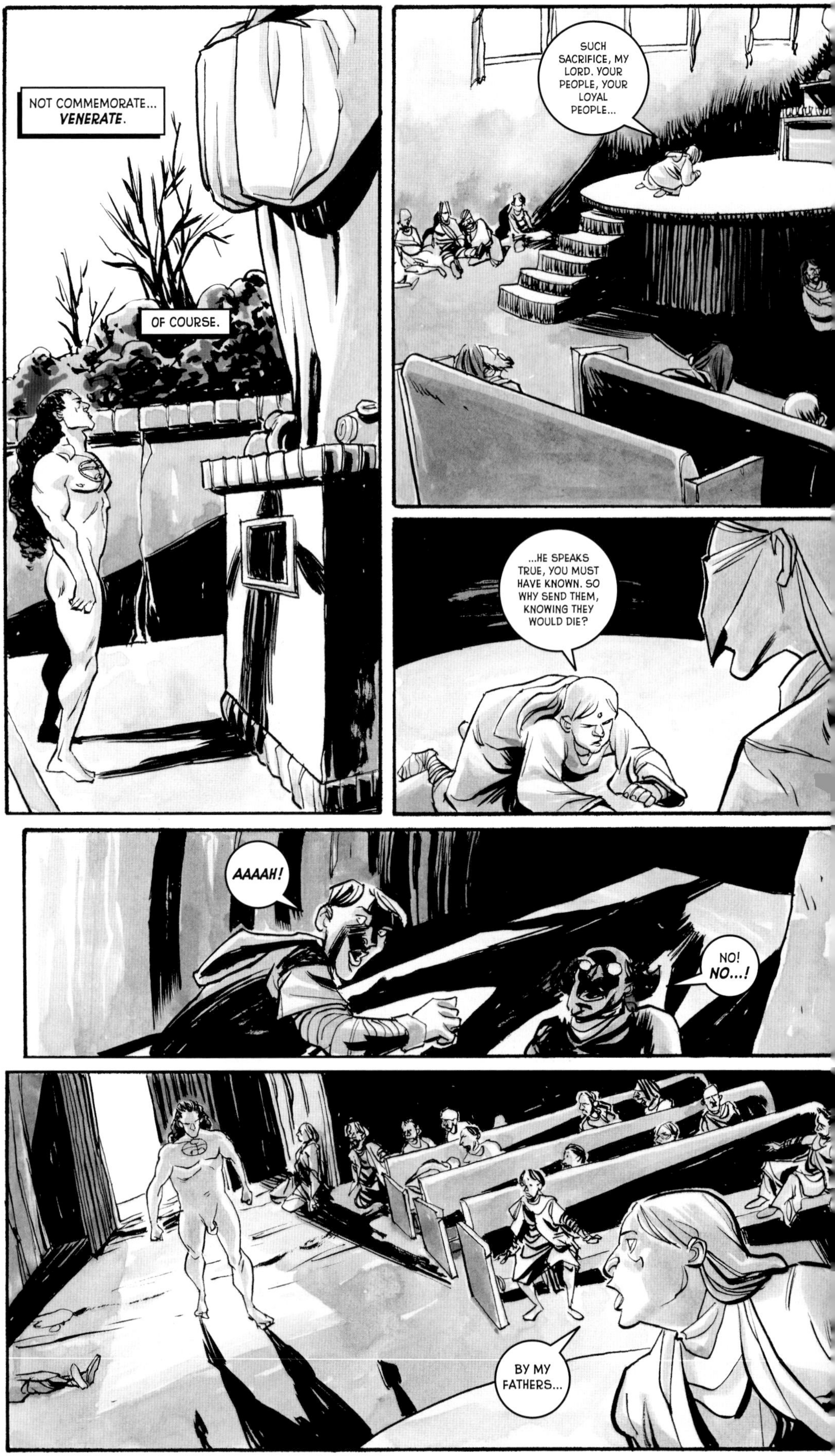
NOT COMMEMORATE... ***VENERATE***.
OF COURSE.
SUCH SACRIFICE, MY LORD. YOUR PEOPLE, YOUR LOYAL PEOPLE...
...HE SPEAKS TRUE, YOU MUST HAVE KNOWN. SO WHY SEND THEM, KNOWING THEY WOULD DIE?
AAAAH!
NO! ***NO...!***
BY MY FATHERS...

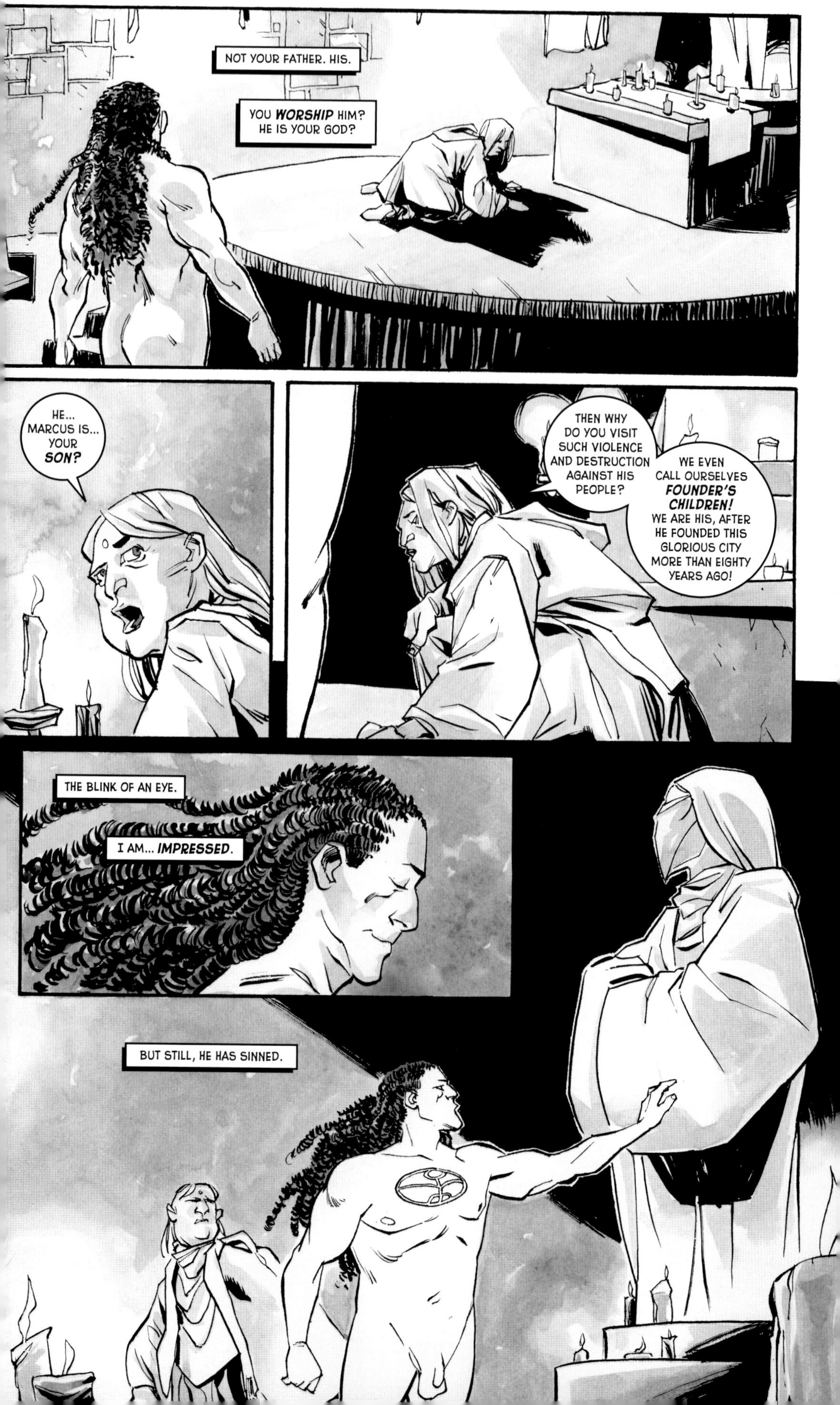
NOT YOUR FATHER. HIS.
YOU WORSHIP HIM? HE IS YOUR GOD?
HE... MARCUS IS... YOUR SON?
THEN WHY DO YOU VISIT SUCH VIOLENCE AND DESTRUCTION AGAINST HIS PEOPLE?
WE EVEN CALL OURSELVES FOUNDER'S CHILDREN! WE ARE HIS, AFTER HE FOUNDED THIS GLORIOUS CITY MORE THAN EIGHTY YEARS AGO!
THE BLINK OF AN EYE.
I AM... IMPRESSED.
BUT STILL, HE HAS SINNED.

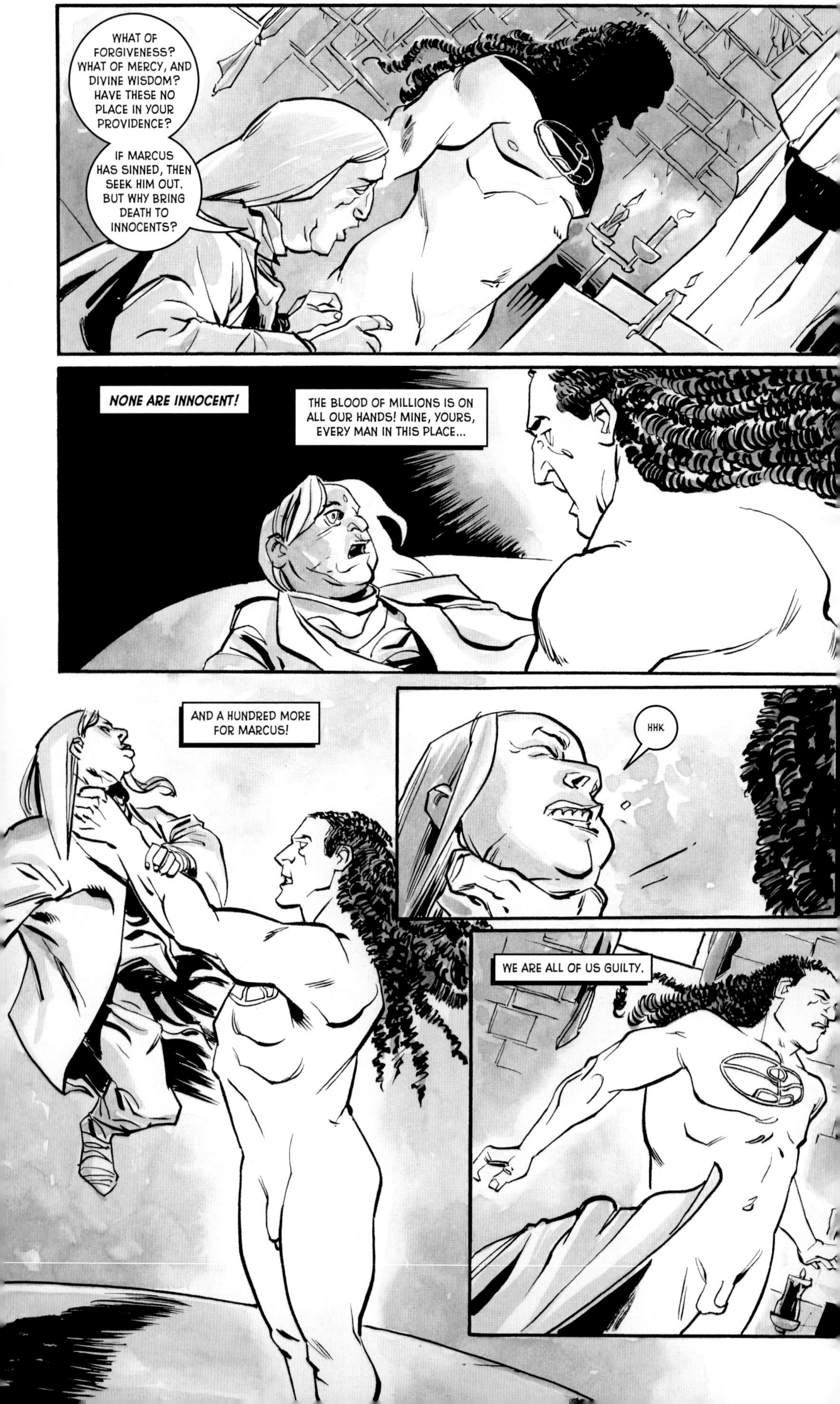
WHAT OF FORGIVENESS? WHAT OF MERCY, AND DIVINE WISDOM? HAVE THESE NO PLACE IN YOUR PROVIDENCE?
IF MARCUS HAS SINNED, THEN SEEK HIM OUT. BUT WHY BRING DEATH TO INNOCENTS?
NONE ARE INNOCENT!
THE BLOOD OF MILLIONS IS ON ALL OUR HANDS! MINE, YOURS, EVERY MAN IN THIS PLACE...
AND A HUNDRED MORE FOR MARCUS!
HHK
WE ARE ALL OF US GUILTY.

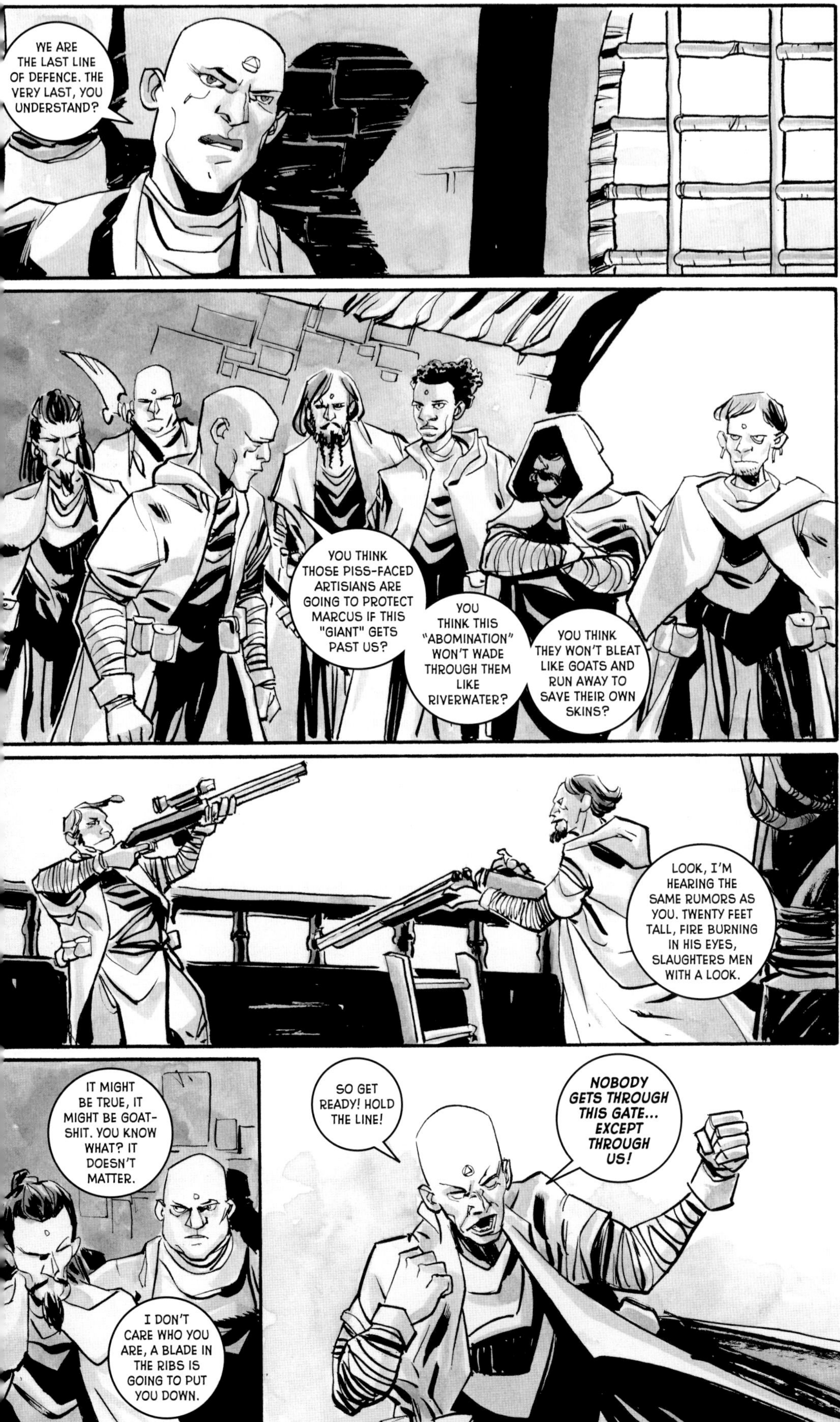
WE ARE THE LAST LINE OF DEFENCE. THE VERY LAST, YOU UNDERSTAND?
YOU THINK THOSE PISS-FACED ARTISIANS ARE GOING TO PROTECT MARCUS IF THIS "GIANT" GETS PAST US?
YOU THINK THIS "ABOMINATION" WON'T WADE THROUGH THEM LIKE RIVERWATER?
YOU THINK THEY WON'T BLEAT LIKE GOATS AND RUN AWAY TO SAVE THEIR OWN SKINS?
LOOK, I'M HEARING THE SAME RUMORS AS YOU. TWENTY FEET TALL, FIRE BURNING IN HIS EYES, SLAUGHTERS MEN WITH A LOOK.
IT MIGHT BE TRUE, IT MIGHT BE GOAT-SHIT. YOU KNOW WHAT? IT DOESN'T MATTER.
I DON'T CARE WHO YOU ARE, A BLADE IN THE RIBS IS GOING TO PUT YOU DOWN.
SO GET READY! HOLD THE LINE!
NOBODY GETS THROUGH THIS GATE... EXCEPT THROUGH US!

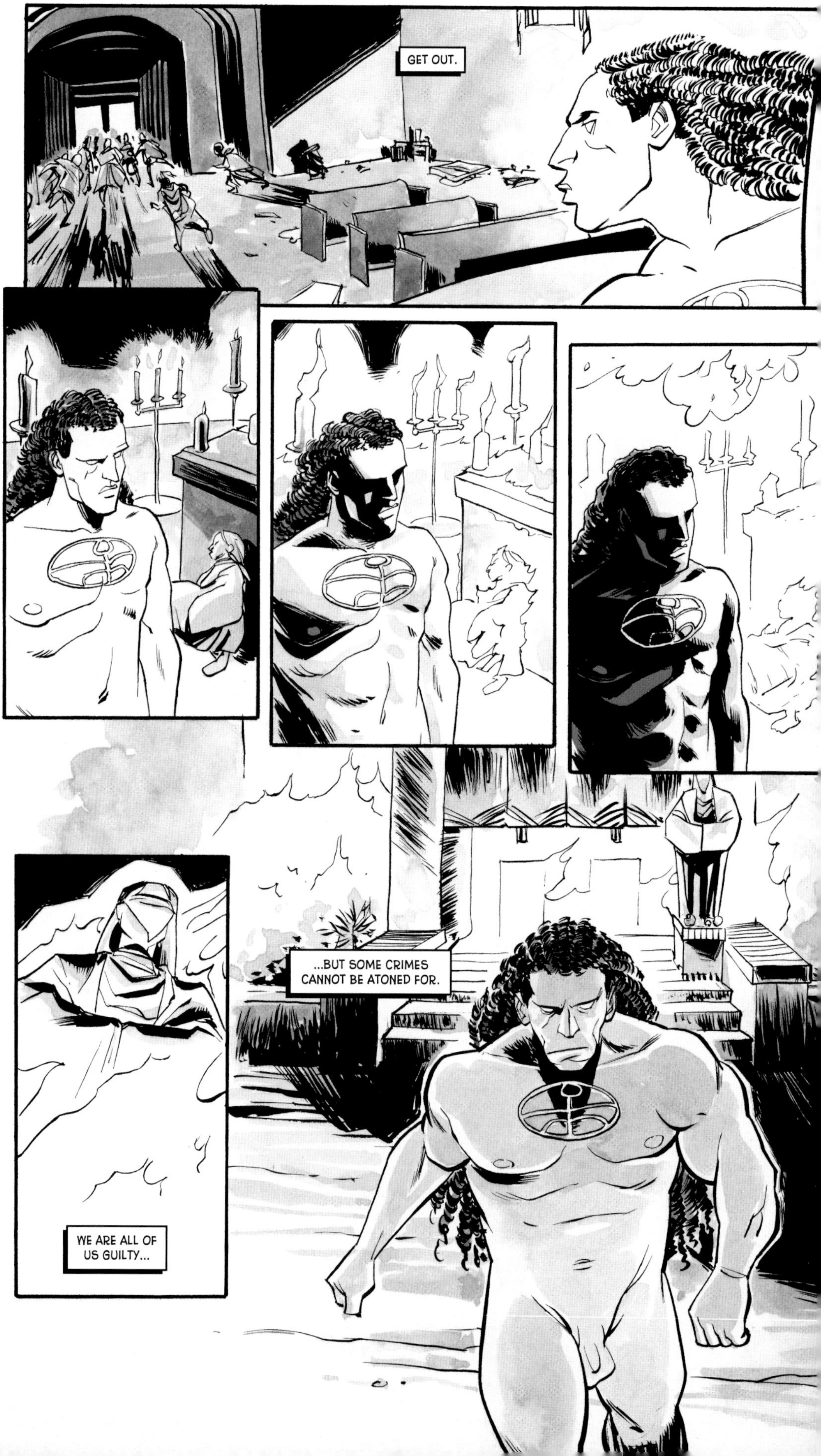
GET OUT.
WE ARE ALL OF US GUILTY...
...BUT SOME CRIMES CANNOT BE ATONED FOR.

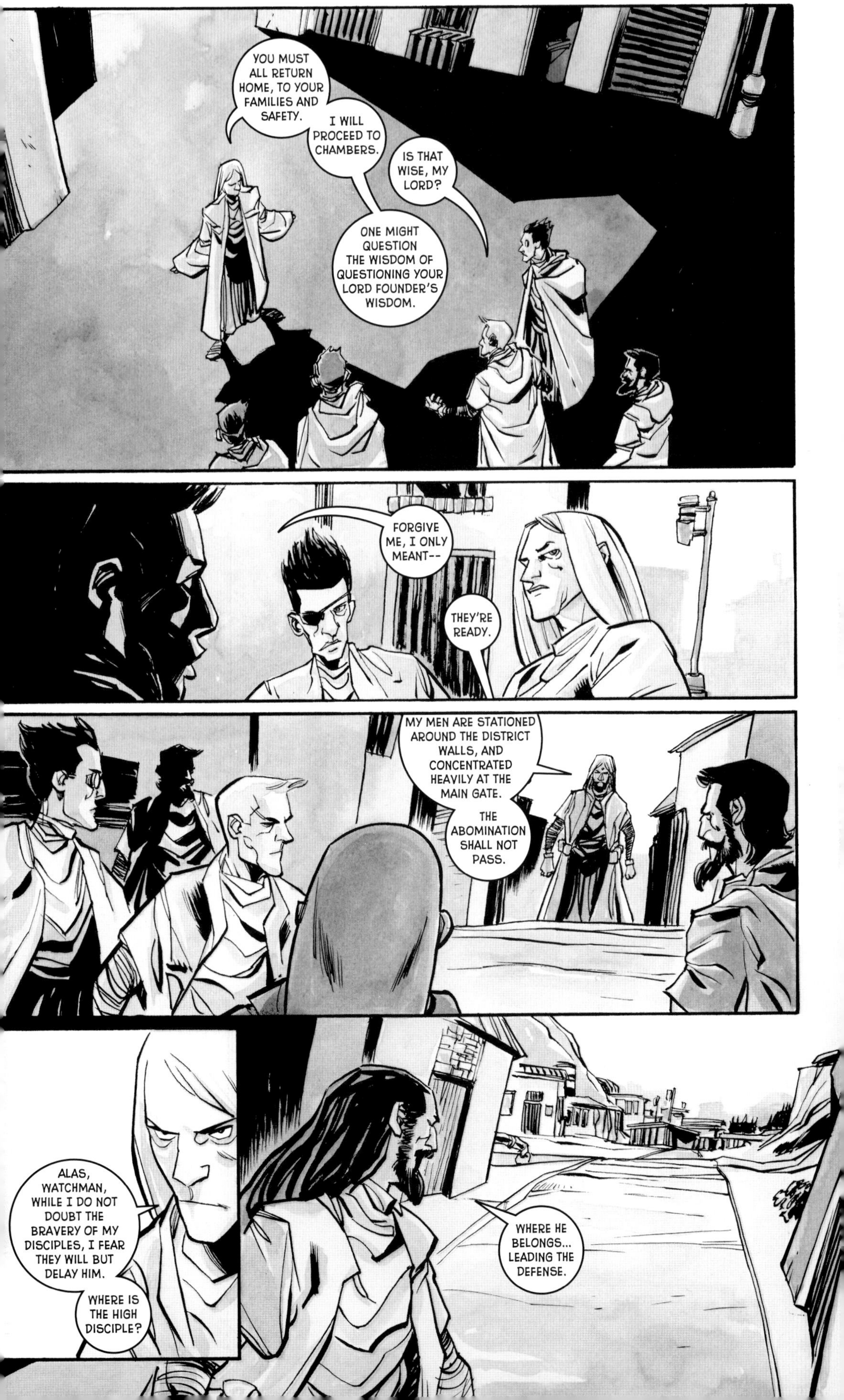
YOU MUST ALL RETURN HOME, TO YOUR FAMILIES AND SAFETY.
I WILL PROCEED TO CHAMBERS.
IS THAT WISE, MY LORD?
ONE MIGHT QUESTION THE WISDOM OF QUESTIONING YOUR LORD FOUNDER'S WISDOM.
FORGIVE ME, I ONLY MEANT--
THEY'RE READY.
MY MEN ARE STATIONED AROUND THE DISTRICT WALLS, AND CONCENTRATED HEAVILY AT THE MAIN GATE.
THE ABOMINATION SHALL NOT PASS.
ALAS, WATCHMAN, WHILE I DO NOT DOUBT THE BRAVERY OF MY DISCIPLES, I FEAR THEY WILL BUT DELAY HIM.
WHERE IS THE HIGH DISCIPLE?
WHERE HE BELONGS... LEADING THE DEFENSE.

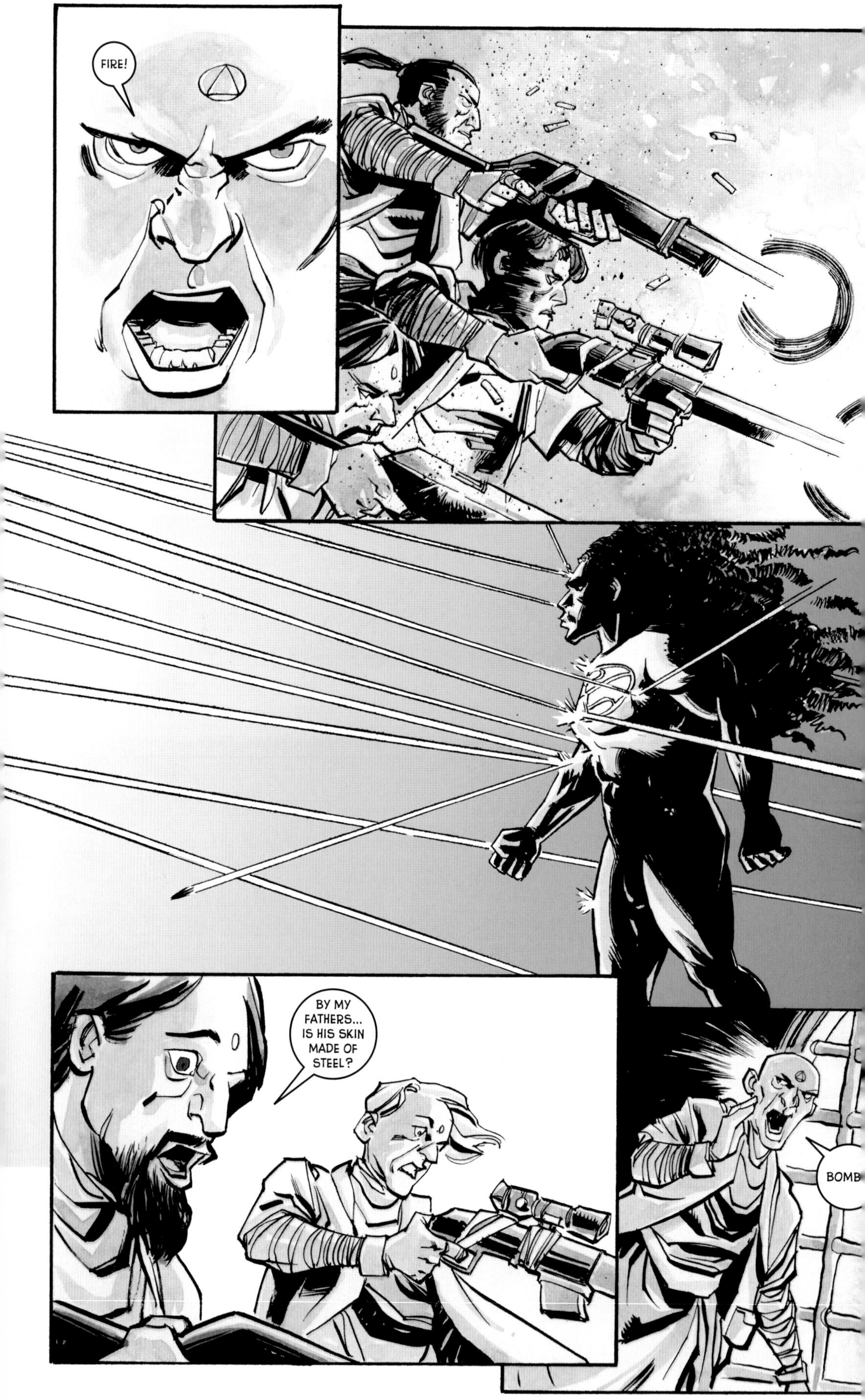
FIRE!
BY MY FATHERS... IS HIS SKIN MADE OF STEEL?
BOMB

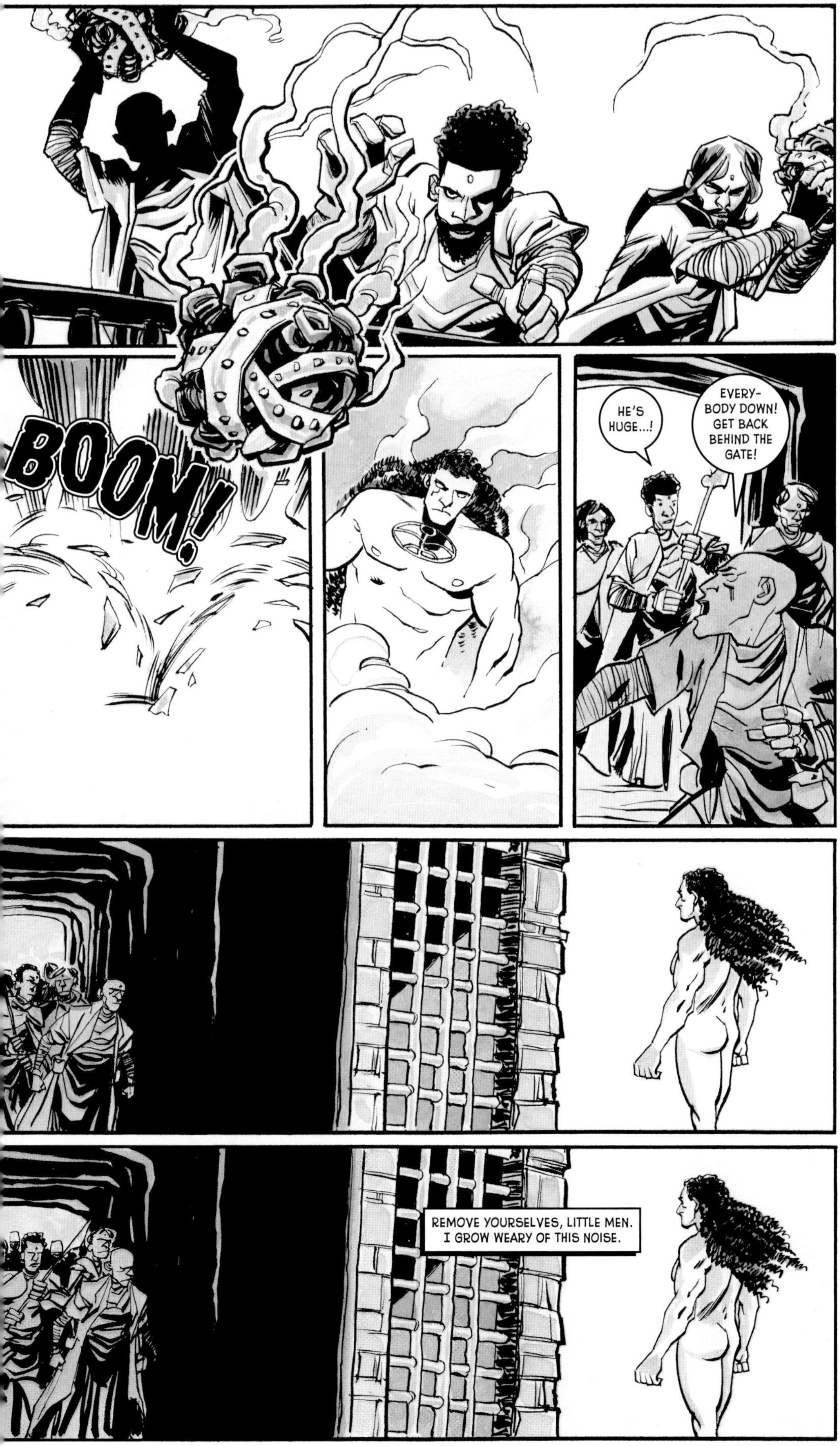
BOOM!
HE'S HUGE...!
EVERY-BODY DOWN! GET BACK BEHIND THE GATE!
REMOVE YOURSELVES, LITTLE MEN. I GROW WEARY OF THIS NOISE.

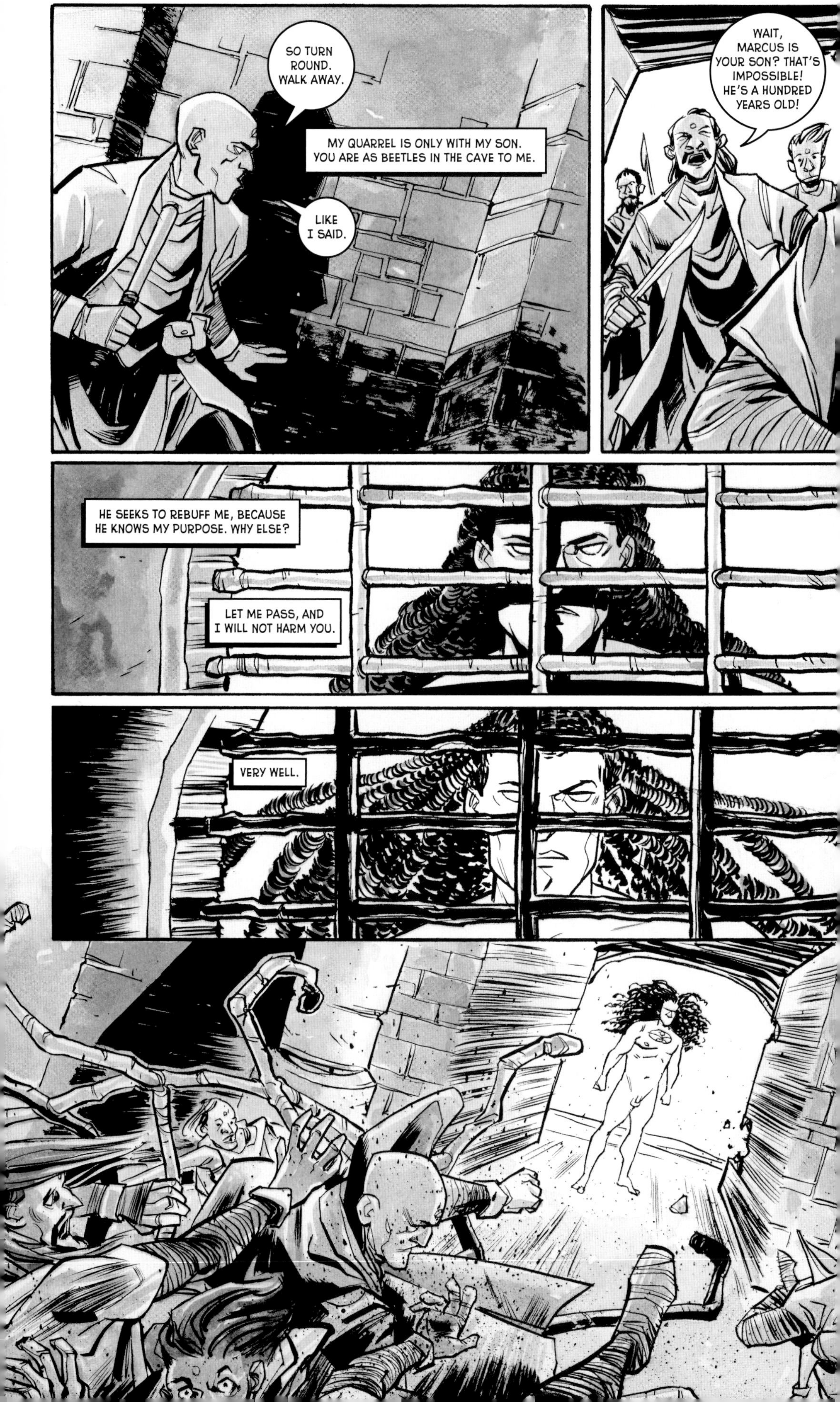
SO TURN ROUND. WALK AWAY.
MY QUARREL IS ONLY WITH MY SON. YOU ARE AS BEETLES IN THE CAVE TO ME.
LIKE I SAID.
WAIT, MARCUS IS YOUR SON? THAT'S IMPOSSIBLE! HE'S A HUNDRED YEARS OLD!
HE SEEKS TO REBUFF ME, BECAUSE HE KNOWS MY PURPOSE. WHY ELSE?
LET ME PASS, AND I WILL NOT HARM YOU.
VERY WELL.

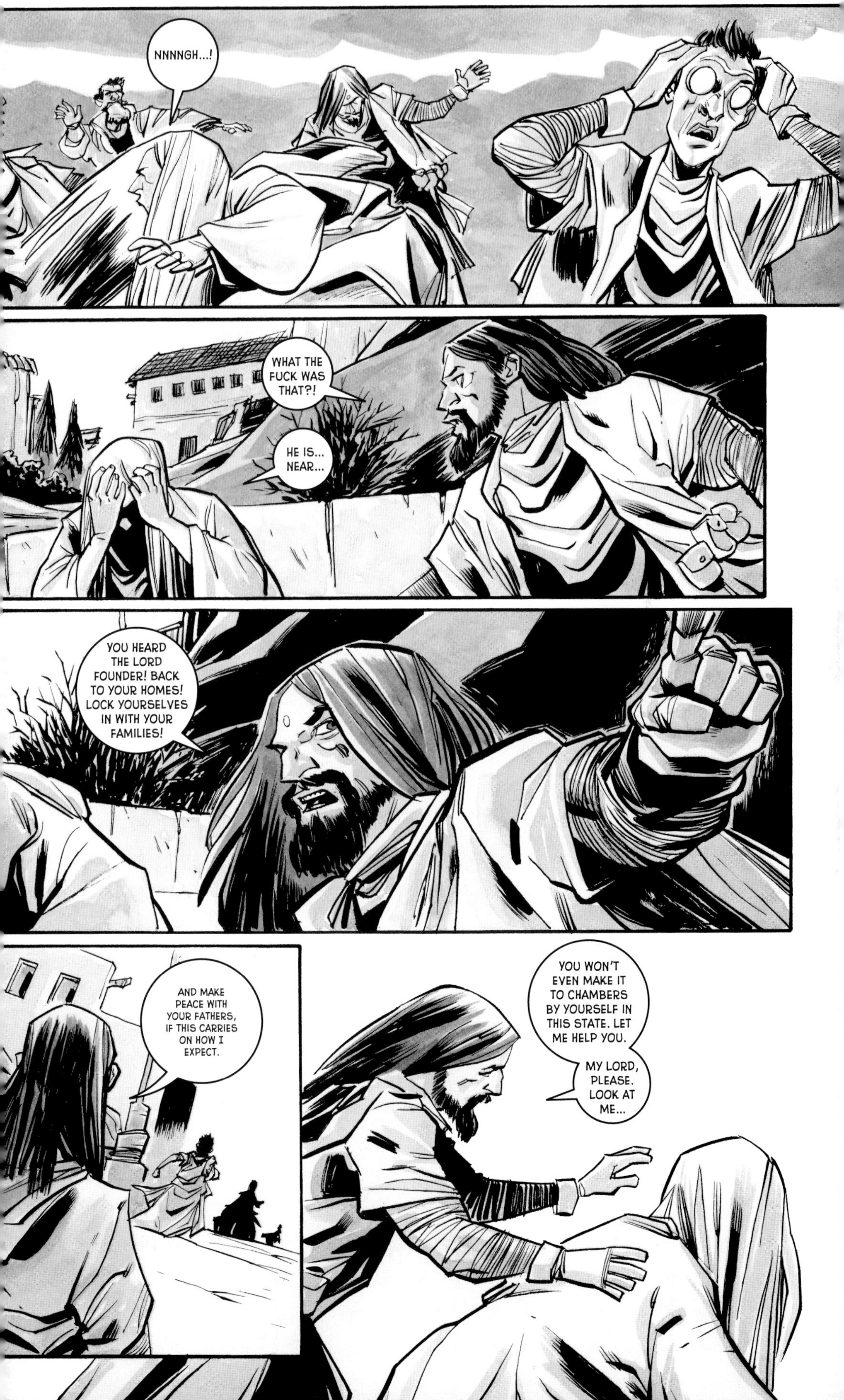
NNNNGH...!
WHAT THE FUCK WAS THAT?!
HE IS... NEAR...
YOU HEARD THE LORD FOUNDER! BACK TO YOUR HOMES! LOCK YOURSELVES IN WITH YOUR FAMILIES!
AND MAKE PEACE WITH YOUR FATHERS, IF THIS CARRIES ON HOW I EXPECT.
YOU WON'T EVEN MAKE IT TO CHAMBERS BY YOURSELF IN THIS STATE. LET ME HELP YOU.
MY LORD, PLEASE. LOOK AT ME...

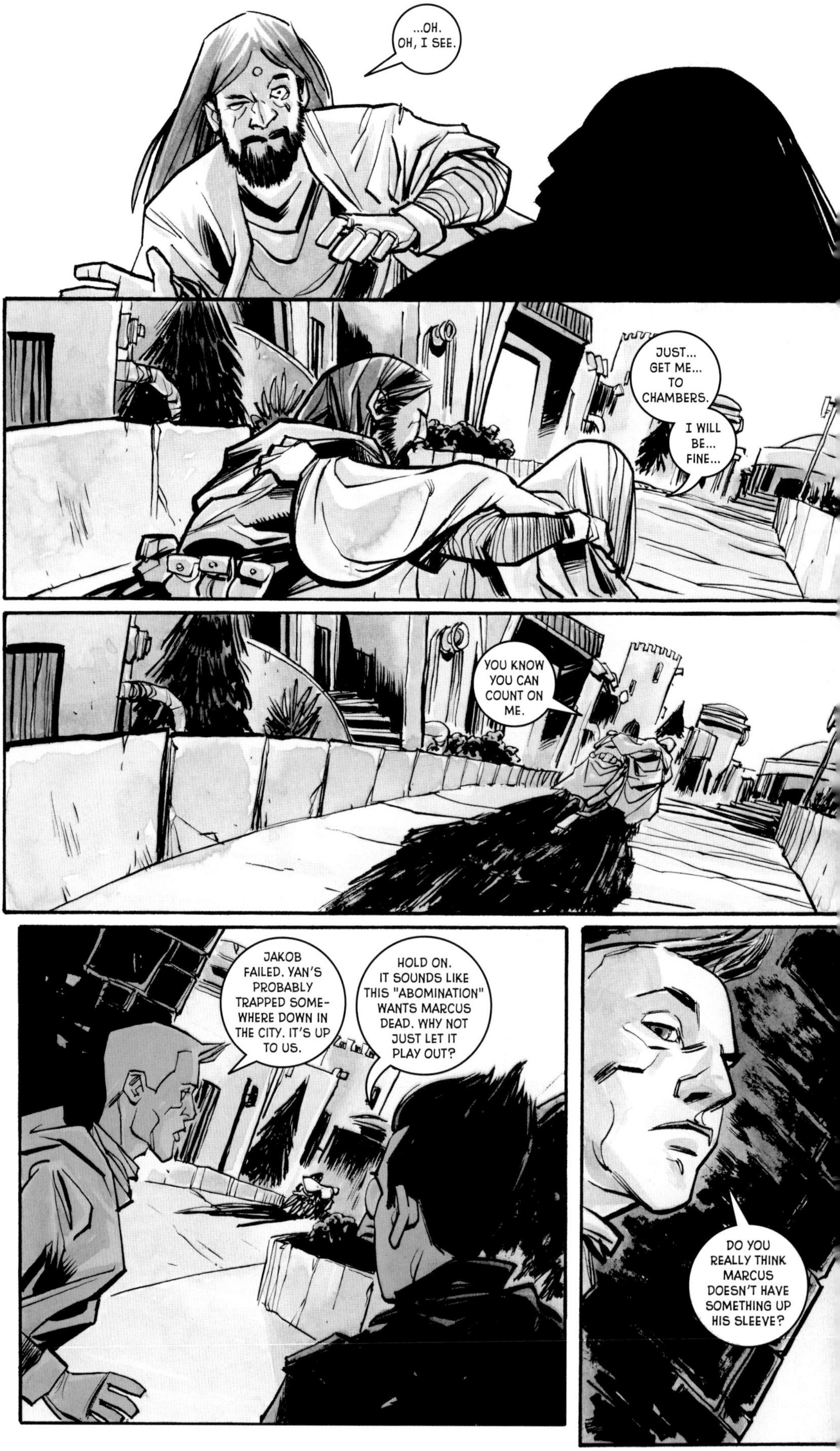
...OH. OH, I SEE.
JUST... GET ME... TO CHAMBERS.
I WILL BE... FINE...
YOU KNOW YOU CAN COUNT ON ME.
JAKOB FAILED. YAN'S PROBABLY TRAPPED SOME-WHERE DOWN IN THE CITY. IT'S UP TO US.
HOLD ON. IT SOUNDS LIKE THIS "ABOMINATION" WANTS MARCUS DEAD. WHY NOT JUST LET IT PLAY OUT?
DO YOU REALLY THINK MARCUS DOESN'T HAVE SOMETHING UP HIS SLEEVE?

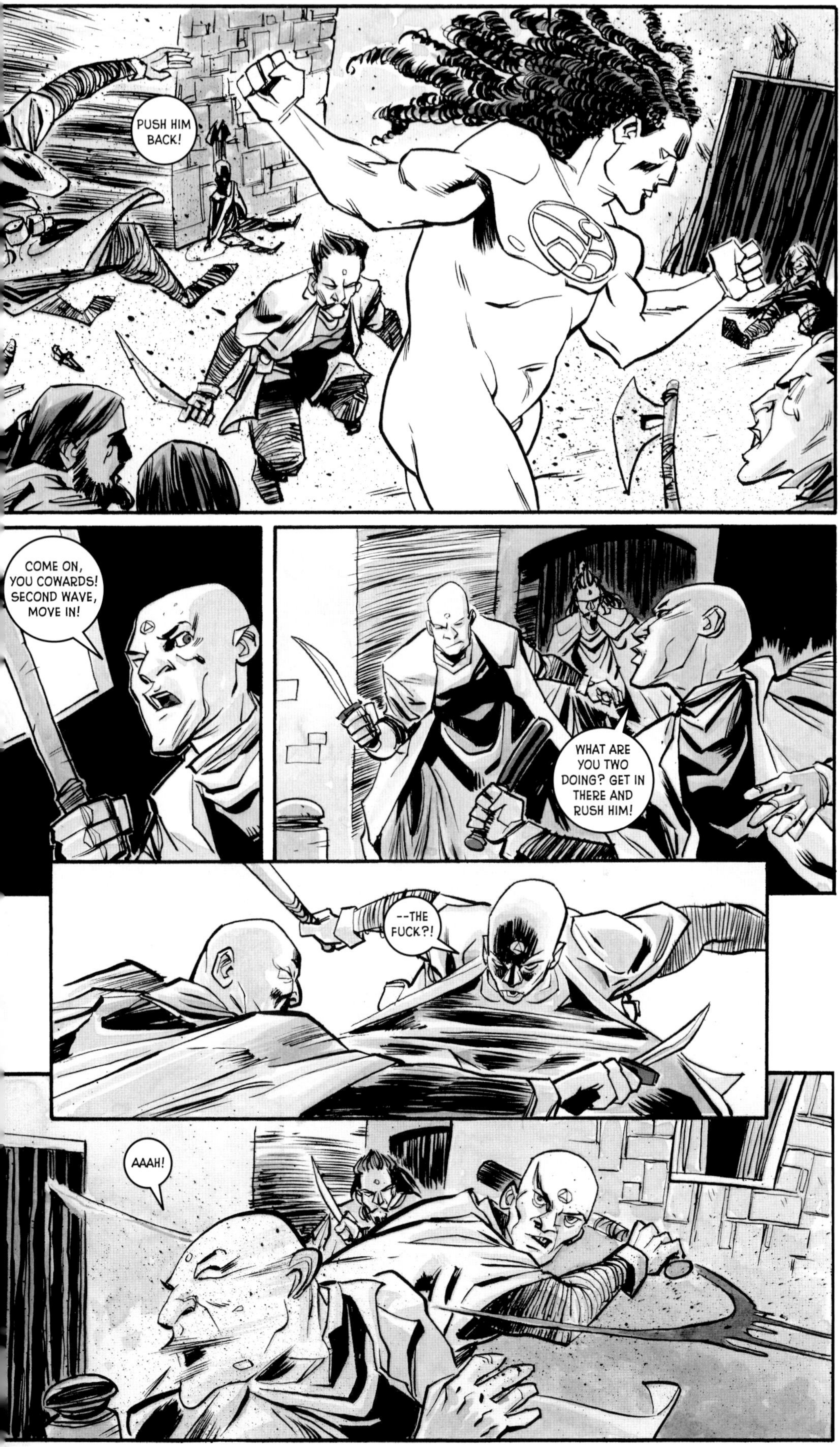
PUSH HIM BACK!
COME ON, YOU COWARDS! SECOND WAVE, MOVE IN!
WHAT ARE YOU TWO DOING? GET IN THERE AND RUSH HIM!
--THE FUCK?!
AAAH!

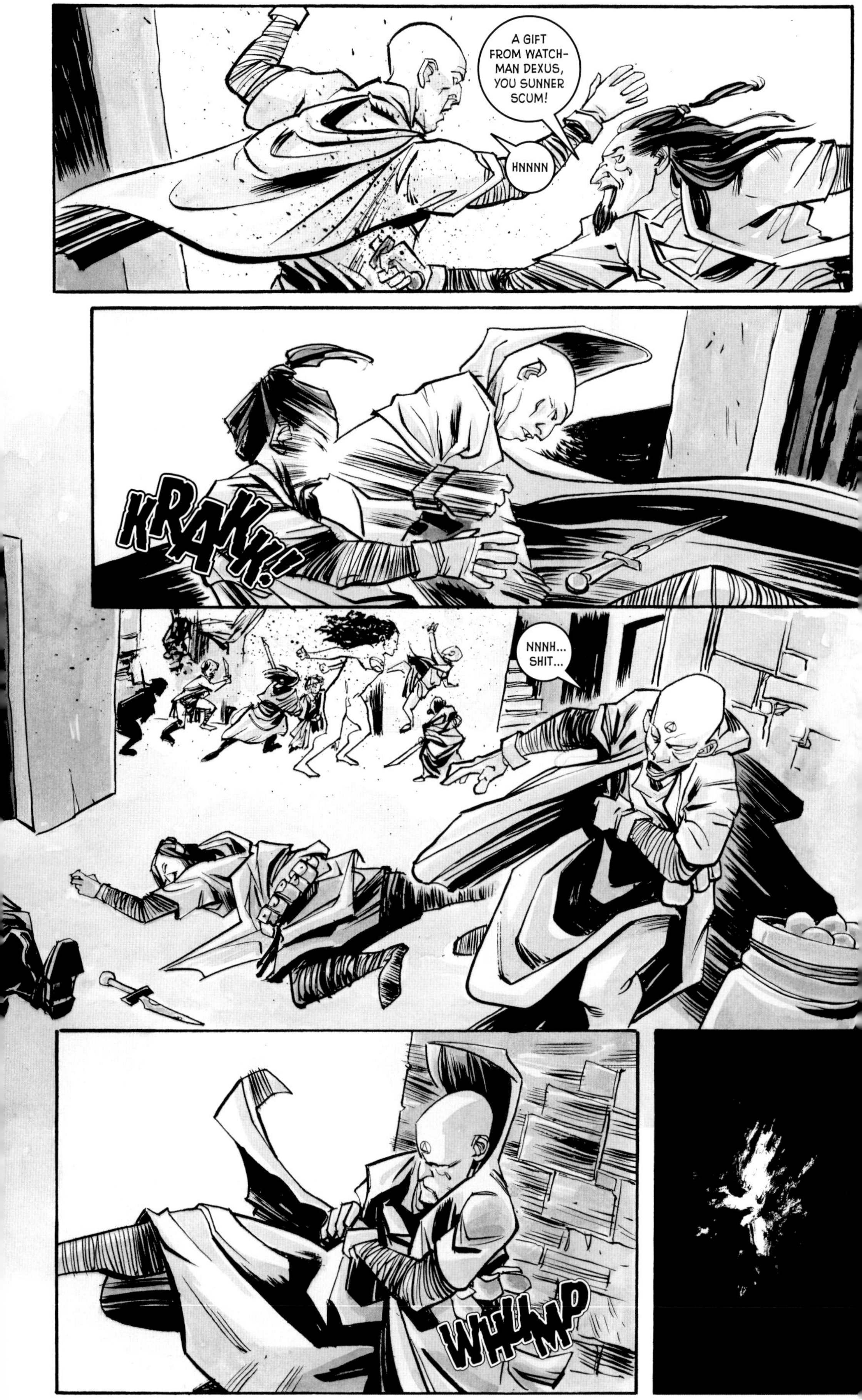

A GIFT FROM WATCH-MAN DEXUS, YOU SUNNER SCUM!
HNNNN
KRAKK!
NNNH... SHIT...
WHUMP

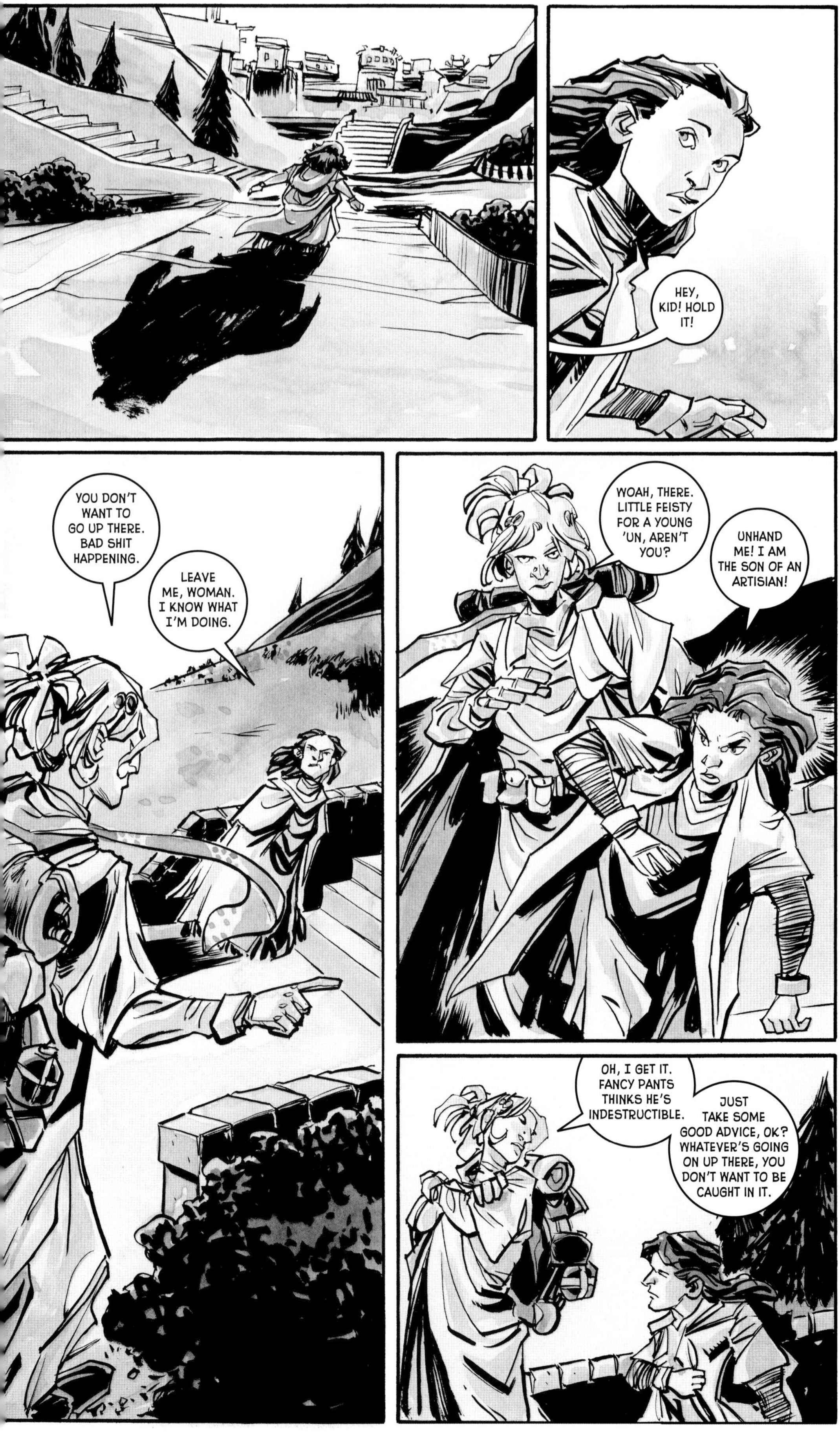
HEY, KID! HOLD IT!
YOU DON'T WANT TO GO UP THERE. BAD SHIT HAPPENING.
LEAVE ME, WOMAN. I KNOW WHAT I'M DOING.
WOAH, THERE. LITTLE FEISTY FOR A YOUNG 'UN, AREN'T YOU?
UNHAND ME! I AM THE SON OF AN ARTISIAN!
OH, I GET IT. FANCY PANTS THINKS HE'S INDESTRUCTIBLE.
JUST TAKE SOME GOOD ADVICE, OK? WHATEVER'S GOING ON UP THERE, YOU DON'T WANT TO BE CAUGHT IN IT.

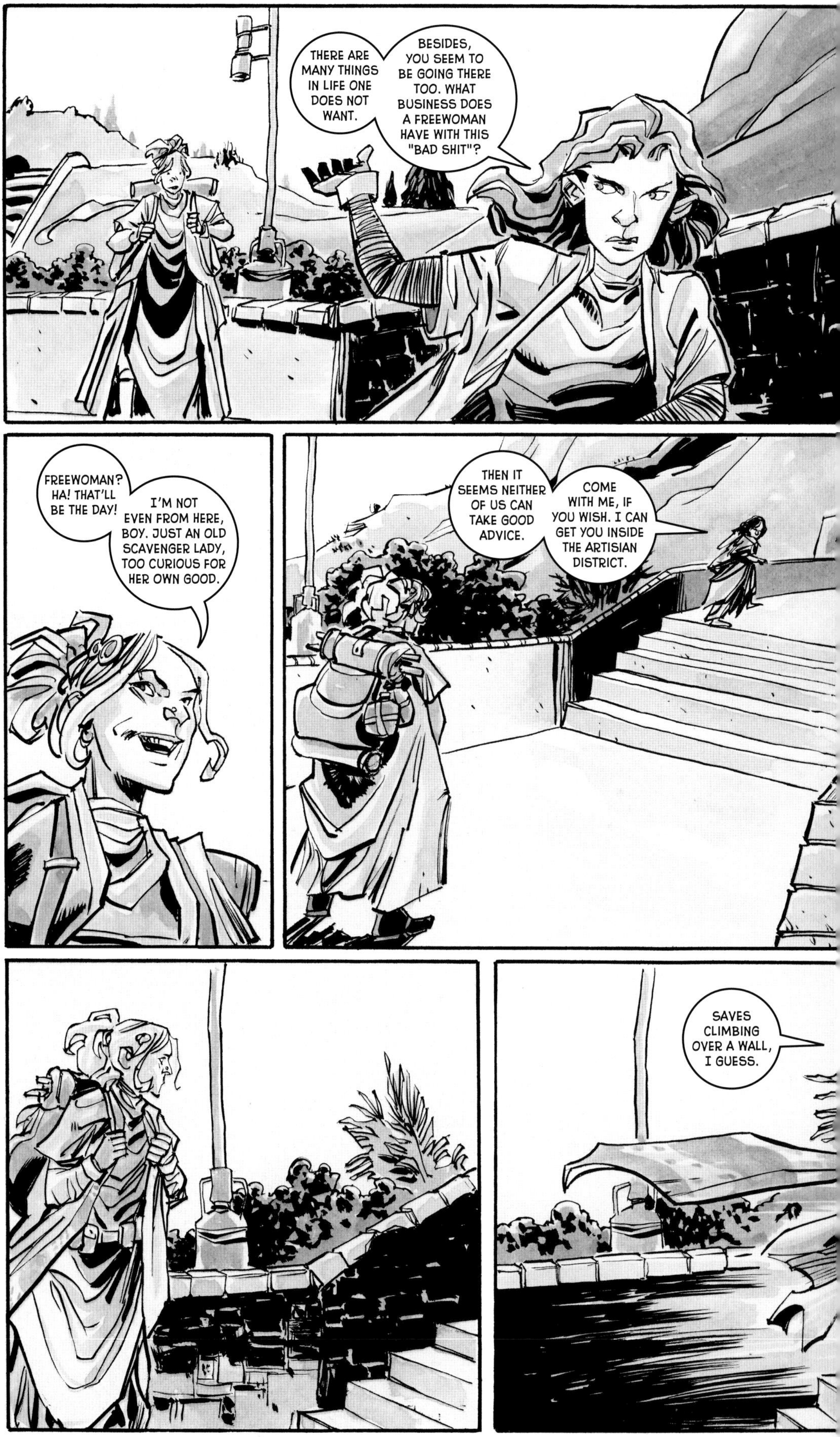
THERE ARE MANY THINGS IN LIFE ONE DOES NOT WANT.
BESIDES, YOU SEEM TO BE GOING THERE TOO. WHAT BUSINESS DOES A FREEWOMAN HAVE WITH THIS "BAD SHIT"?
FREEWOMAN? HA! THAT'LL BE THE DAY!
I'M NOT EVEN FROM HERE, BOY. JUST AN OLD SCAVENGER LADY, TOO CURIOUS FOR HER OWN GOOD.
THEN IT SEEMS NEITHER OF US CAN TAKE GOOD ADVICE.
COME WITH ME, IF YOU WISH. I CAN GET YOU INSIDE THE ARTISIAN DISTRICT.
SAVES CLIMBING OVER A WALL, I GUESS.

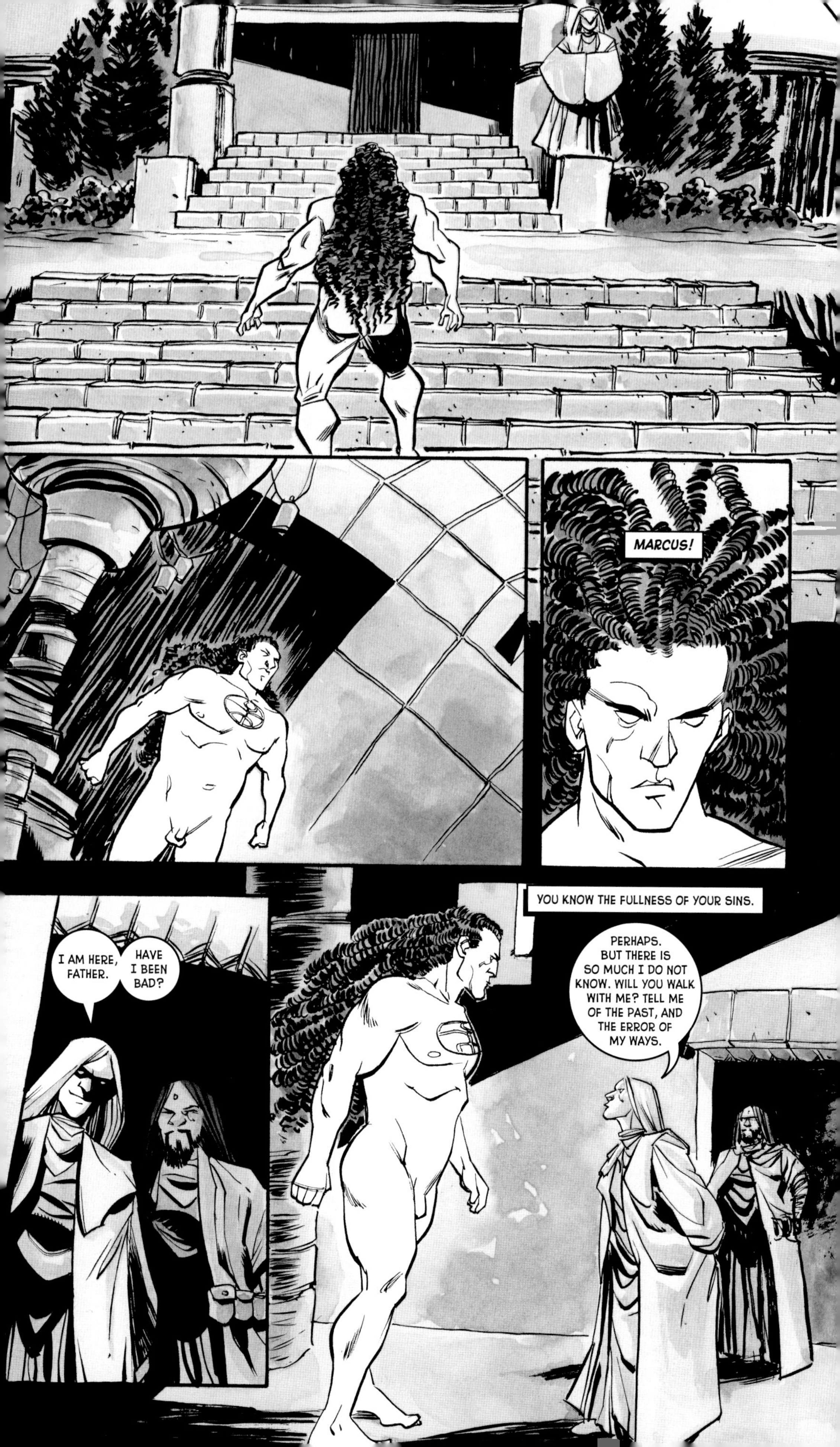
MARCUS!
YOU KNOW THE FULLNESS OF YOUR SINS.
I AM HERE, FATHER.
HAVE I BEEN BAD?
PERHAPS. BUT THERE IS SO MUCH I DO NOT KNOW. WILL YOU WALK WITH ME? TELL ME OF THE PAST, AND THE ERROR OF MY WAYS.

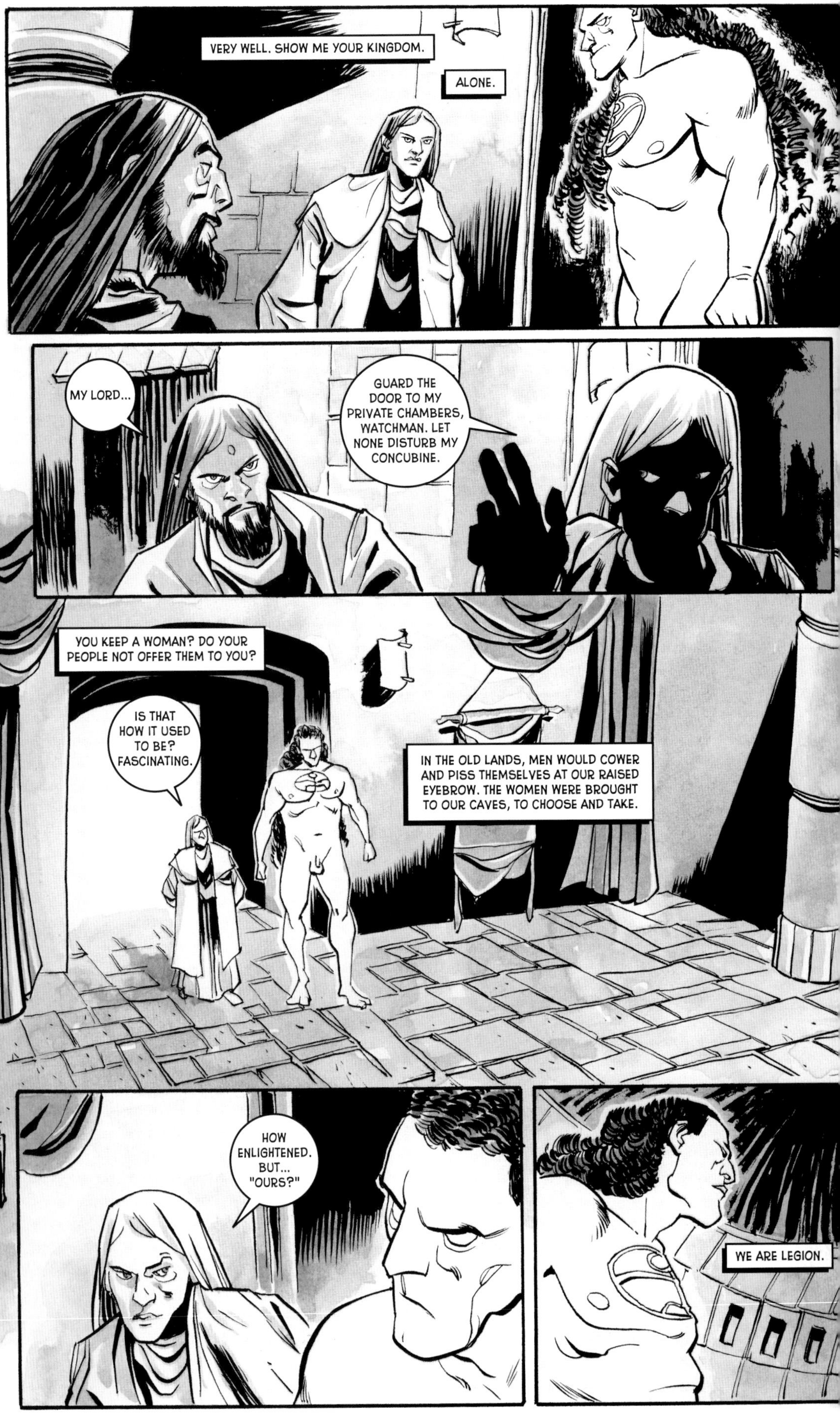
VERY WELL. SHOW ME YOUR KINGDOM.
ALONE.
MY LORD...
GUARD THE DOOR TO MY PRIVATE CHAMBERS, WATCHMAN. LET NONE DISTURB MY CONCUBINE.
YOU KEEP A WOMAN? DO YOUR PEOPLE NOT OFFER THEM TO YOU?
IS THAT HOW IT USED TO BE? FASCINATING.
IN THE OLD LANDS, MEN WOULD COWER AND PISS THEMSELVES AT OUR RAISED EYEBROW. THE WOMEN WERE BROUGHT TO OUR CAVES, TO CHOOSE AND TAKE.
HOW ENLIGHTENED. BUT... "OURS?"
WE ARE LEGION.

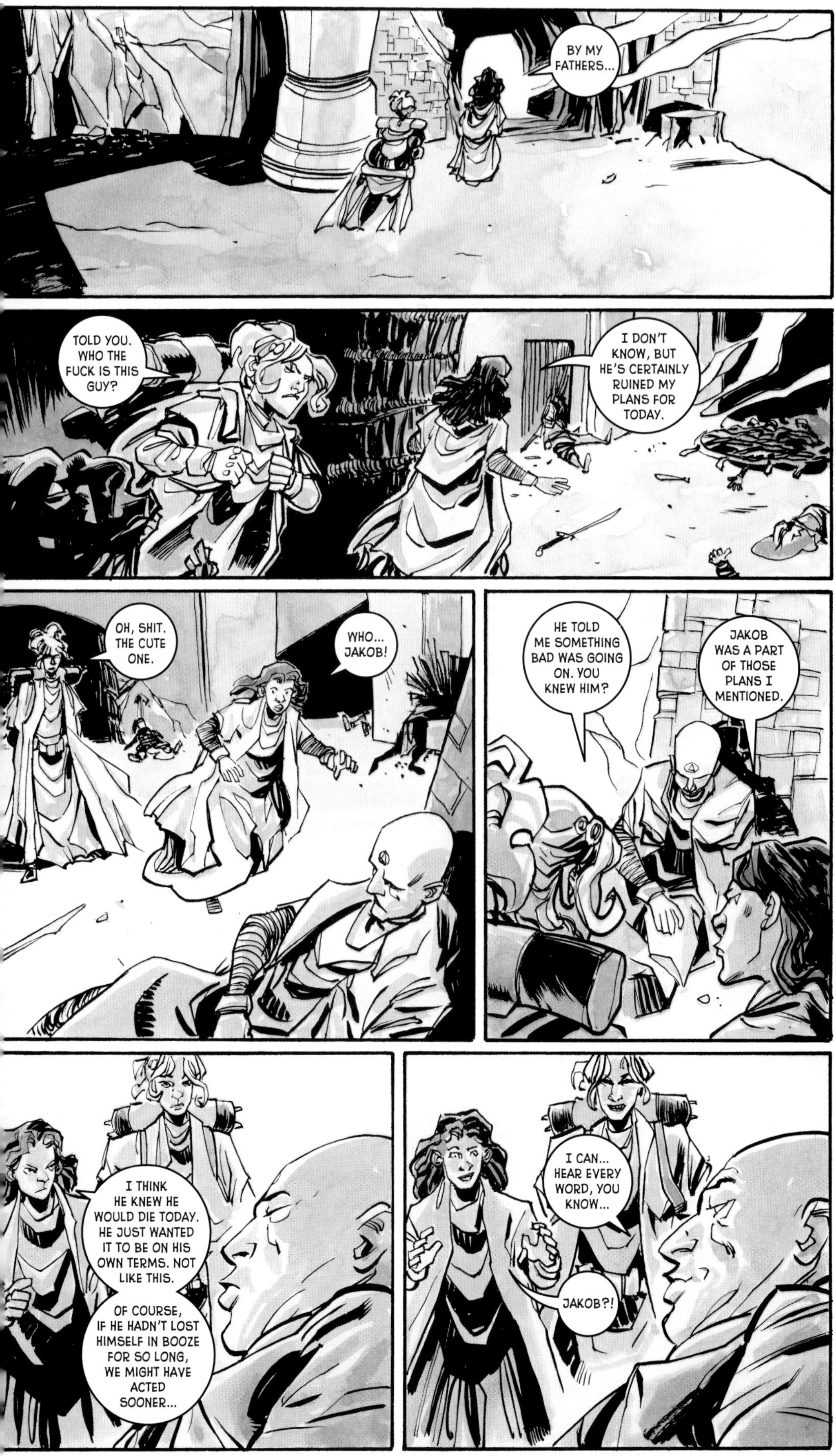

BY MY FATHERS...
TOLD YOU. WHO THE FUCK IS THIS GUY?
I DON'T KNOW, BUT HE'S CERTAINLY RUINED MY PLANS FOR TODAY.
OH, SHIT. THE CUTE ONE.
WHO... JAKOB!
HE TOLD ME SOMETHING BAD WAS GOING ON. YOU KNEW HIM?
JAKOB WAS A PART OF THOSE PLANS I MENTIONED.
I THINK HE KNEW HE WOULD DIE TODAY. HE JUST WANTED IT TO BE ON HIS OWN TERMS. NOT LIKE THIS.
OF COURSE, IF HE HADN'T LOST HIMSELF IN BOOZE FOR SO LONG, WE MIGHT HAVE ACTED SOONER...
I CAN... HEAR EVERY WORD, YOU KNOW...
JAKOB?!

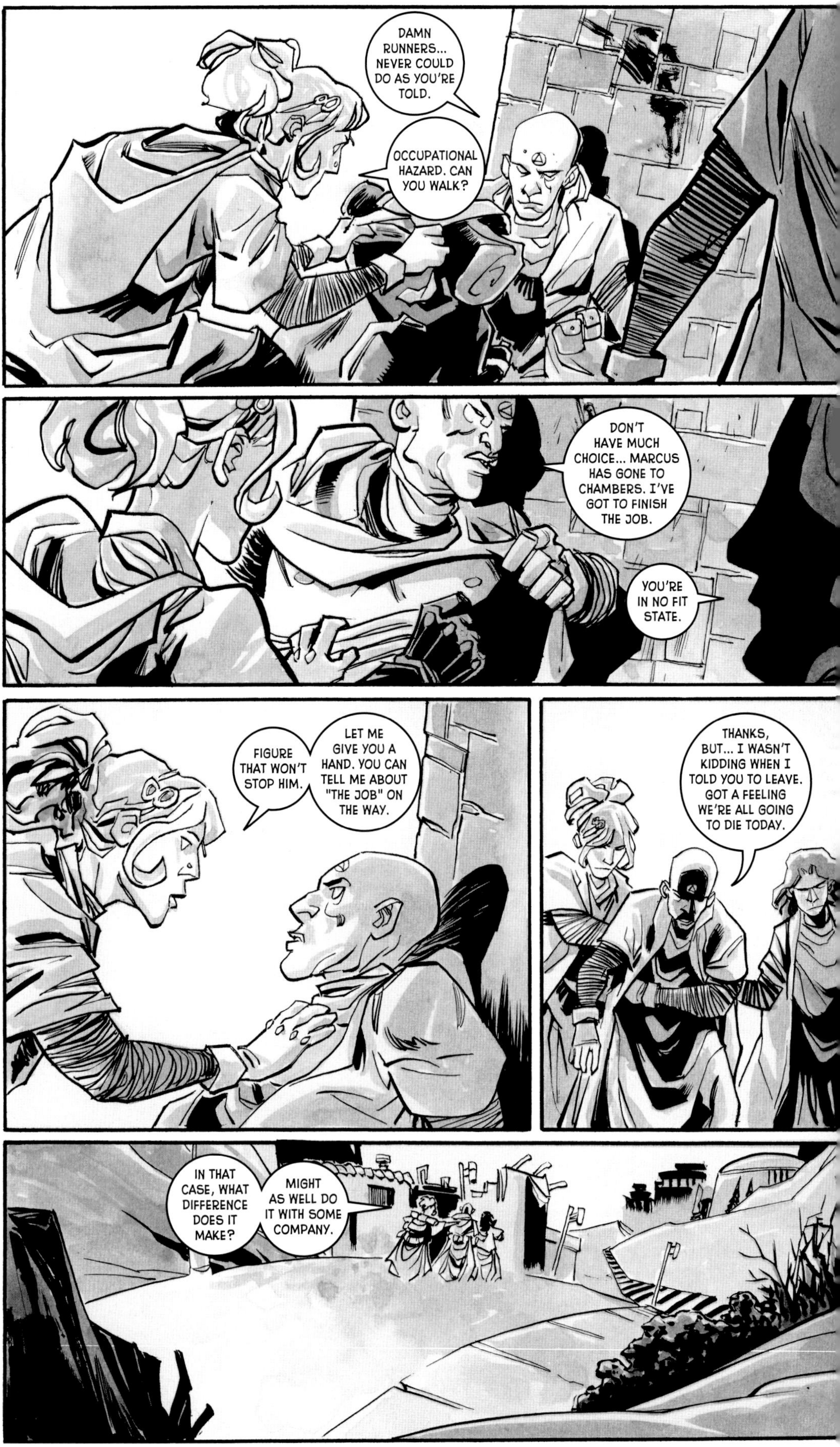
DAMN RUNNERS... NEVER COULD DO AS YOU'RE TOLD.
OCCUPATIONAL HAZARD. CAN YOU WALK?
DON'T HAVE MUCH CHOICE... MARCUS HAS GONE TO CHAMBERS. I'VE GOT TO FINISH THE JOB.
YOU'RE IN NO FIT STATE.
FIGURE THAT WON'T STOP HIM.
LET ME GIVE YOU A HAND. YOU CAN TELL ME ABOUT "THE JOB" ON THE WAY.
THANKS, BUT... I WASN'T KIDDING WHEN I TOLD YOU TO LEAVE. GOT A FEELING WE'RE ALL GOING TO DIE TODAY.
IN THAT CASE, WHAT DIFFERENCE DOES IT MAKE?
MIGHT AS WELL DO IT WITH SOME COMPANY.

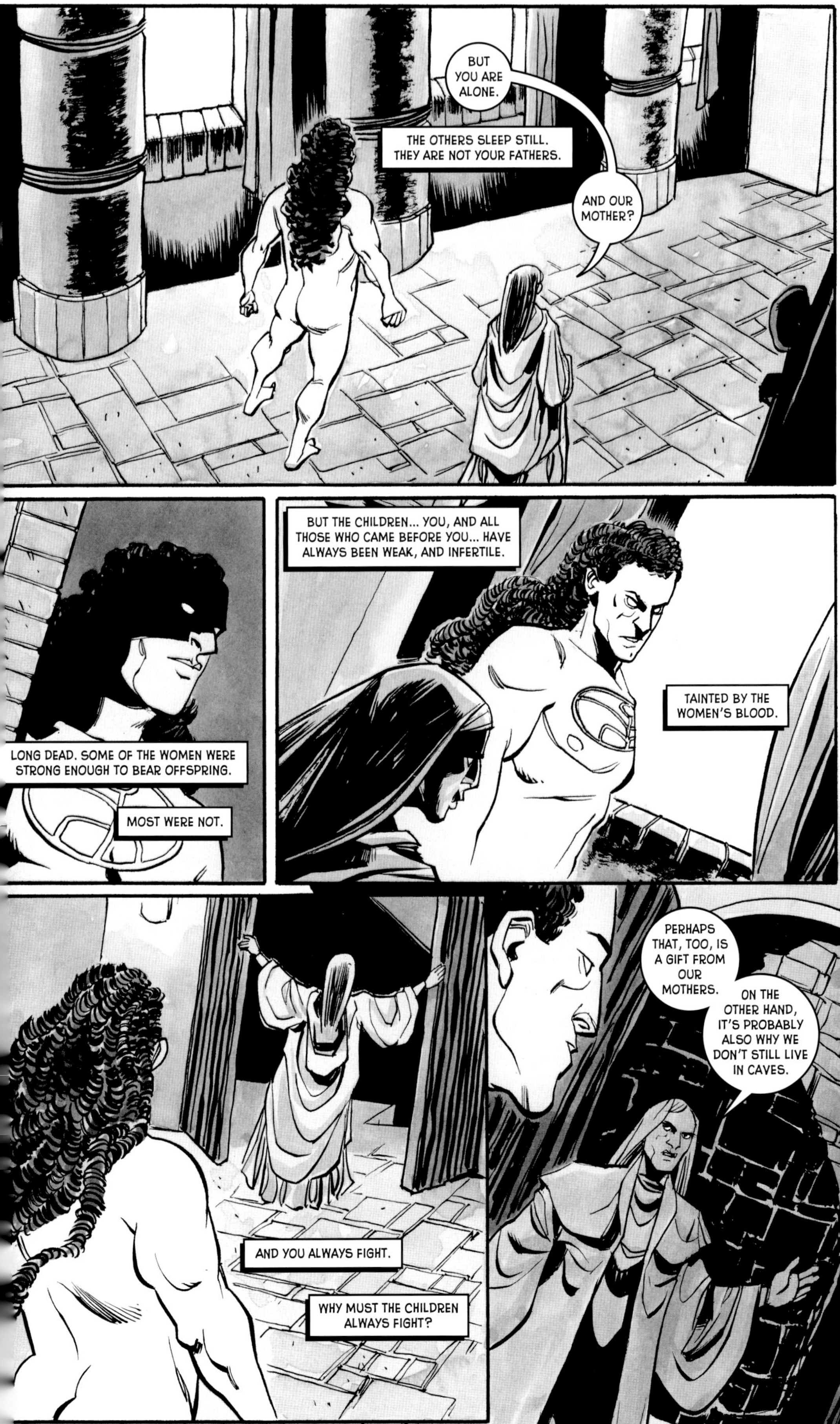
BUT YOU ARE ALONE.
THE OTHERS SLEEP STILL. THEY ARE NOT YOUR FATHERS.
AND OUR MOTHER?
LONG DEAD. SOME OF THE WOMEN WERE STRONG ENOUGH TO BEAR OFFSPRING.
MOST WERE NOT.
BUT THE CHILDREN... YOU, AND ALL THOSE WHO CAME BEFORE YOU... HAVE ALWAYS BEEN WEAK, AND INFERTILE.
TAINTED BY THE WOMEN'S BLOOD.
AND YOU ALWAYS FIGHT.
WHY MUST THE CHILDREN ALWAYS FIGHT?
PERHAPS THAT, TOO, IS A GIFT FROM OUR MOTHERS.
ON THE OTHER HAND, IT'S PROBABLY ALSO WHY WE DON'T STILL LIVE IN CAVES.

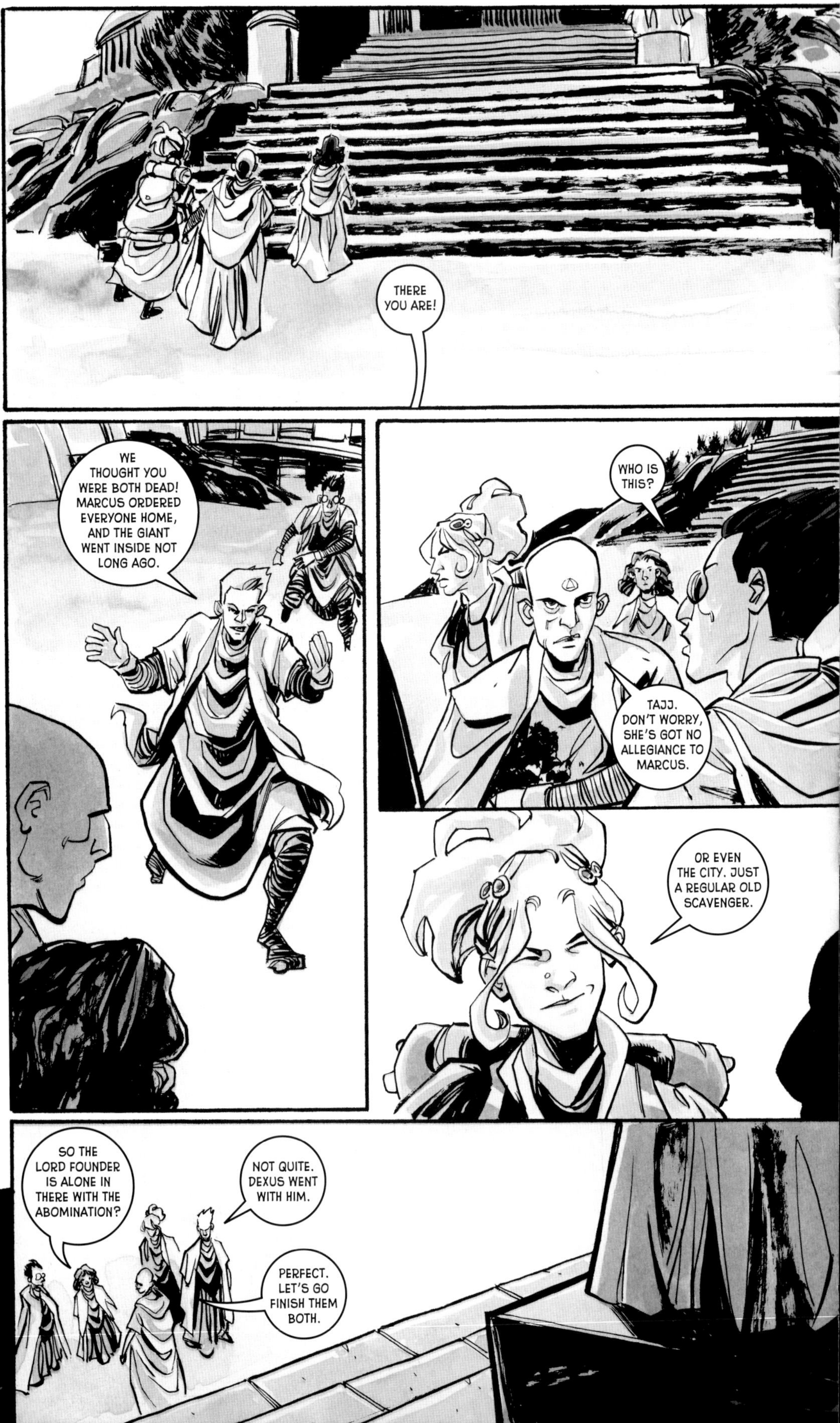
THERE YOU ARE!
WE THOUGHT YOU WERE BOTH DEAD! MARCUS ORDERED EVERYONE HOME, AND THE GIANT WENT INSIDE NOT LONG AGO.
WHO IS THIS?
TAJJ. DON'T WORRY, SHE'S GOT NO ALLEGIANCE TO MARCUS.
OR EVEN THE CITY. JUST A REGULAR OLD SCAVENGER.
SO THE LORD FOUNDER IS ALONE IN THERE WITH THE ABOMINATION?
NOT QUITE. DEXUS WENT WITH HIM.
PERFECT. LET'S GO FINISH THEM BOTH.

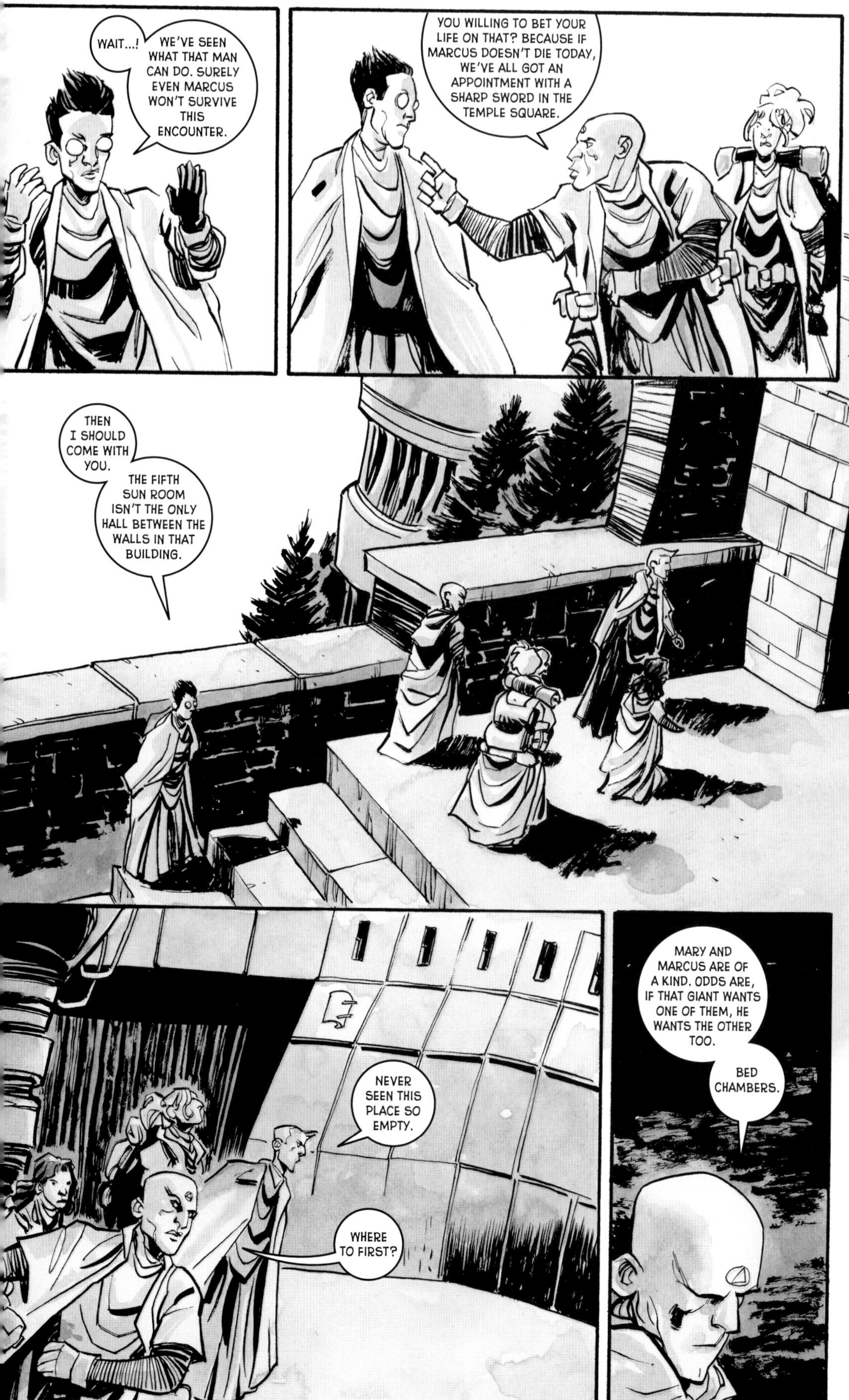
WAIT...!
WE'VE SEEN WHAT THAT MAN CAN DO. SURELY EVEN MARCUS WON'T SURVIVE THIS ENCOUNTER.
YOU WILLING TO BET YOUR LIFE ON THAT? BECAUSE IF MARCUS DOESN'T DIE TODAY, WE'VE ALL GOT AN APPOINTMENT WITH A SHARP SWORD IN THE TEMPLE SQUARE.
THEN I SHOULD COME WITH YOU.
THE FIFTH SUN ROOM ISN'T THE ONLY HALL BETWEEN THE WALLS IN THAT BUILDING.
NEVER SEEN THIS PLACE SO EMPTY.
WHERE TO FIRST?
MARY AND MARCUS ARE OF A KIND. ODDS ARE, IF THAT GIANT WANTS ONE OF THEM, HE WANTS THE OTHER TOO.
BED CHAMBERS.

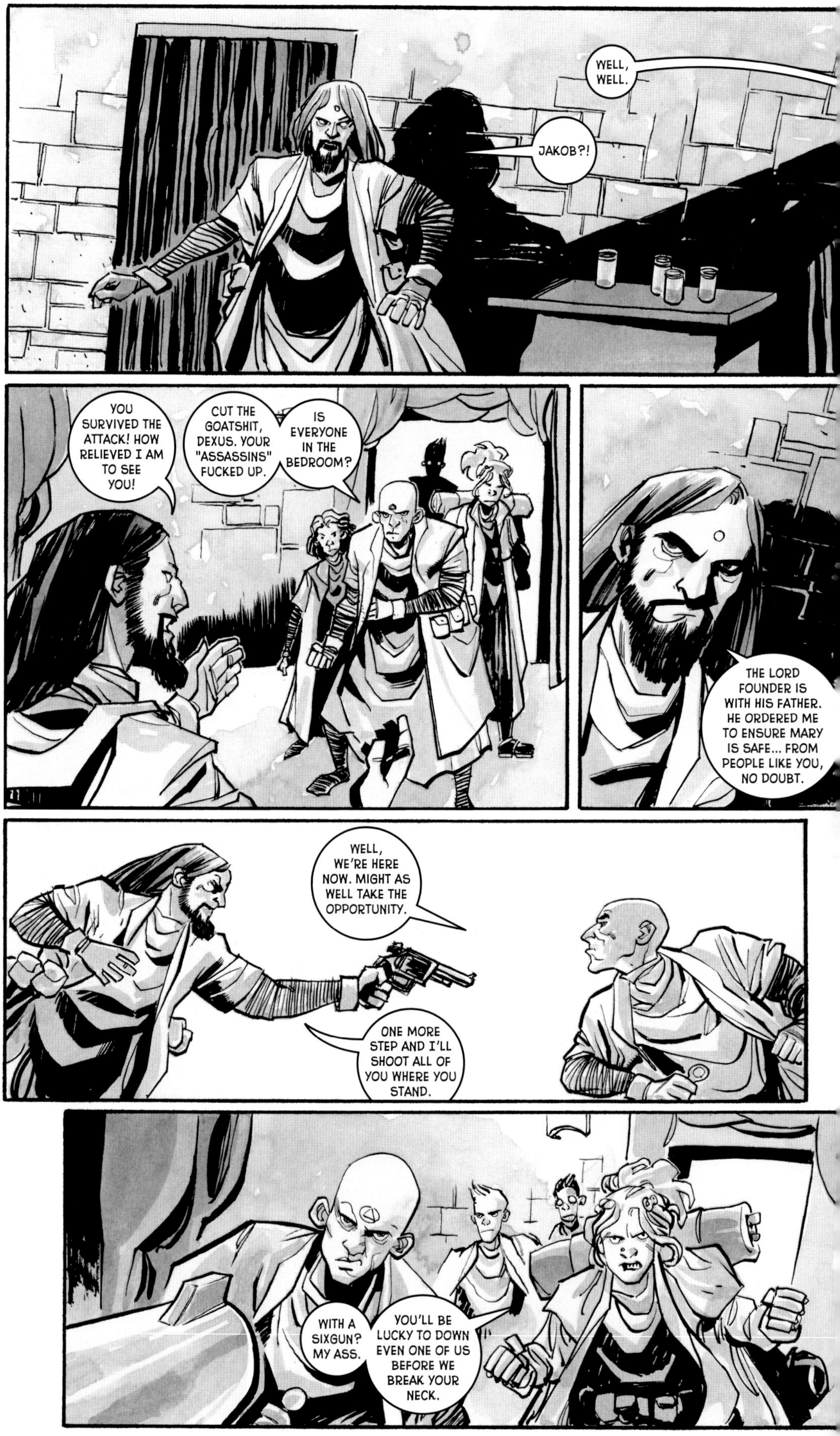
WELL, WELL.
JAKOB?!
YOU SURVIVED THE ATTACK! HOW RELIEVED I AM TO SEE YOU!
CUT THE GOATSHIT, DEXUS. YOUR "ASSASSINS" FUCKED UP.
IS EVERYONE IN THE BEDROOM?
THE LORD FOUNDER IS WITH HIS FATHER. HE ORDERED ME TO ENSURE MARY IS SAFE... FROM PEOPLE LIKE YOU, NO DOUBT.
WELL, WE'RE HERE NOW. MIGHT AS WELL TAKE THE OPPORTUNITY.
ONE MORE STEP AND I'LL SHOOT ALL OF YOU WHERE YOU STAND.
WITH A SIXGUN? MY ASS.
YOU'LL BE LUCKY TO DOWN EVEN ONE OF US BEFORE WE BREAK YOUR NECK.

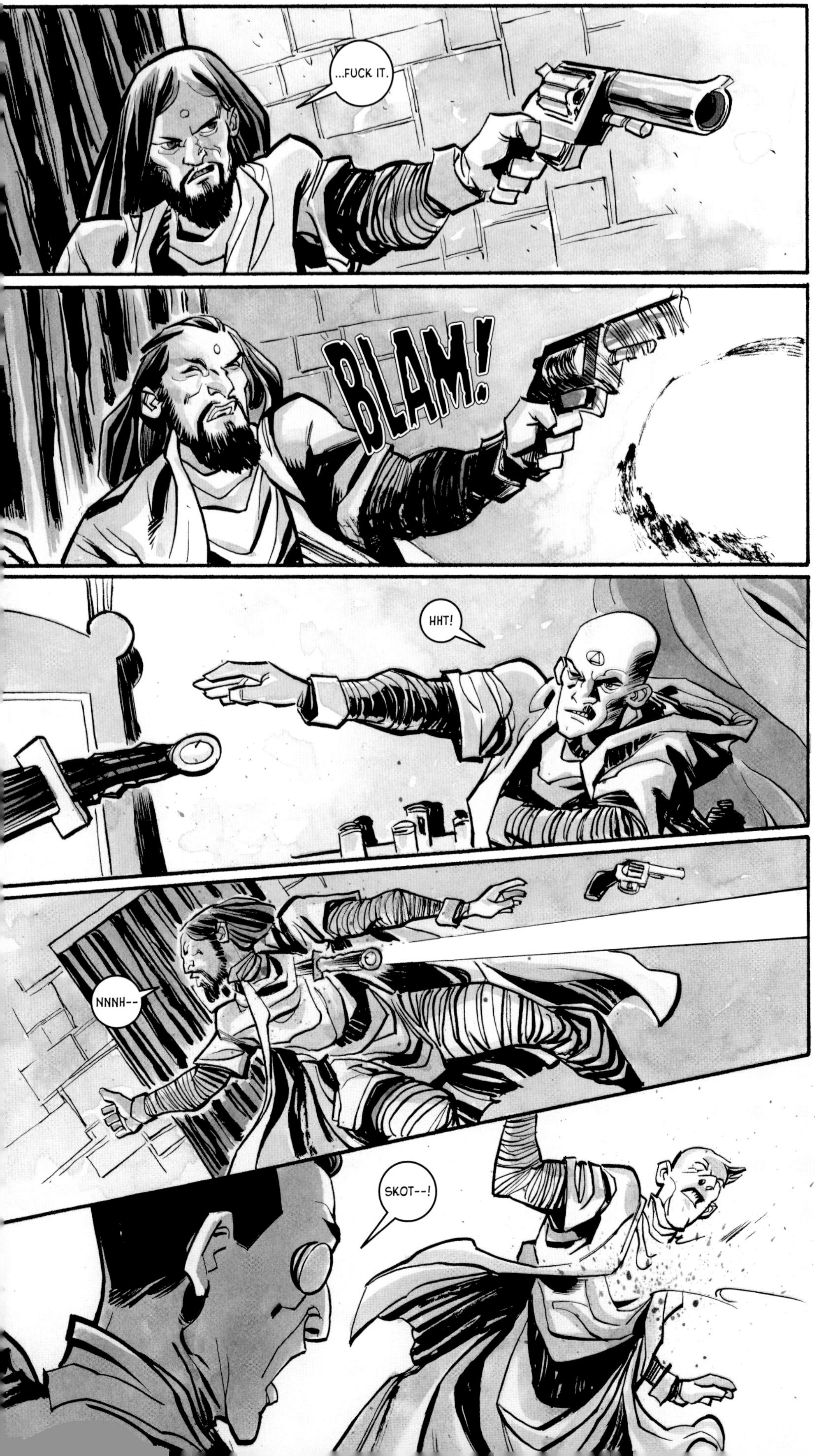
...FUCK IT.
BLAM!
HHT!
NNNH--
SKOT--!

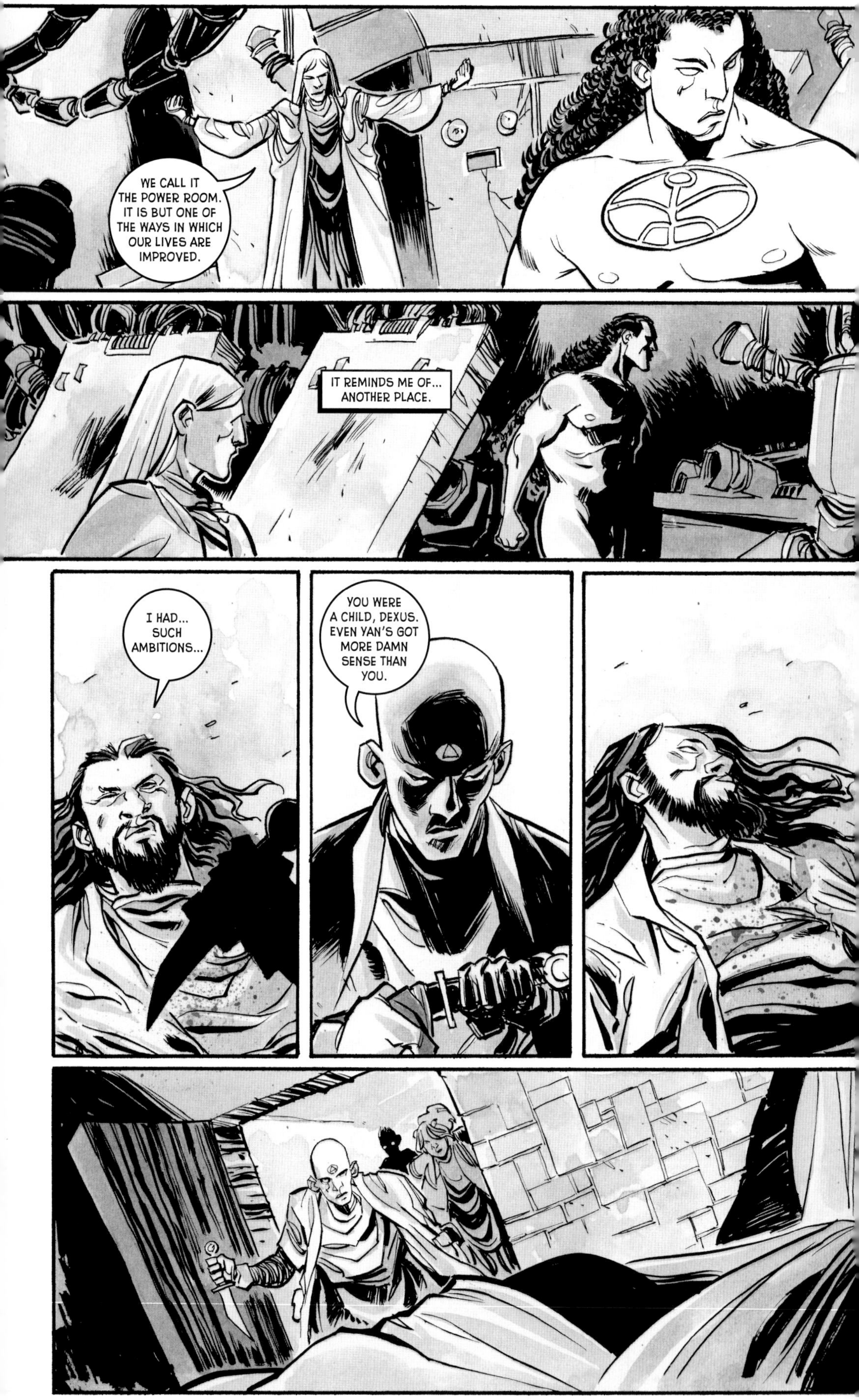
WE CALL IT THE POWER ROOM. IT IS BUT ONE OF THE WAYS IN WHICH OUR LIVES ARE IMPROVED.
IT REMINDS ME OF... ANOTHER PLACE.
I HAD... SUCH AMBITIONS...
YOU WERE A CHILD, DEXUS. EVEN YAN'S GOT MORE DAMN SENSE THAN YOU.

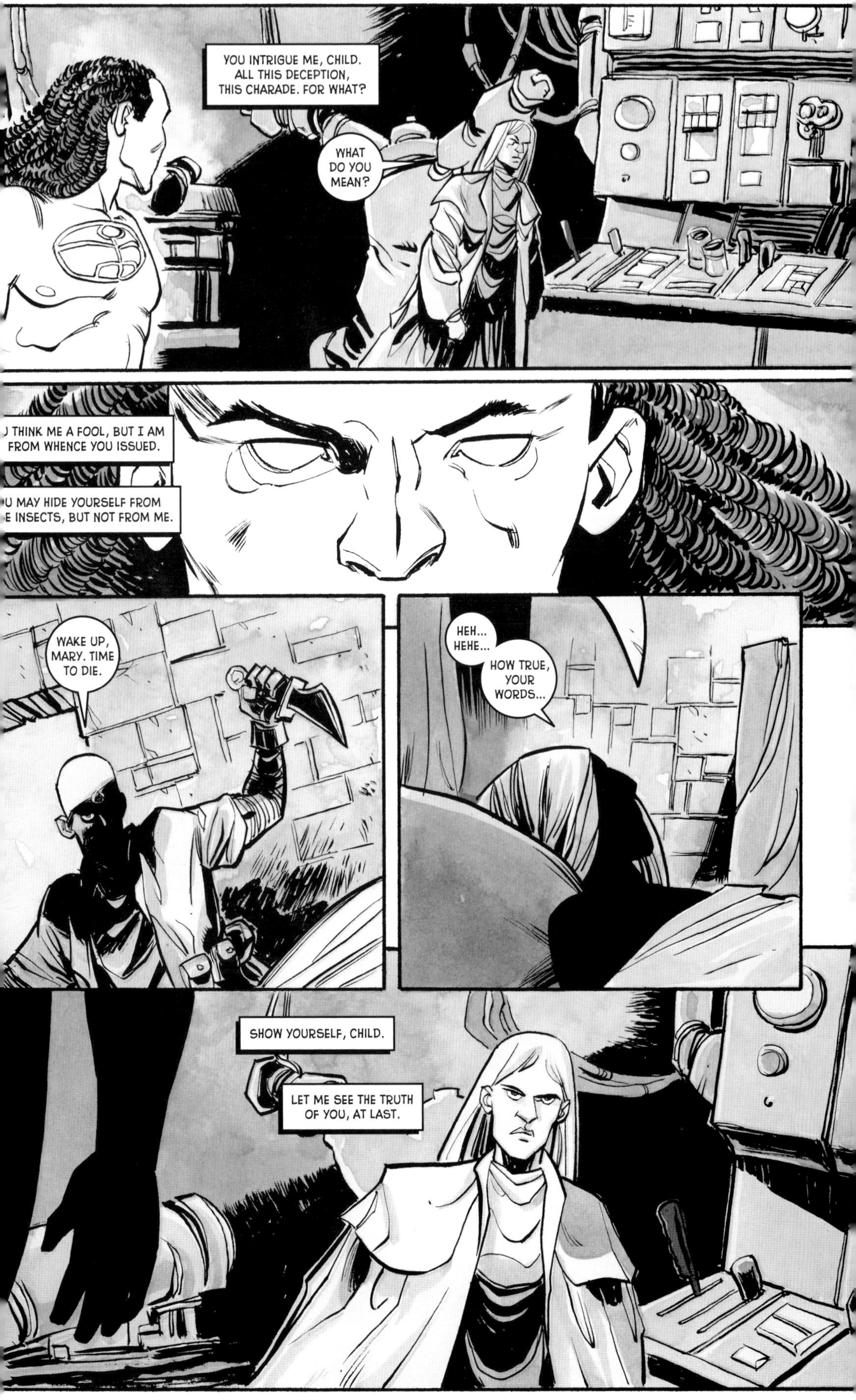
YOU INTRIGUE ME, CHILD. ALL THIS DECEPTION, THIS CHARADE. FOR WHAT?
WHAT DO YOU MEAN?
U THINK ME A FOOL, BUT I AM FROM WHENCE YOU ISSUED.
U MAY HIDE YOURSELF FROM E INSECTS, BUT NOT FROM ME.
WAKE UP, MARY. TIME TO DIE.
HEH... HEHE...
HOW TRUE, YOUR WORDS...
SHOW YOURSELF, CHILD.
LET ME SEE THE TRUTH OF YOU, AT LAST.

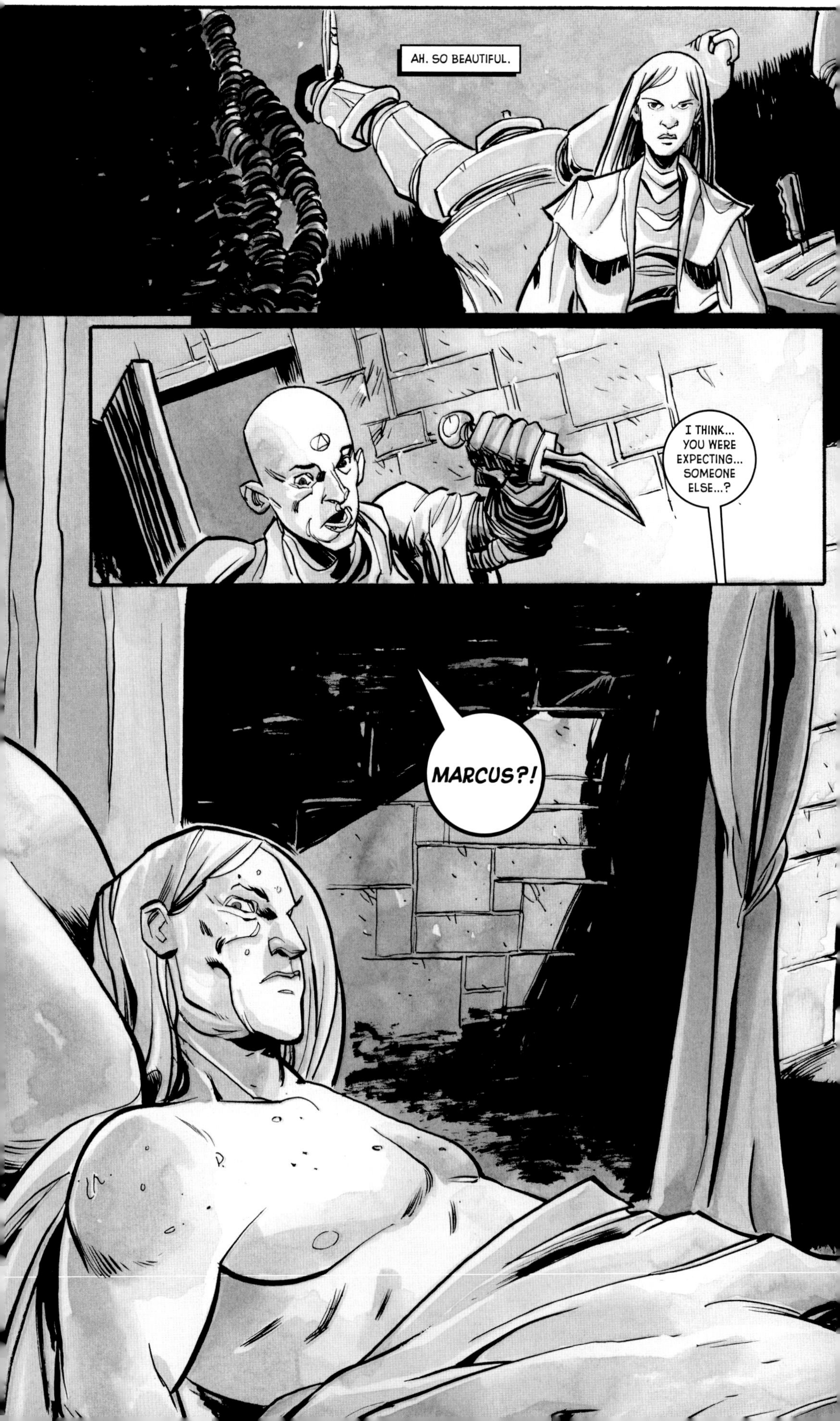
AH. SO BEAUTIFUL.
I THINK... YOU WERE EXPECTING... SOMEONE ELSE...?
MARCUS?!

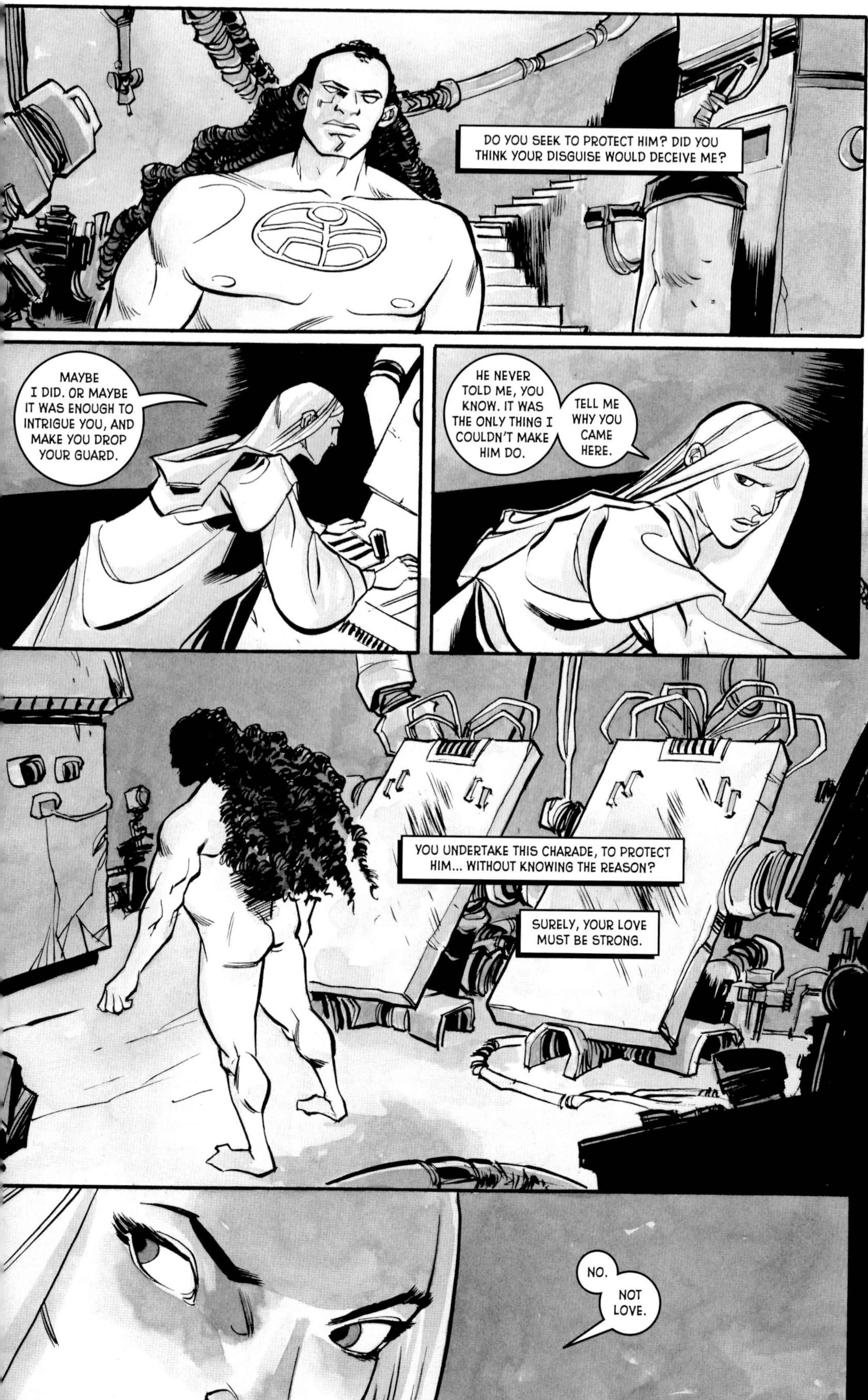
DO YOU SEEK TO PROTECT HIM? DID YOU THINK YOUR DISGUISE WOULD DECEIVE ME?
MAYBE I DID. OR MAYBE IT WAS ENOUGH TO INTRIGUE YOU, AND MAKE YOU DROP YOUR GUARD.
HE NEVER TOLD ME, YOU KNOW. IT WAS THE ONLY THING I COULDN'T MAKE HIM DO.
TELL ME WHY YOU CAME HERE.
YOU UNDERTAKE THIS CHARADE, TO PROTECT HIM... WITHOUT KNOWING THE REASON?
SURELY, YOUR LOVE MUST BE STRONG.
NO.
NOT LOVE.

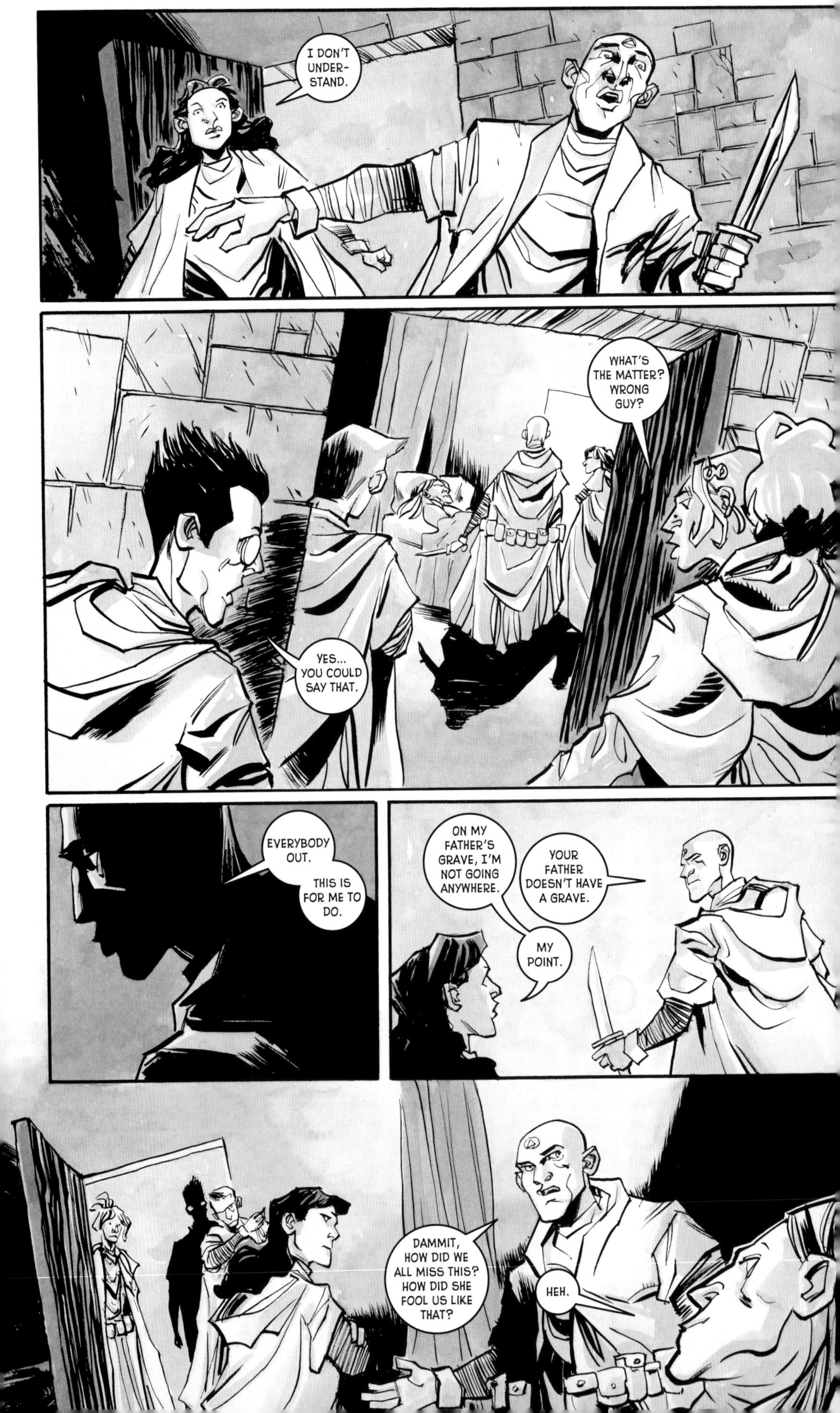
I DON'T UNDER-STAND.
WHAT'S THE MATTER? WRONG GUY?
YES... YOU COULD SAY THAT.
EVERYBODY OUT.
THIS IS FOR ME TO DO.
ON MY FATHER'S GRAVE, I'M NOT GOING ANYWHERE.
YOUR FATHER DOESN'T HAVE A GRAVE.
MY POINT.
DAMMIT, HOW DID WE ALL MISS THIS? HOW DID SHE FOOL US LIKE THAT?
HEH.

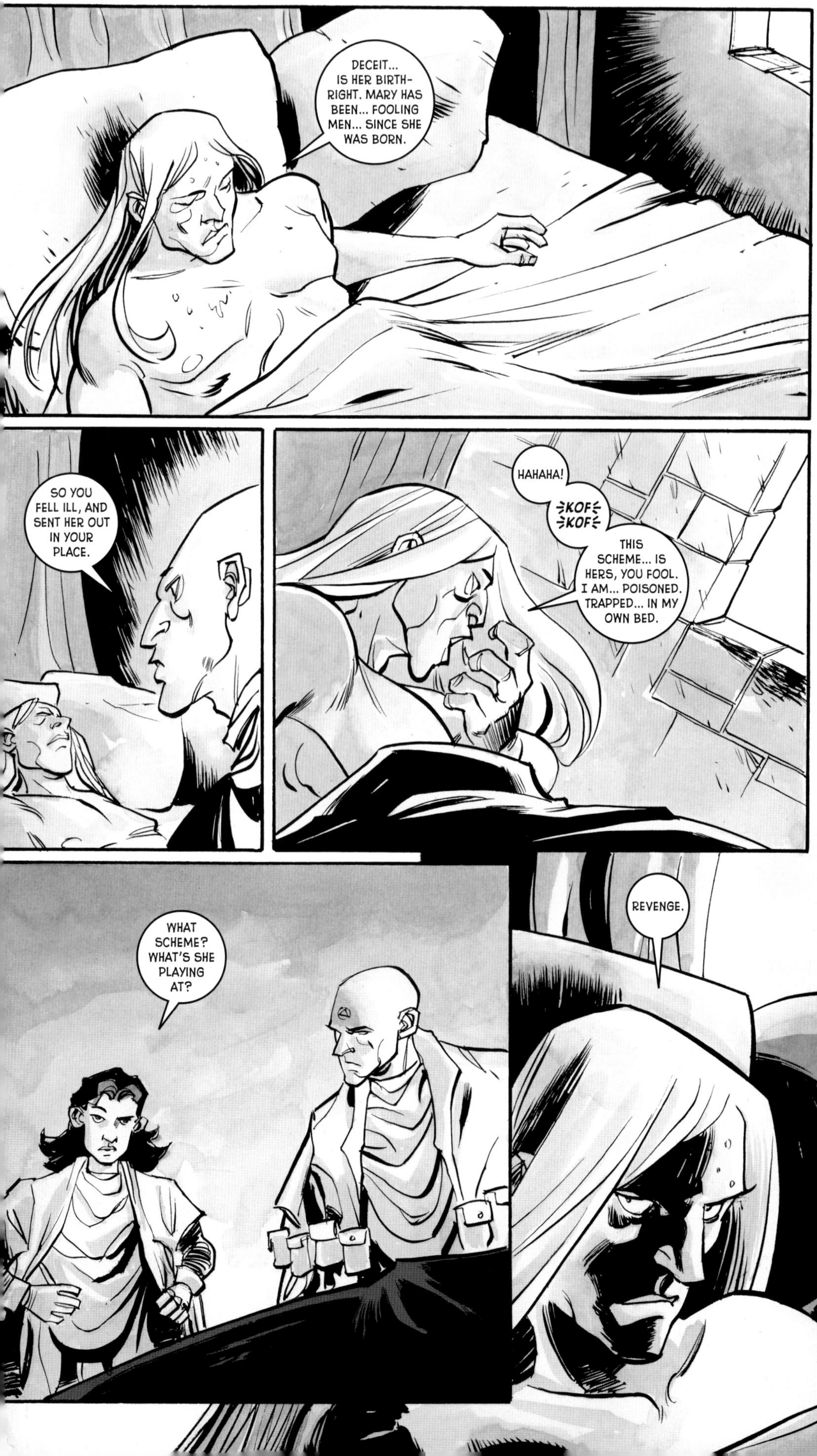
DECEIT... IS HER BIRTH-RIGHT. MARY HAS BEEN... FOOLING MEN... SINCE SHE WAS BORN.
SO YOU FELL ILL, AND SENT HER OUT IN YOUR PLACE.
HAHAHA!
KOF KOF
THIS SCHEME... IS HERS, YOU FOOL. I AM... POISONED. TRAPPED... IN MY OWN BED.
WHAT SCHEME? WHAT'S SHE PLAYING AT?
REVENGE.

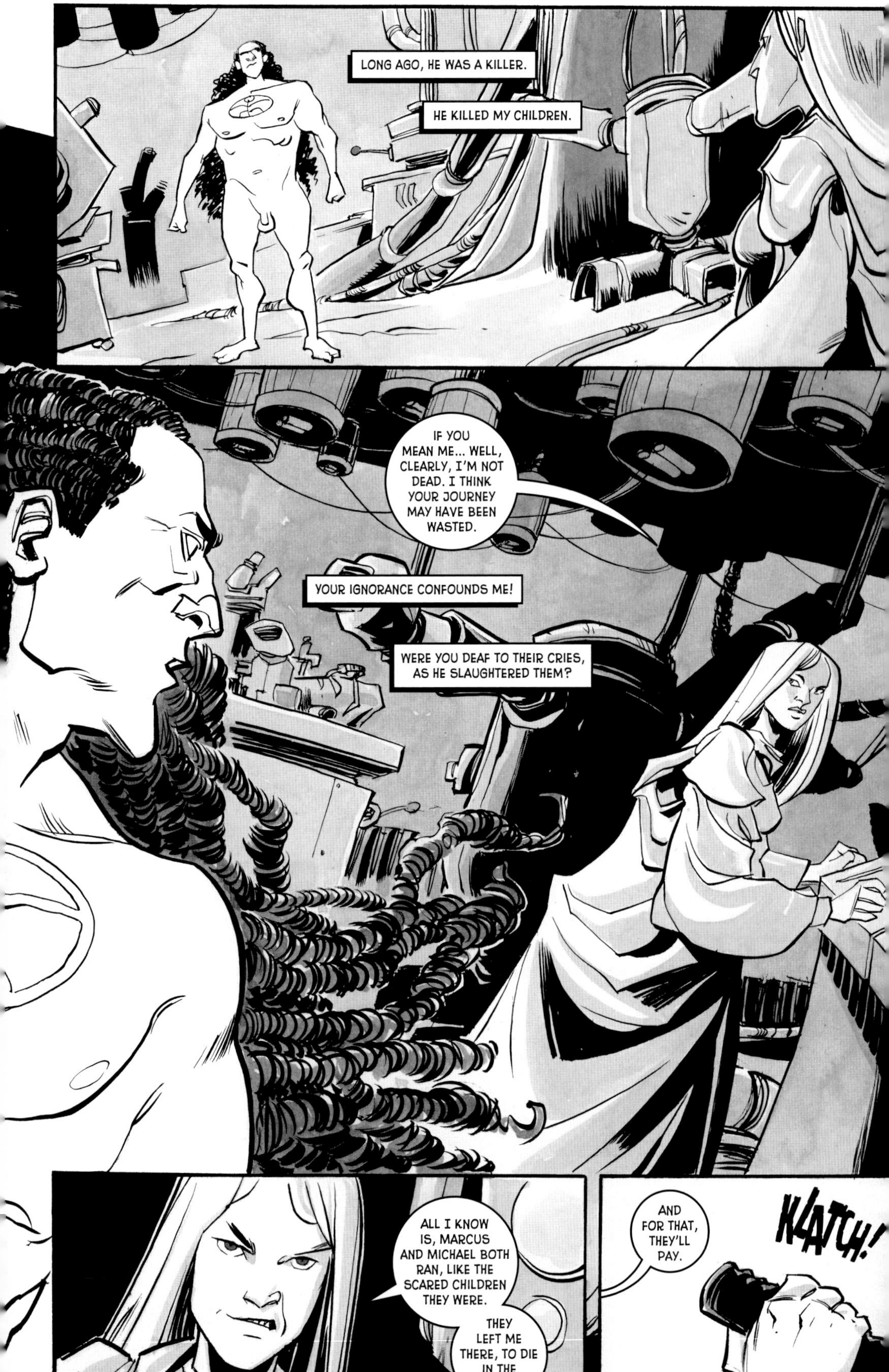
LONG AGO, HE WAS A KILLER.
HE KILLED MY CHILDREN.
IF YOU MEAN ME... WELL, CLEARLY, I'M NOT DEAD. I THINK YOUR JOURNEY MAY HAVE BEEN WASTED.
YOUR IGNORANCE CONFOUNDS ME!
WERE YOU DEAF TO THEIR CRIES, AS HE SLAUGHTERED THEM?
ALL I KNOW IS, MARCUS AND MICHAEL BOTH RAN, LIKE THE SCARED CHILDREN THEY WERE.
THEY LEFT ME THERE, TO DIE IN THE DESERT.
AND FOR THAT, THEY'LL PAY.
KLATCH!

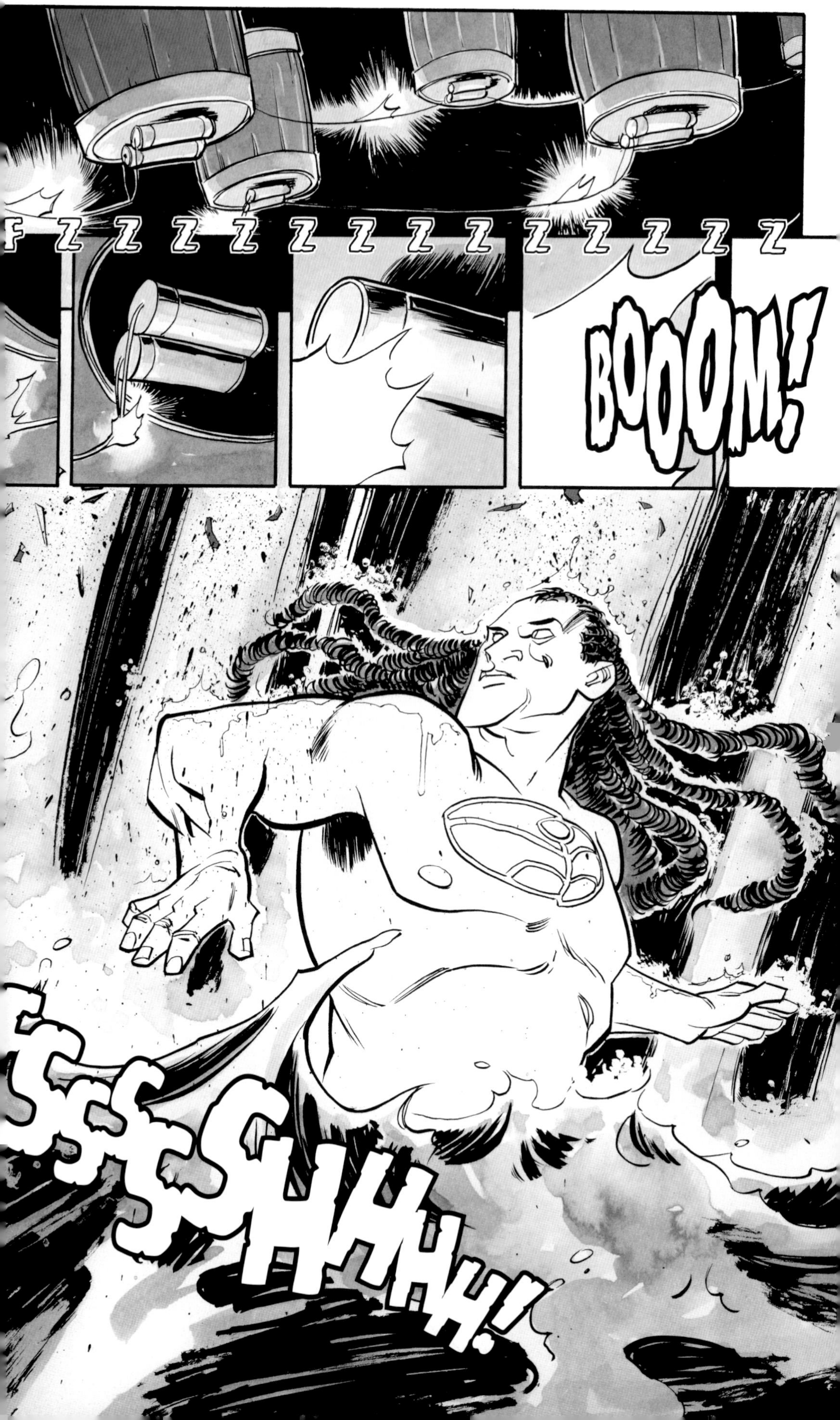
FZZZZZZZZZZZZ
BOOOM!
SSSSHHHHH!

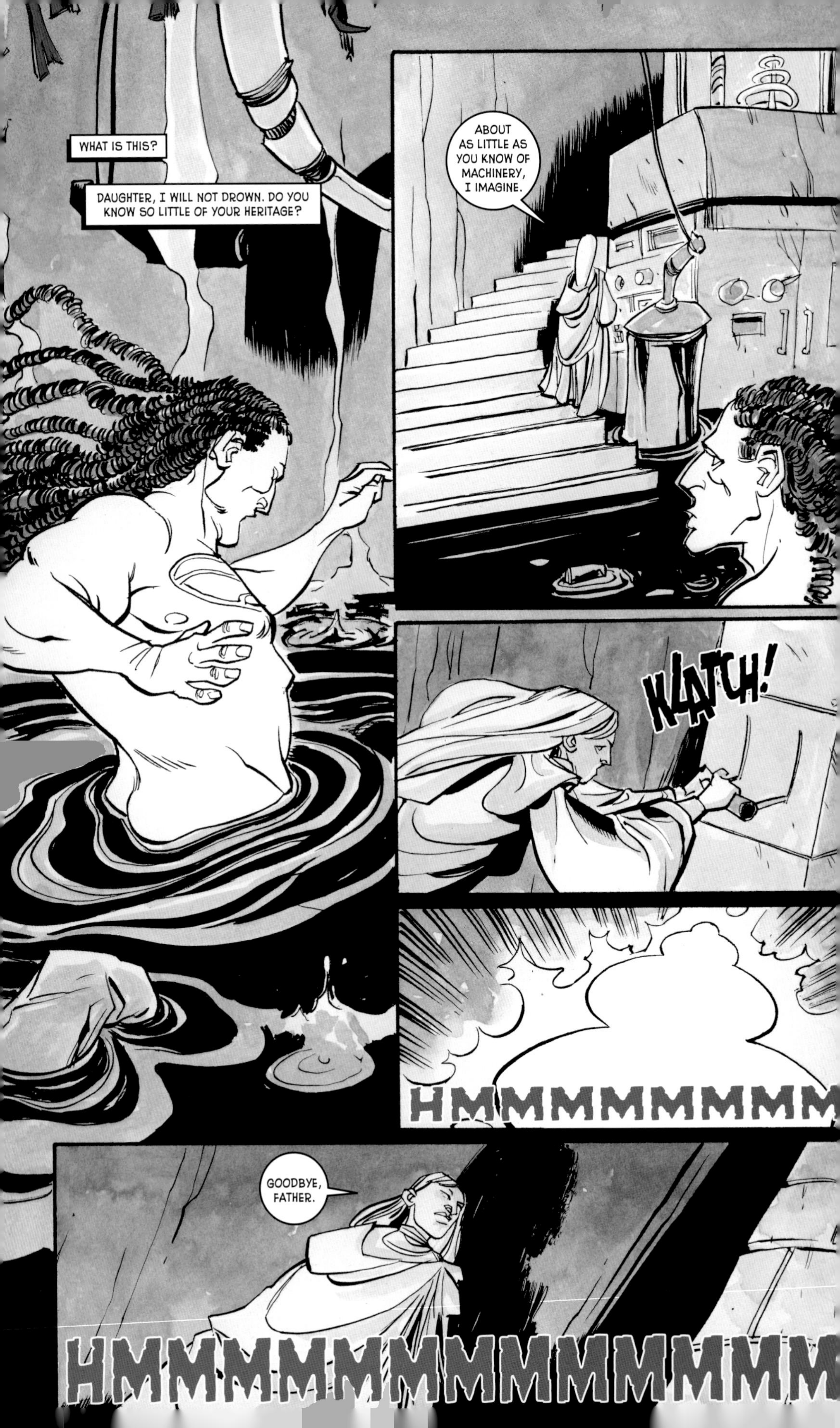
WHAT IS THIS?
DAUGHTER, I WILL NOT DROWN. DO YOU KNOW SO LITTLE OF YOUR HERITAGE?
ABOUT AS LITTLE AS YOU KNOW OF MACHINERY, I IMAGINE.
KLATCH!
HMMMMMMMMM
GOODBYE, FATHER.
HMMMMMMMMMMMMM

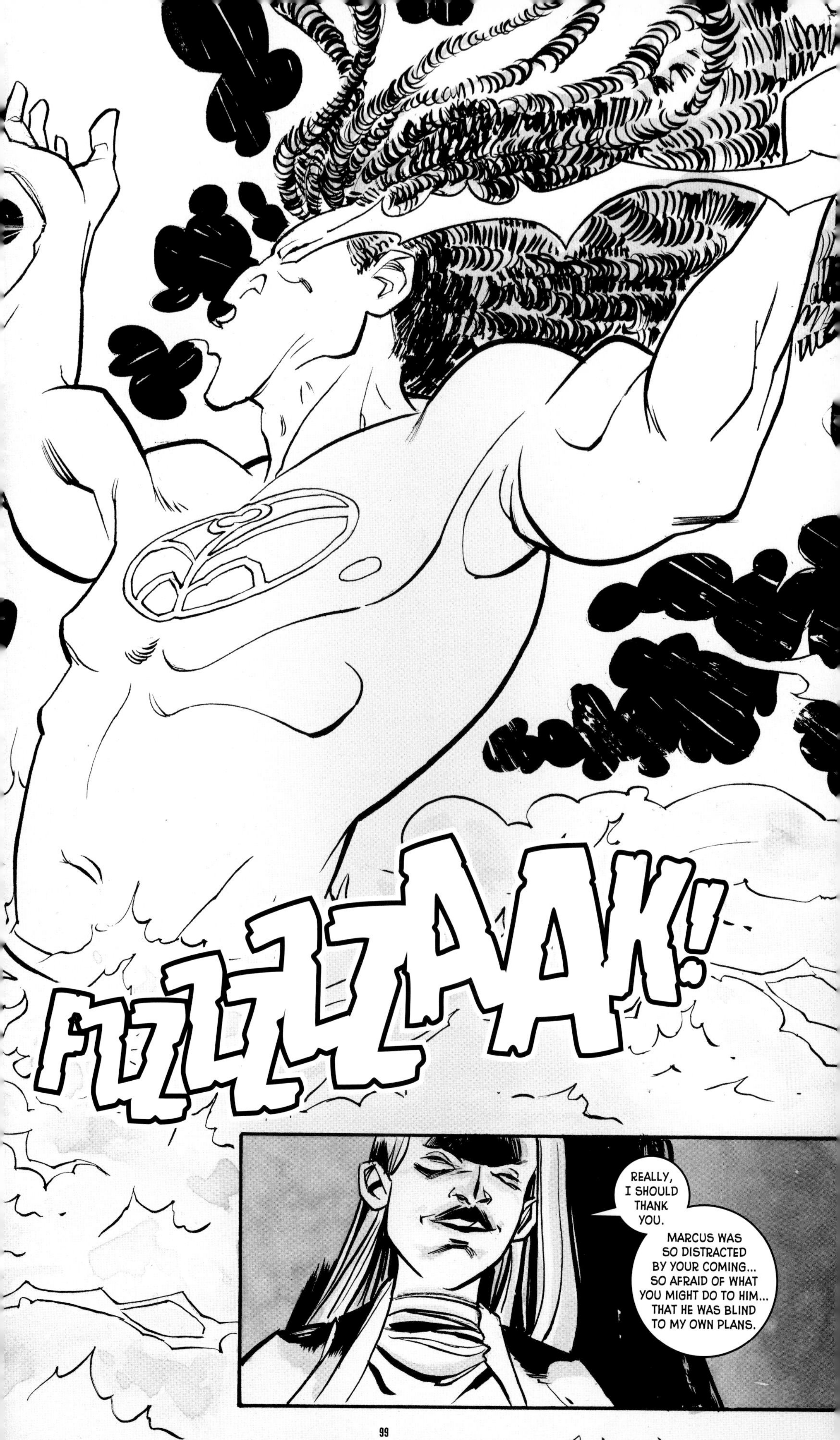
FZZZZZAAK!
REALLY, I SHOULD THANK YOU.
MARCUS WAS SO DISTRACTED BY YOUR COMING... SO AFRAID OF WHAT YOU MIGHT DO TO HIM... THAT HE WAS BLIND TO MY OWN PLANS.

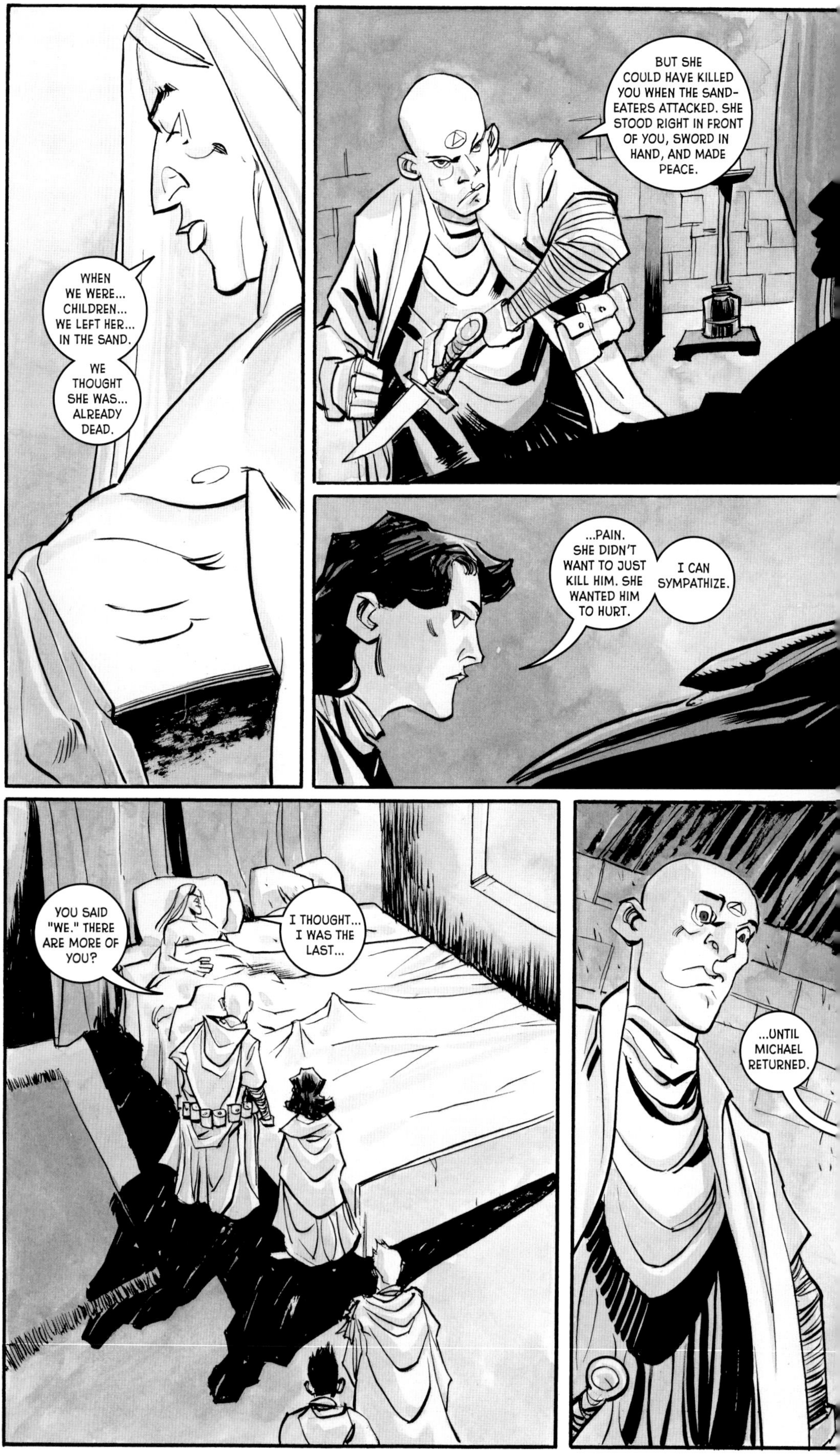
WHEN WE WERE... CHILDREN... WE LEFT HER... IN THE SAND.
WE THOUGHT SHE WAS... ALREADY DEAD.
BUT SHE COULD HAVE KILLED YOU WHEN THE SAND-EATERS ATTACKED. SHE STOOD RIGHT IN FRONT OF YOU, SWORD IN HAND, AND MADE PEACE.
...PAIN. SHE DIDN'T WANT TO JUST KILL HIM. SHE WANTED HIM TO HURT.
I CAN SYMPATHIZE.
YOU SAID "WE." THERE ARE MORE OF YOU?
I THOUGHT... I WAS THE LAST...
...UNTIL MICHAEL RETURNED.

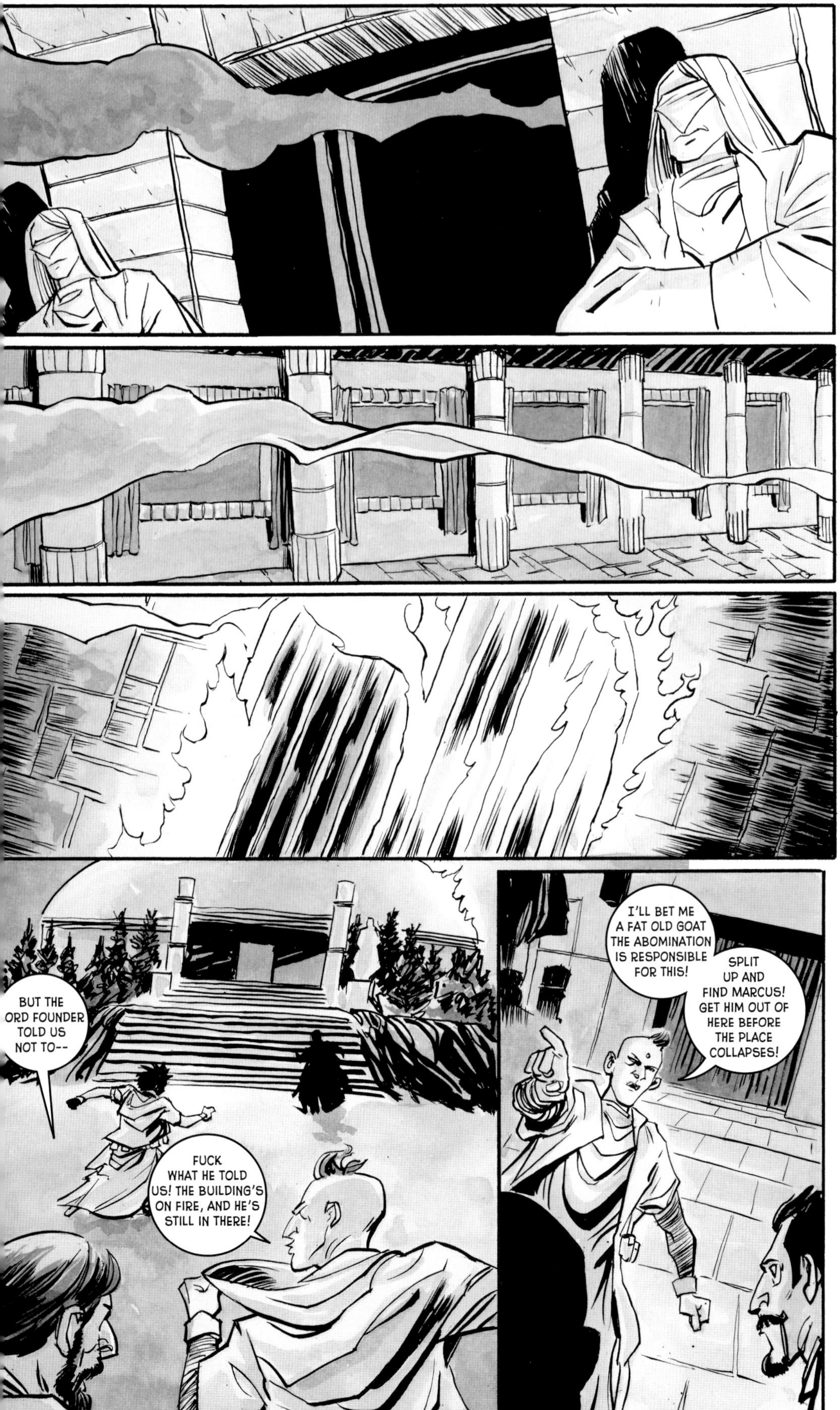
BUT THE ORD FOUNDER TOLD US NOT TO--
FUCK WHAT HE TOLD US! THE BUILDING'S ON FIRE, AND HE'S STILL IN THERE!
I'LL BET ME A FAT OLD GOAT THE ABOMINATION IS RESPONSIBLE FOR THIS!
SPLIT UP AND FIND MARCUS! GET HIM OUT OF HERE BEFORE THE PLACE COLLAPSES!

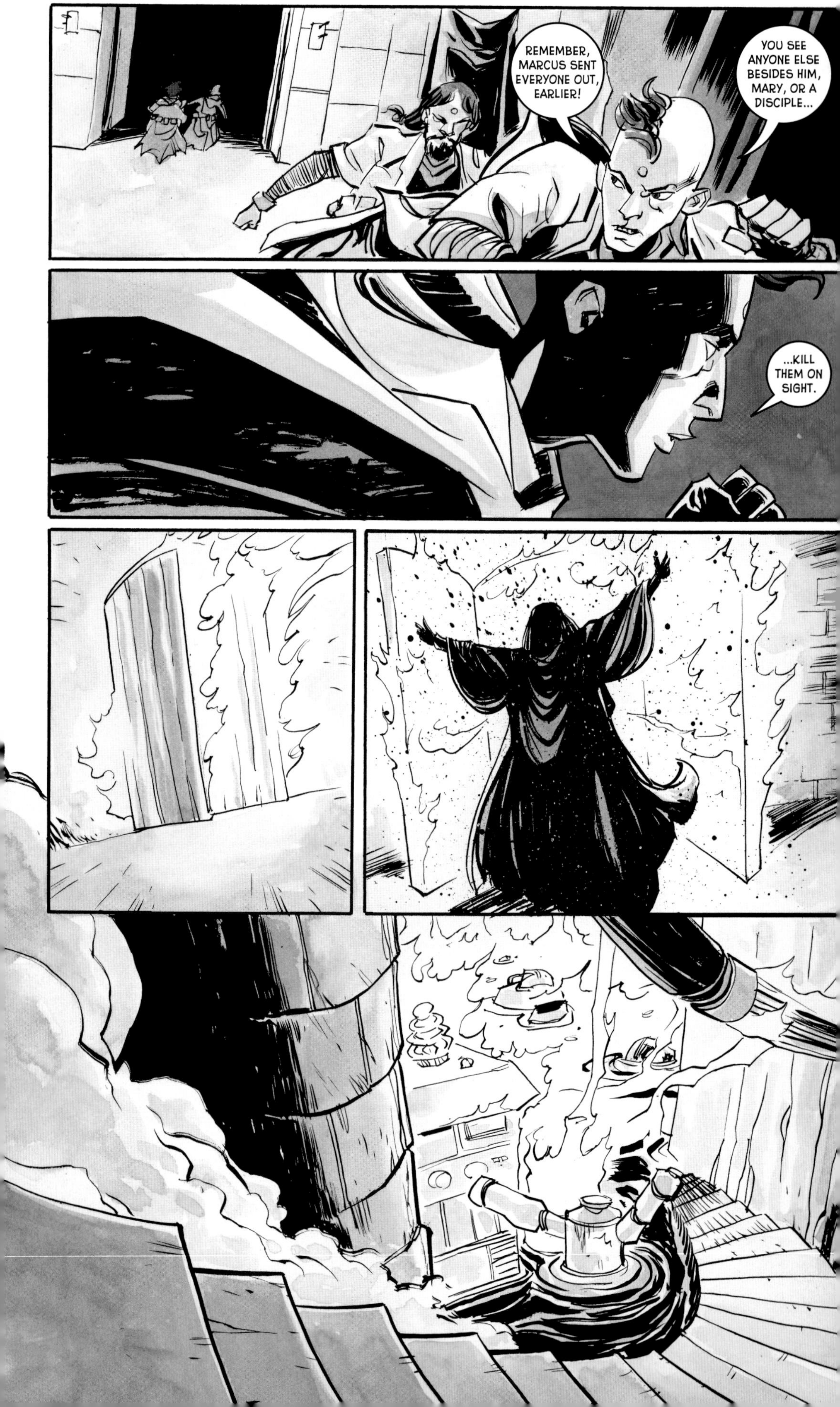
REMEMBER, MARCUS SENT EVERYONE OUT, EARLIER!
YOU SEE ANYONE ELSE BESIDES HIM, MARY, OR A DISCIPLE...
...KILL THEM ON SIGHT.

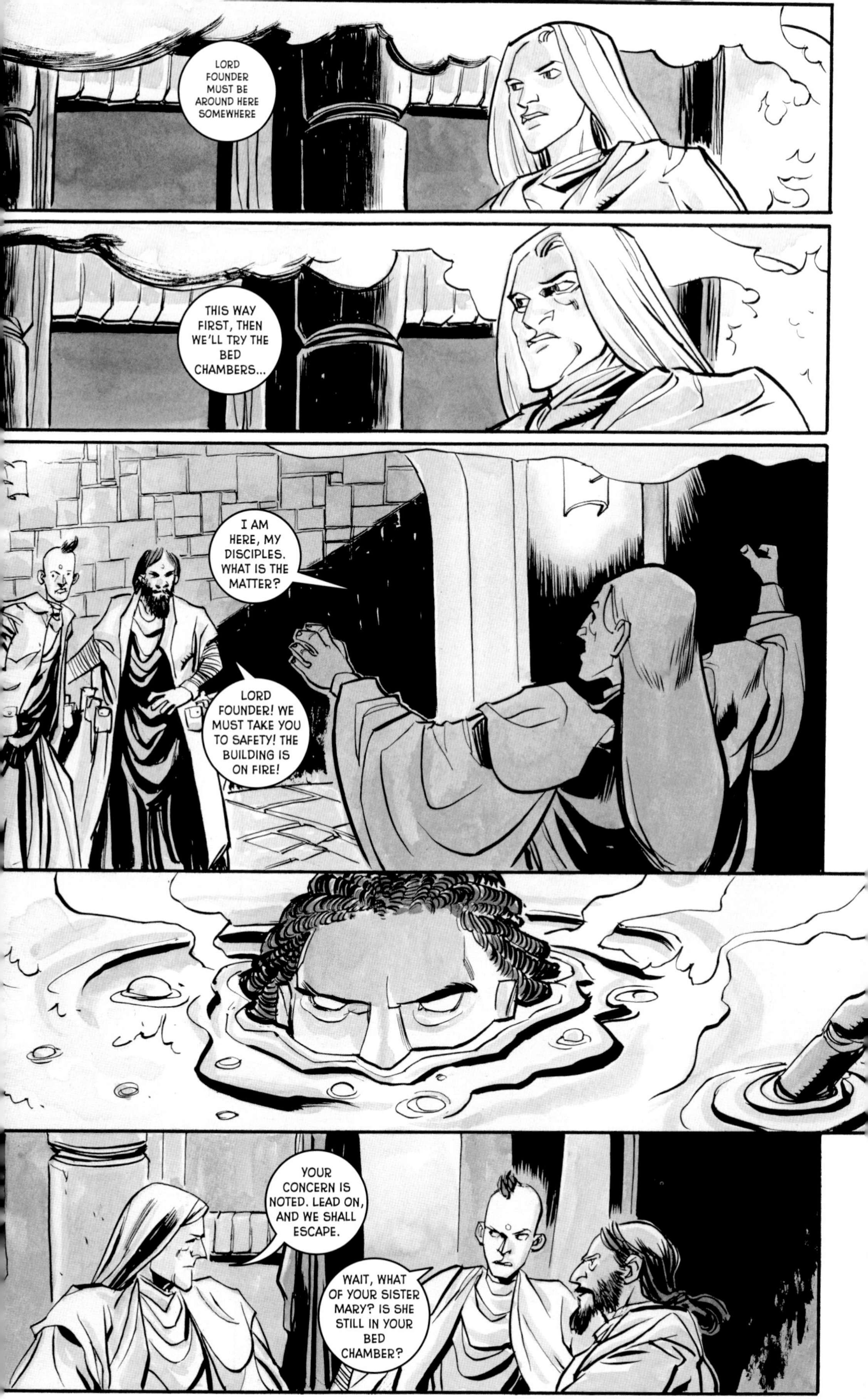
LORD FOUNDER MUST BE AROUND HERE SOMEWHERE
THIS WAY FIRST, THEN WE'LL TRY THE BED CHAMBERS...
I AM HERE, MY DISCIPLES. WHAT IS THE MATTER?
LORD FOUNDER! WE MUST TAKE YOU TO SAFETY! THE BUILDING IS ON FIRE!
YOUR CONCERN IS NOTED. LEAD ON, AND WE SHALL ESCAPE.
WAIT, WHAT OF YOUR SISTER MARY? IS SHE STILL IN YOUR BED CHAMBER?

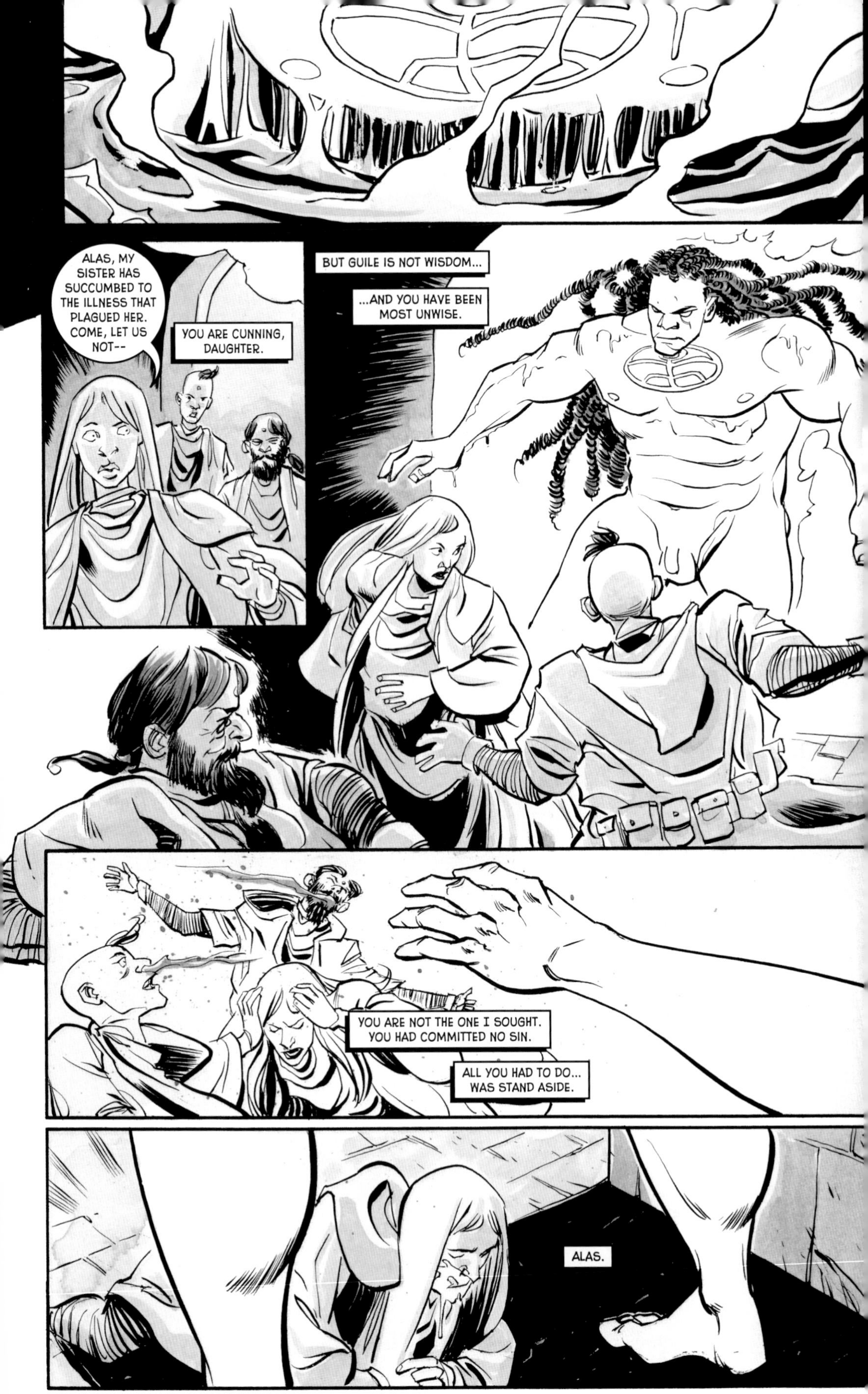
ALAS, MY SISTER HAS SUCCUMBED TO THE ILLNESS THAT PLAGUED HER. COME, LET US NOT--
YOU ARE CUNNING, DAUGHTER.
BUT GUILE IS NOT WISDOM...
...AND YOU HAVE BEEN MOST UNWISE.
YOU ARE NOT THE ONE I SOUGHT. YOU HAD COMMITTED NO SIN.
ALL YOU HAD TO DO... WAS STAND ASIDE.
ALAS.

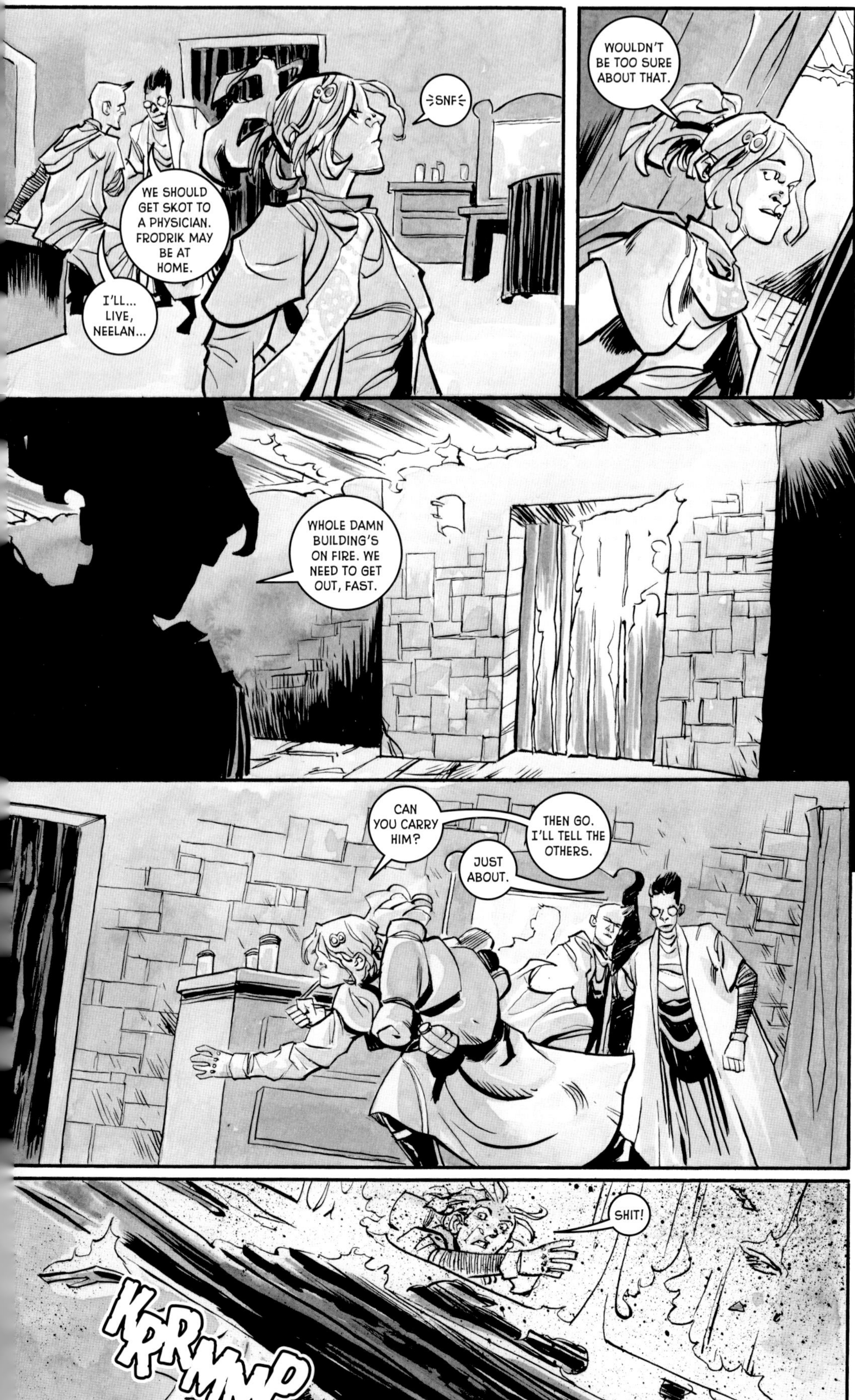

WE SHOULD GET SKOT TO A PHYSICIAN. FRODRIK MAY BE AT HOME.
I'LL... LIVE, NEELAN...
SNF
WOULDN'T BE TOO SURE ABOUT THAT.
WHOLE DAMN BUILDING'S ON FIRE. WE NEED TO GET OUT, FAST.
CAN YOU CARRY HIM?
JUST ABOUT.
THEN GO. I'LL TELL THE OTHERS.
SHIT!
KRRMMP

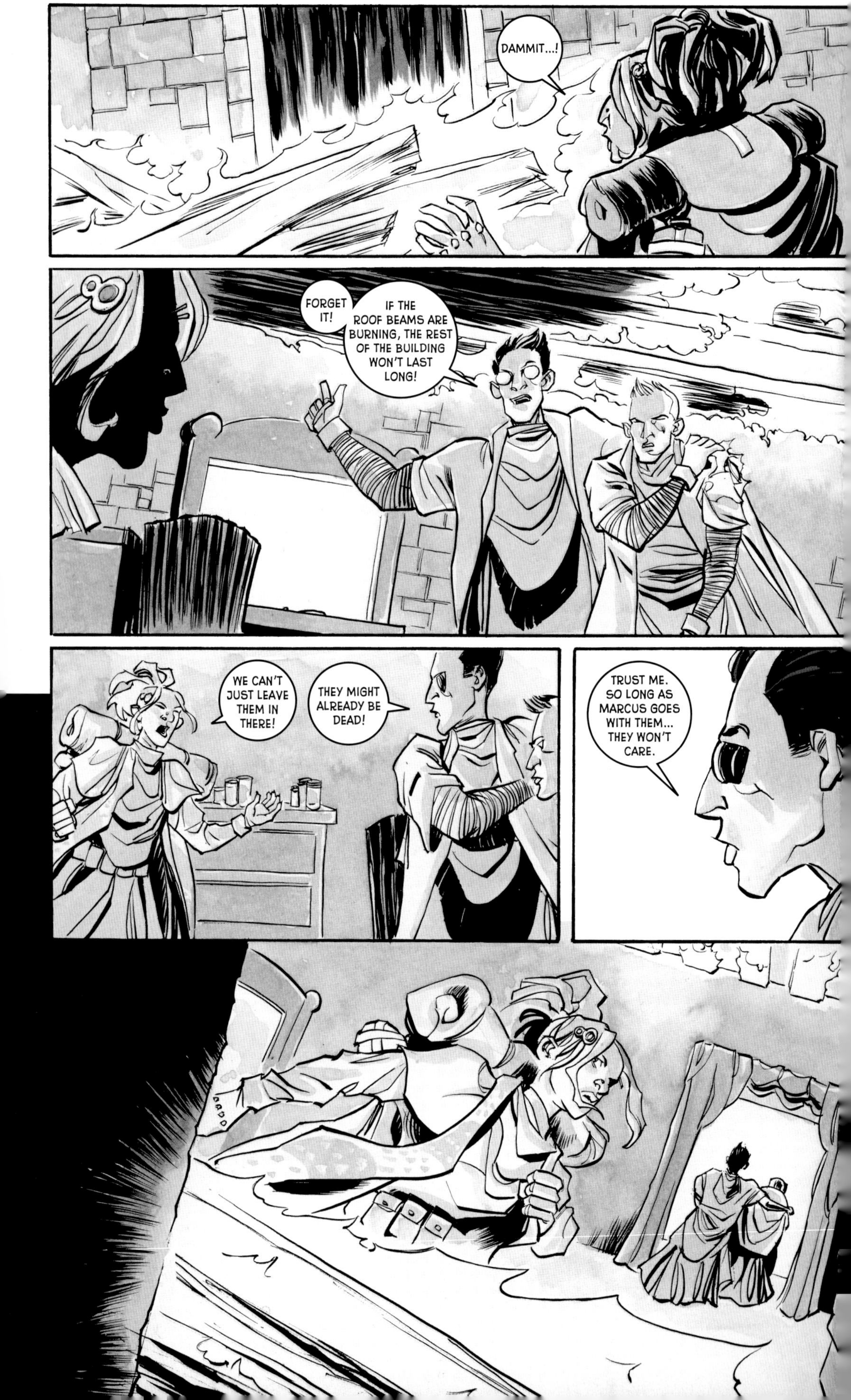
DAMMIT...!
FORGET IT!
IF THE ROOF BEAMS ARE BURNING, THE REST OF THE BUILDING WON'T LAST LONG!
WE CAN'T JUST LEAVE THEM IN THERE!
THEY MIGHT ALREADY BE DEAD!
TRUST ME. SO LONG AS MARCUS GOES WITH THEM... THEY WON'T CARE.

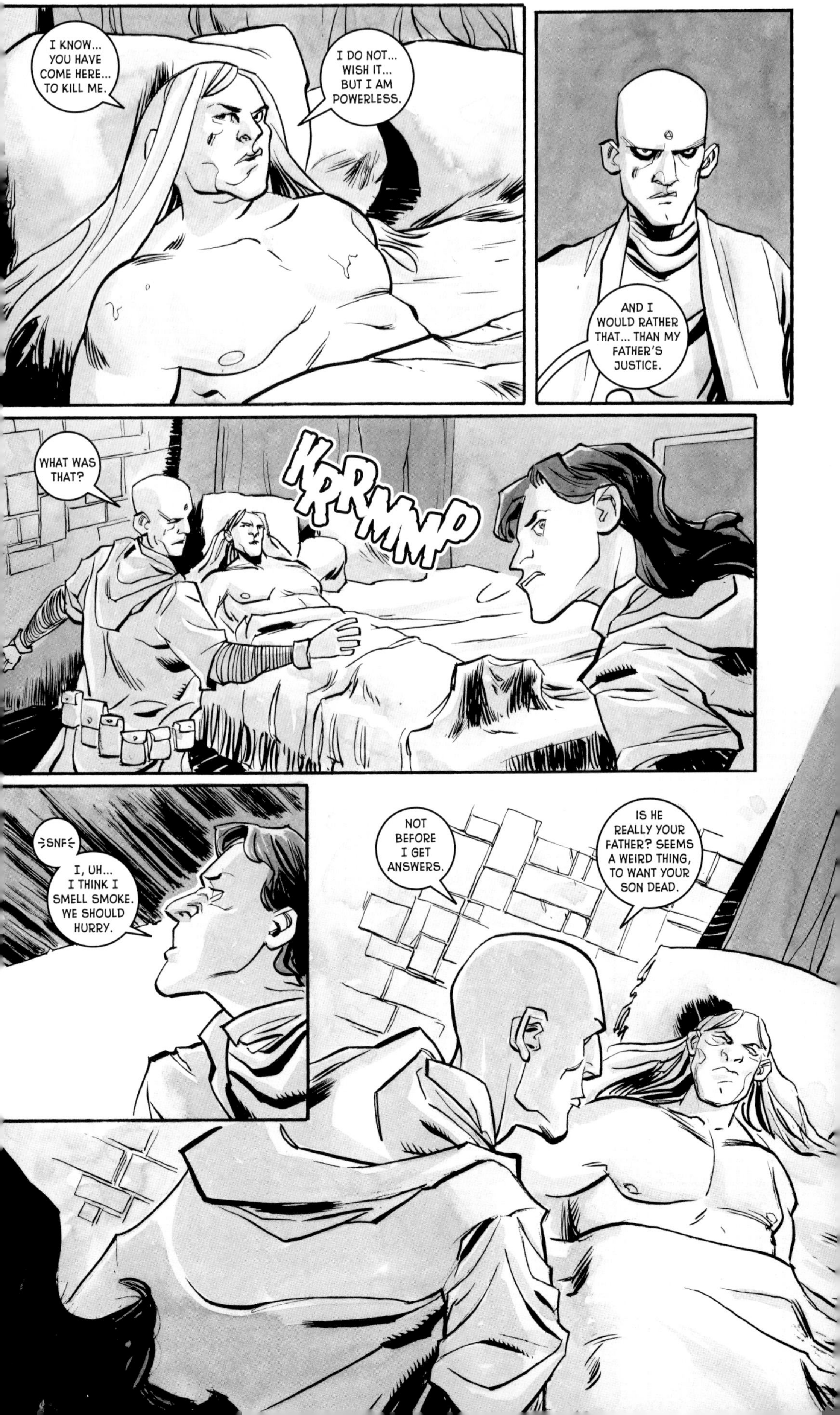
I KNOW... YOU HAVE COME HERE... TO KILL ME.
I DO NOT... WISH IT... BUT I AM POWERLESS.
AND I WOULD RATHER THAT... THAN MY FATHER'S JUSTICE.
WHAT WAS THAT?
KRRMMP
SNF
I, UH... I THINK I SMELL SMOKE. WE SHOULD HURRY.
NOT BEFORE I GET ANSWERS.
IS HE REALLY YOUR FATHER? SEEMS A WEIRD THING, TO WANT YOUR SON DEAD.

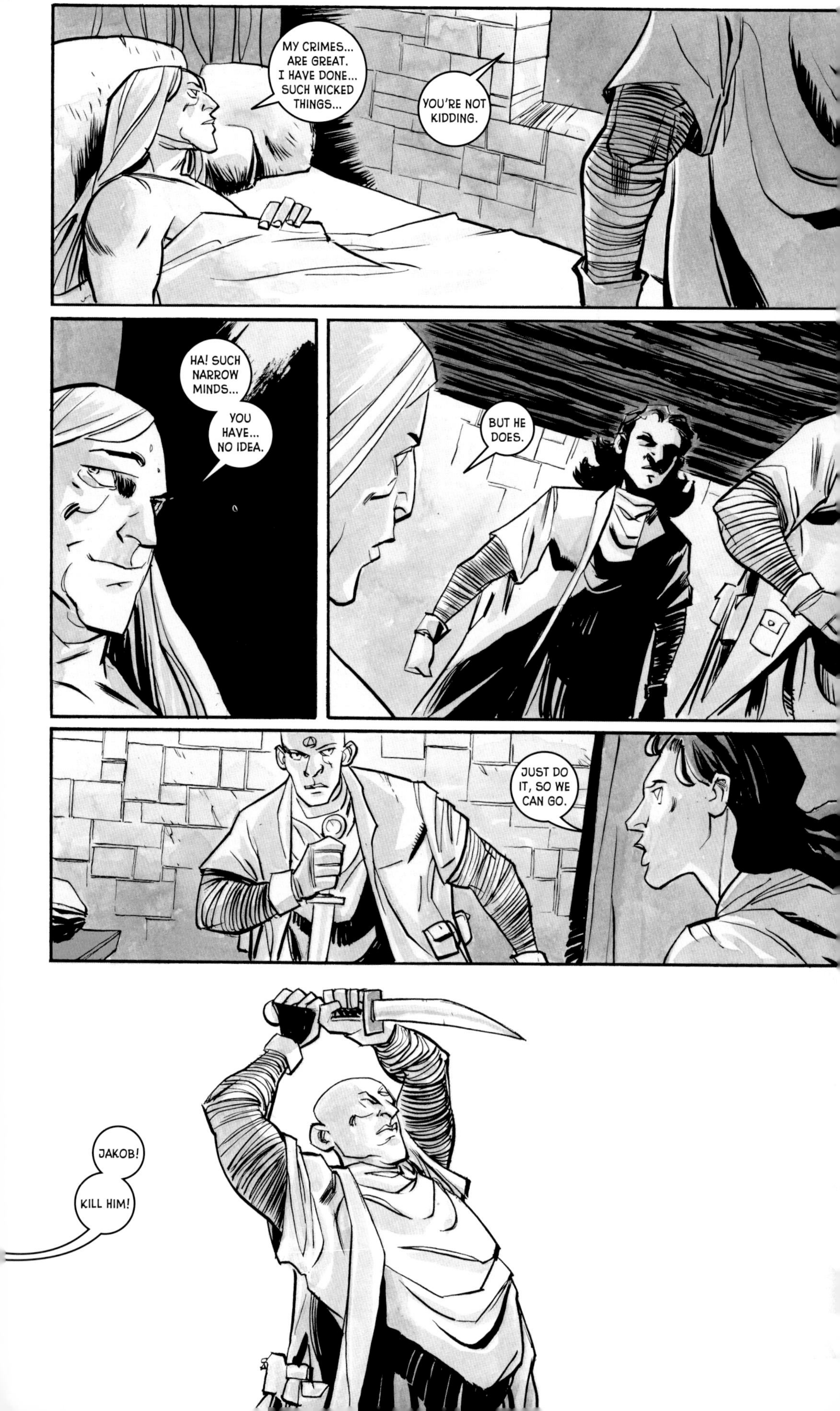
MY CRIMES... ARE GREAT. I HAVE DONE... SUCH WICKED THINGS...
YOU'RE NOT KIDDING.
HA! SUCH NARROW MINDS...
YOU HAVE... NO IDEA.
BUT HE DOES.
JUST DO IT, SO WE CAN GO.
JAKOB!
KILL HIM!

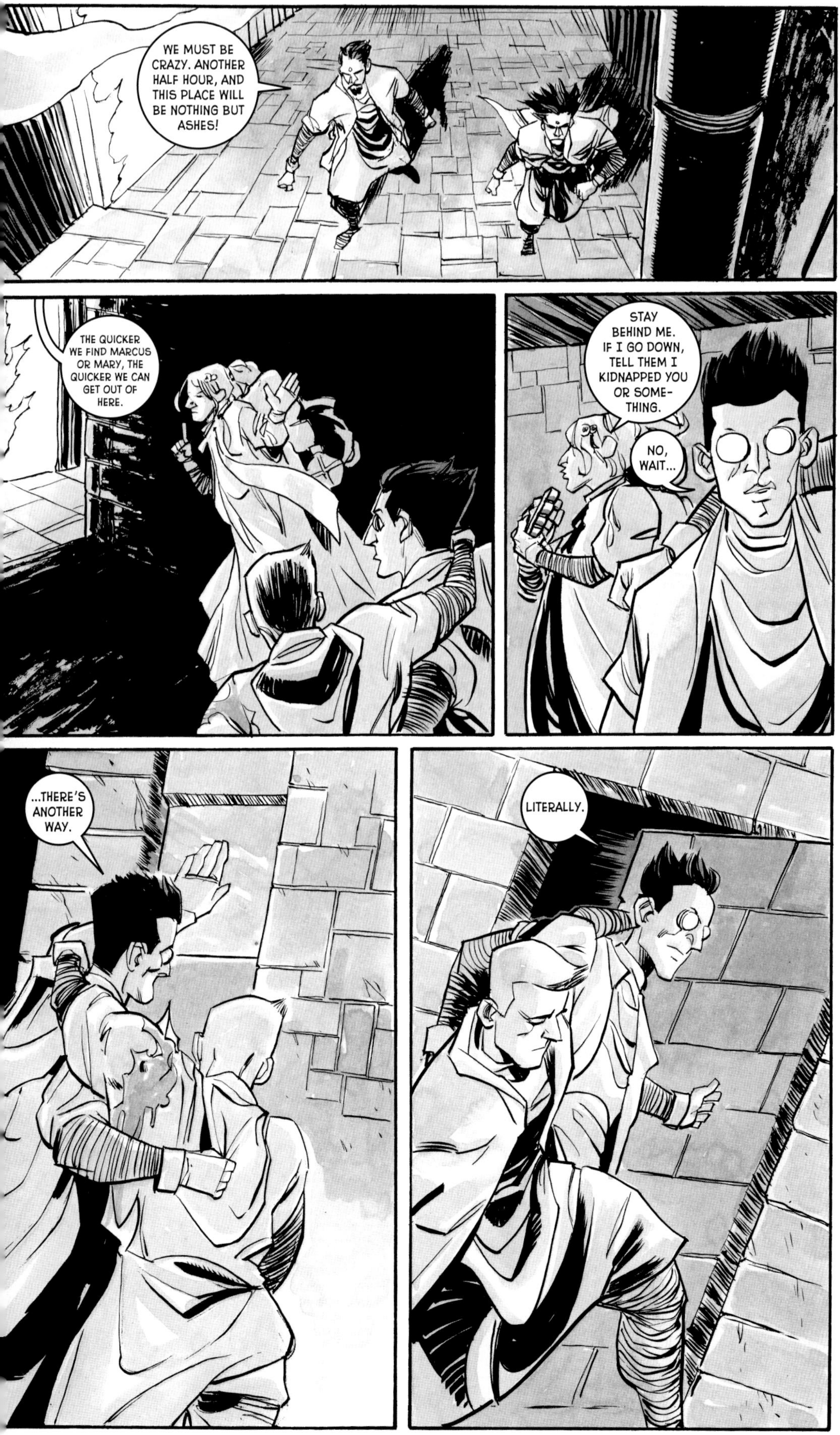
WE MUST BE CRAZY. ANOTHER HALF HOUR, AND THIS PLACE WILL BE NOTHING BUT ASHES!
THE QUICKER WE FIND MARCUS OR MARY, THE QUICKER WE CAN GET OUT OF HERE.
STAY BEHIND ME. IF I GO DOWN, TELL THEM I KIDNAPPED YOU OR SOME-THING.
NO, WAIT...
...THERE'S ANOTHER WAY.
LITERALLY.

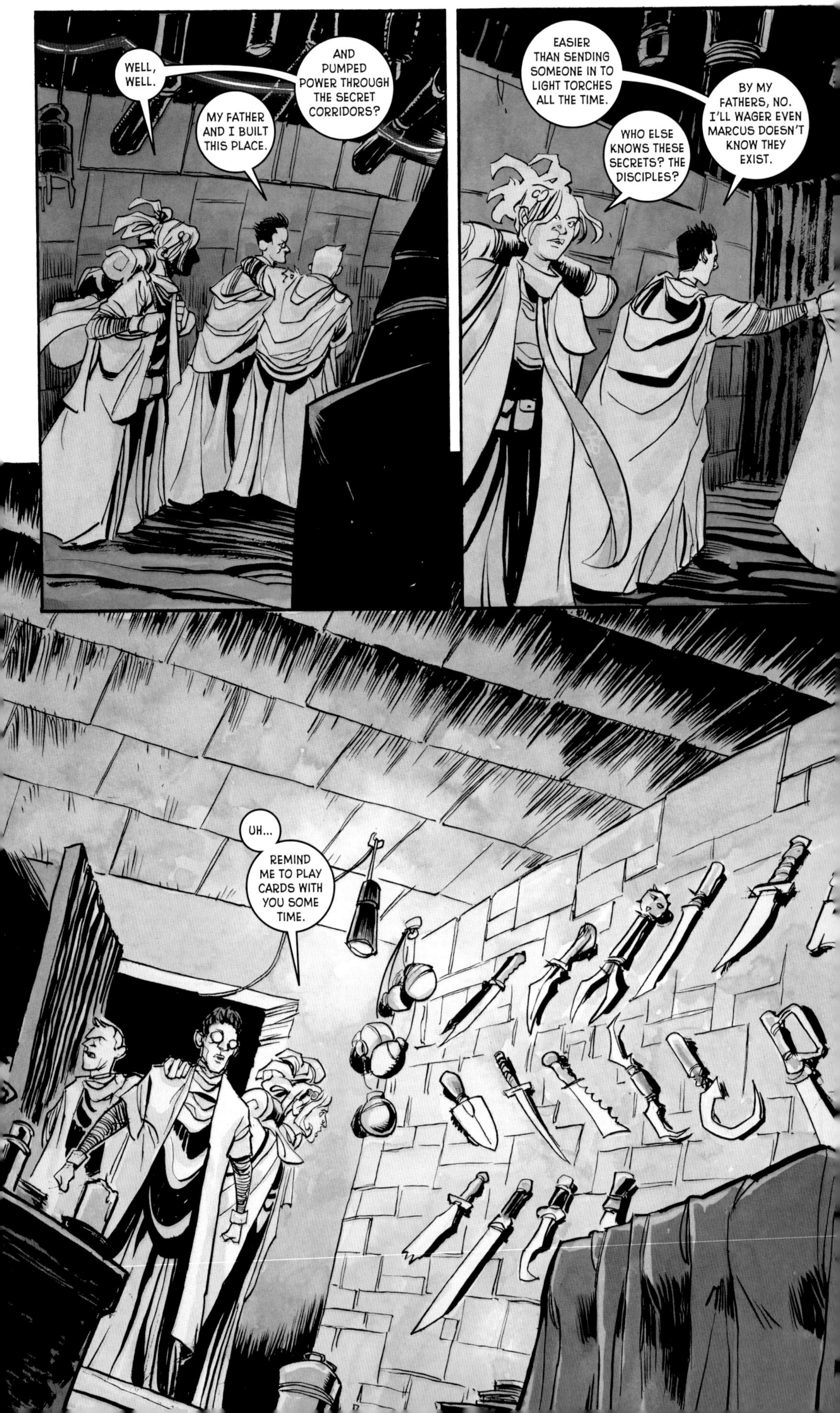
WELL, WELL.
MY FATHER AND I BUILT THIS PLACE.
AND PUMPED POWER THROUGH THE SECRET CORRIDORS?
EASIER THAN SENDING SOMEONE IN TO LIGHT TORCHES ALL THE TIME.
WHO ELSE KNOWS THESE SECRETS? THE DISCIPLES?
BY MY FATHERS, NO. I'LL WAGER EVEN MARCUS DOESN'T KNOW THEY EXIST.
UH...
REMIND ME TO PLAY CARDS WITH YOU SOME TIME.

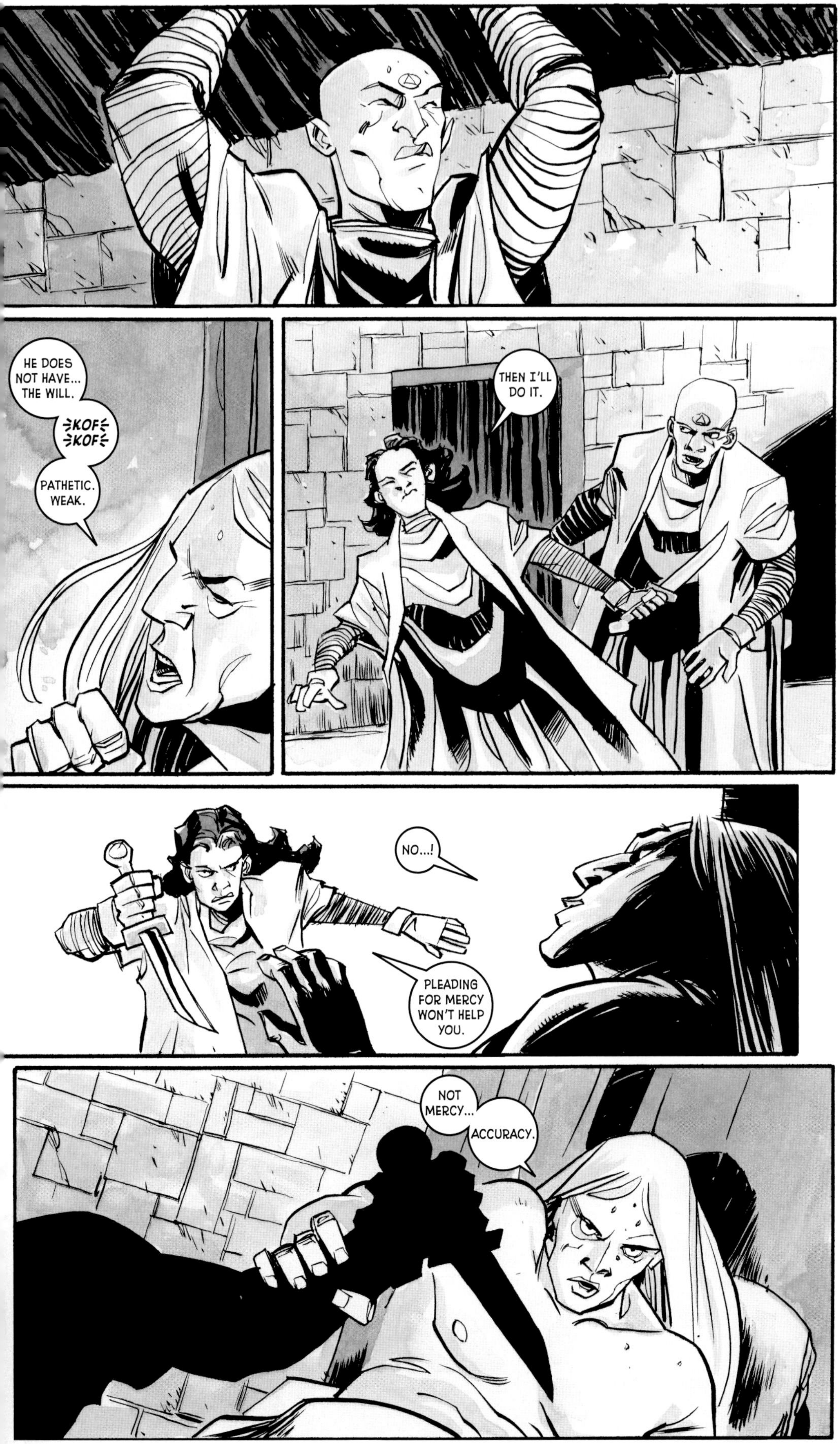
HE DOES NOT HAVE... THE WILL.
KOF KOF
PATHETIC. WEAK.
THEN I'LL DO IT.
NO...!
PLEADING FOR MERCY WON'T HELP YOU.
NOT MERCY...
ACCURACY.

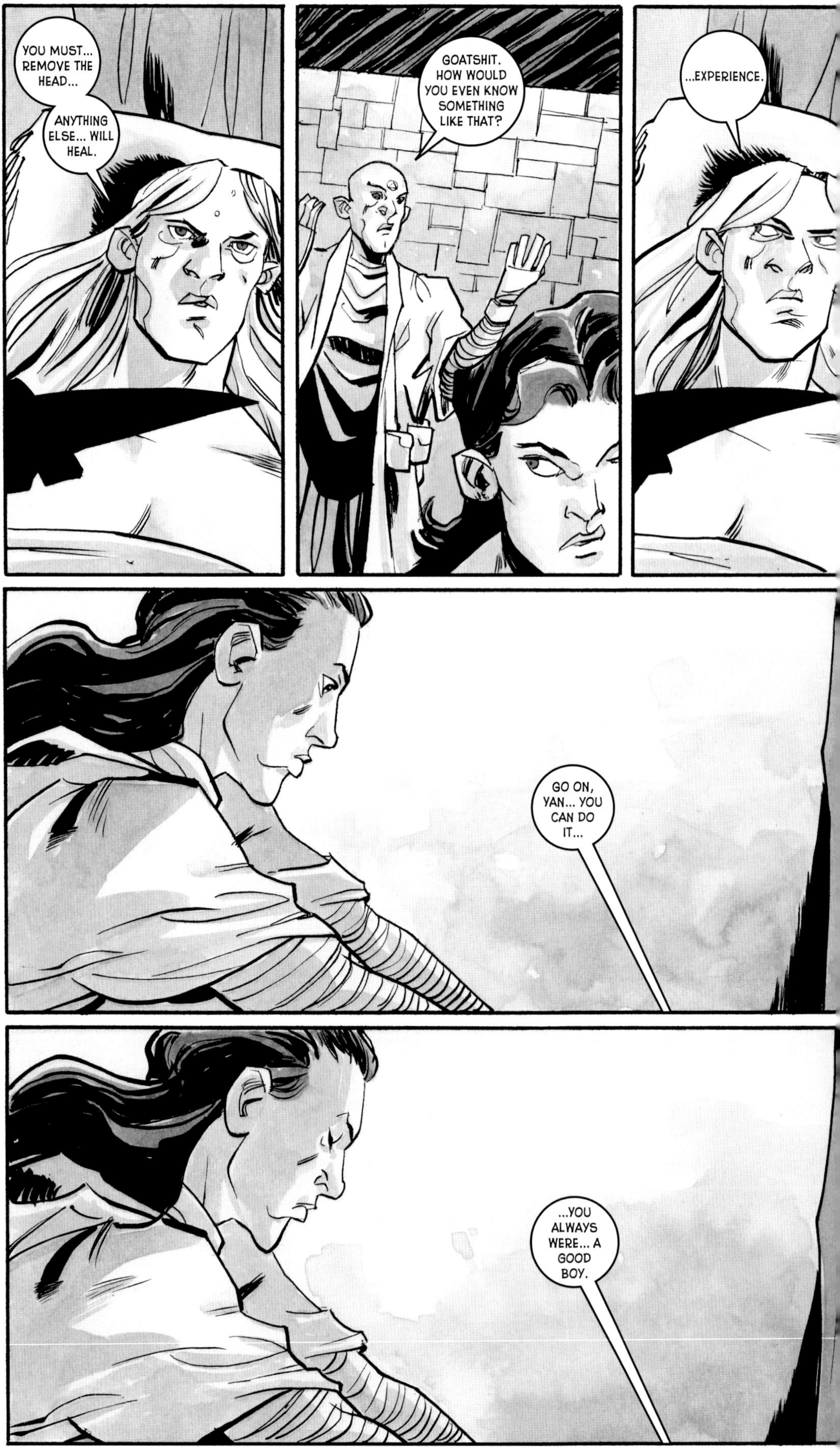
YOU MUST... REMOVE THE HEAD...
ANYTHING ELSE... WILL HEAL.
GOATSHIT. HOW WOULD YOU EVEN KNOW SOMETHING LIKE THAT?
...EXPERIENCE.
GO ON, YAN... YOU CAN DO IT...
...YOU ALWAYS WERE... A GOOD BOY.

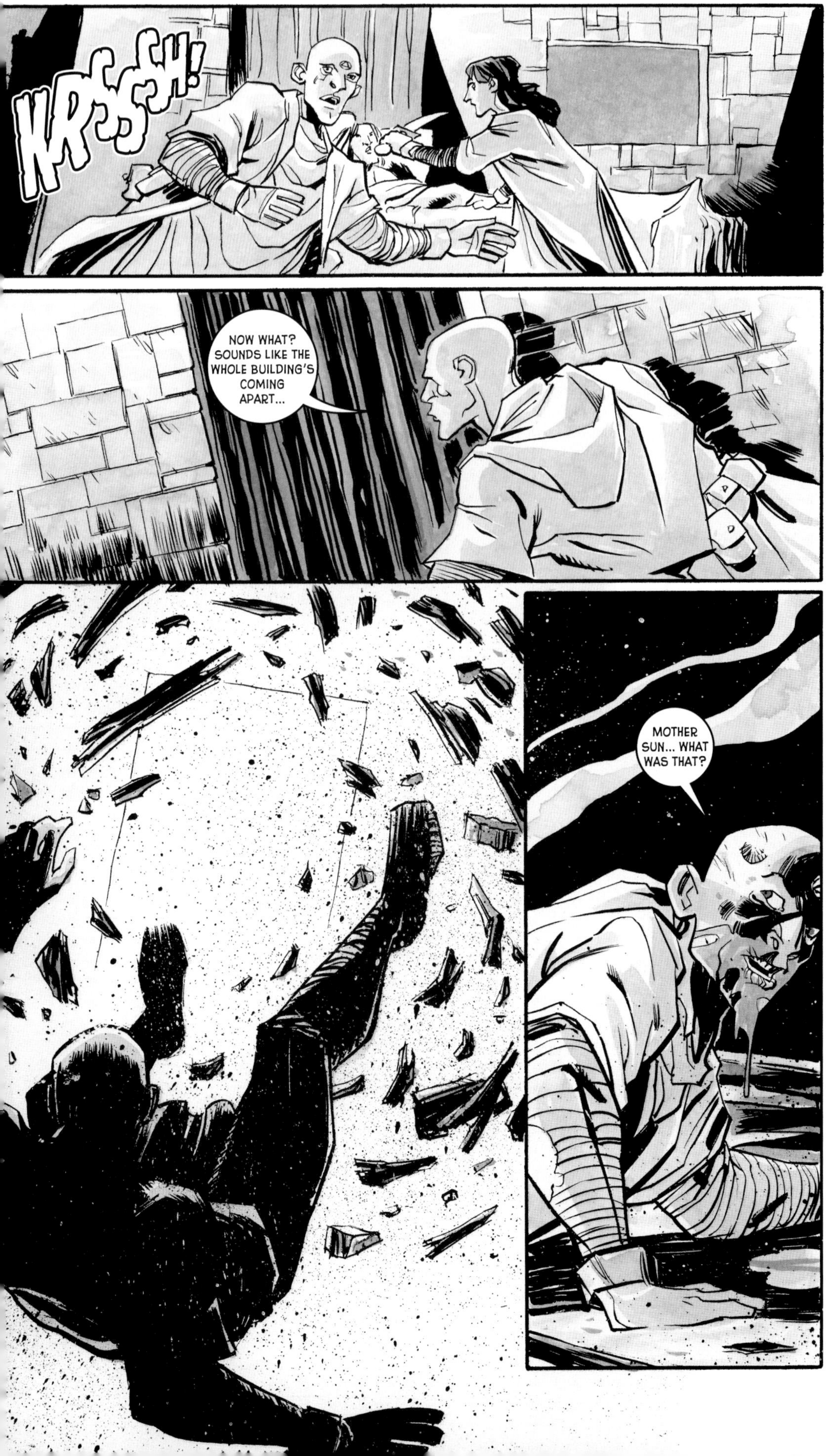
KRSSSH!
NOW WHAT? SOUNDS LIKE THE WHOLE BUILDING'S COMING APART...
MOTHER SUN... WHAT WAS THAT?

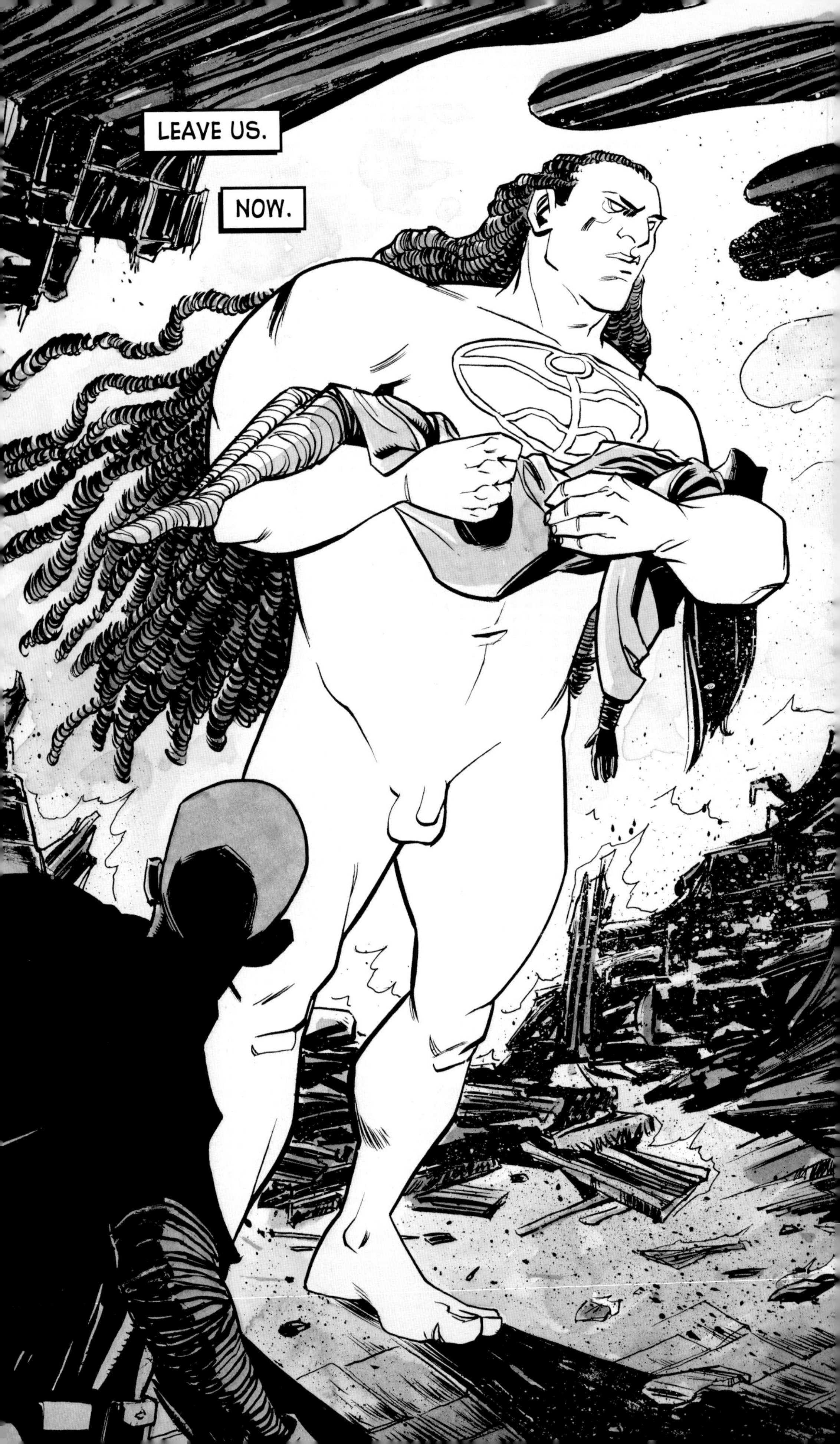
LEAVE US.
NOW.

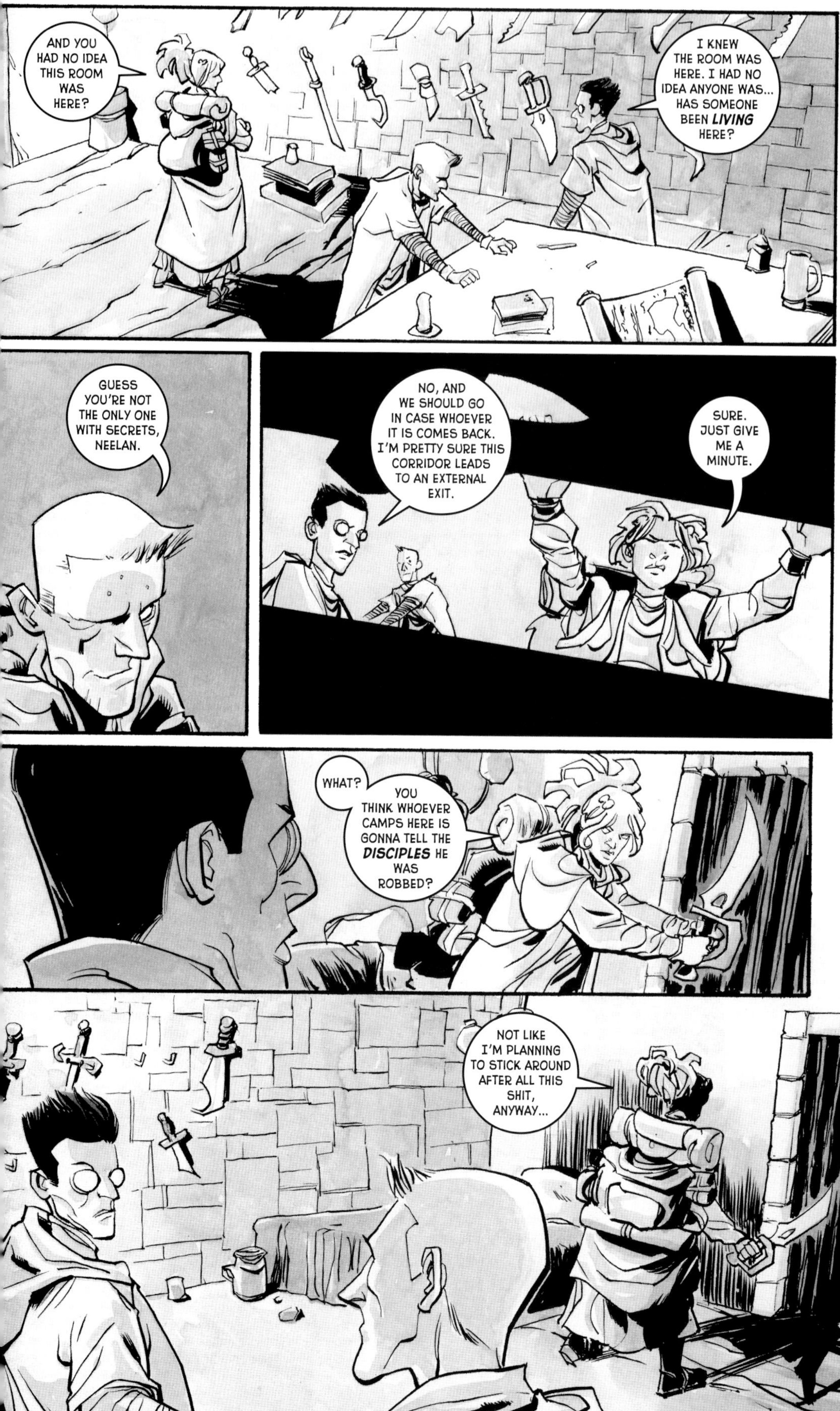
AND YOU HAD NO IDEA THIS ROOM WAS HERE?
I KNEW THE ROOM WAS HERE. I HAD NO IDEA ANYONE WAS... HAS SOMEONE BEEN *LIVING* HERE?
GUESS YOU'RE NOT THE ONLY ONE WITH SECRETS, NEELAN.
NO, AND WE SHOULD GO IN CASE WHOEVER IT IS COMES BACK. I'M PRETTY SURE THIS CORRIDOR LEADS TO AN EXTERNAL EXIT.
SURE. JUST GIVE ME A MINUTE.
WHAT?
YOU THINK WHOEVER CAMPS HERE IS GONNA TELL THE ***DISCIPLES*** HE WAS ROBBED?
NOT LIKE I'M PLANNING TO STICK AROUND AFTER ALL THIS SHIT, ANYWAY...

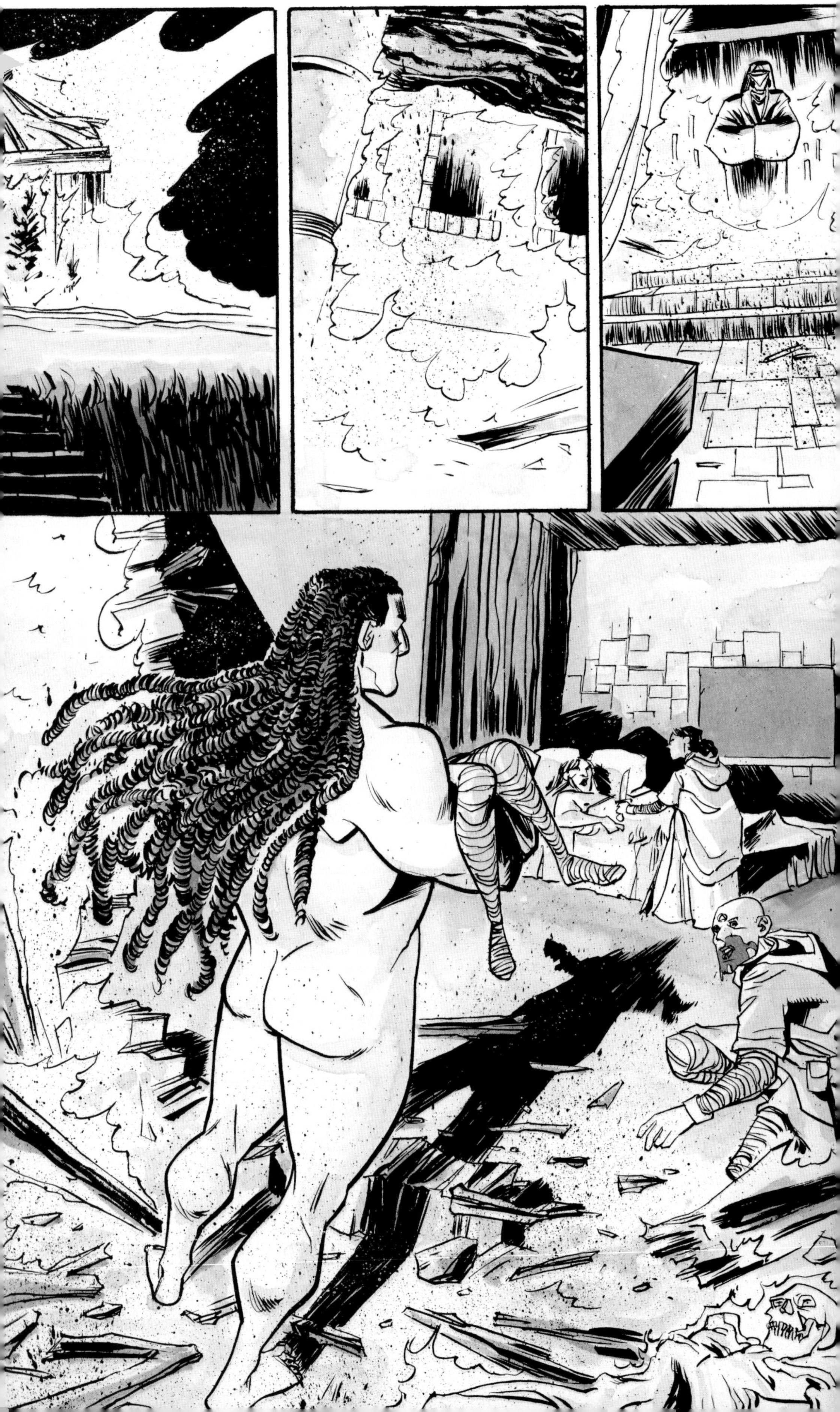

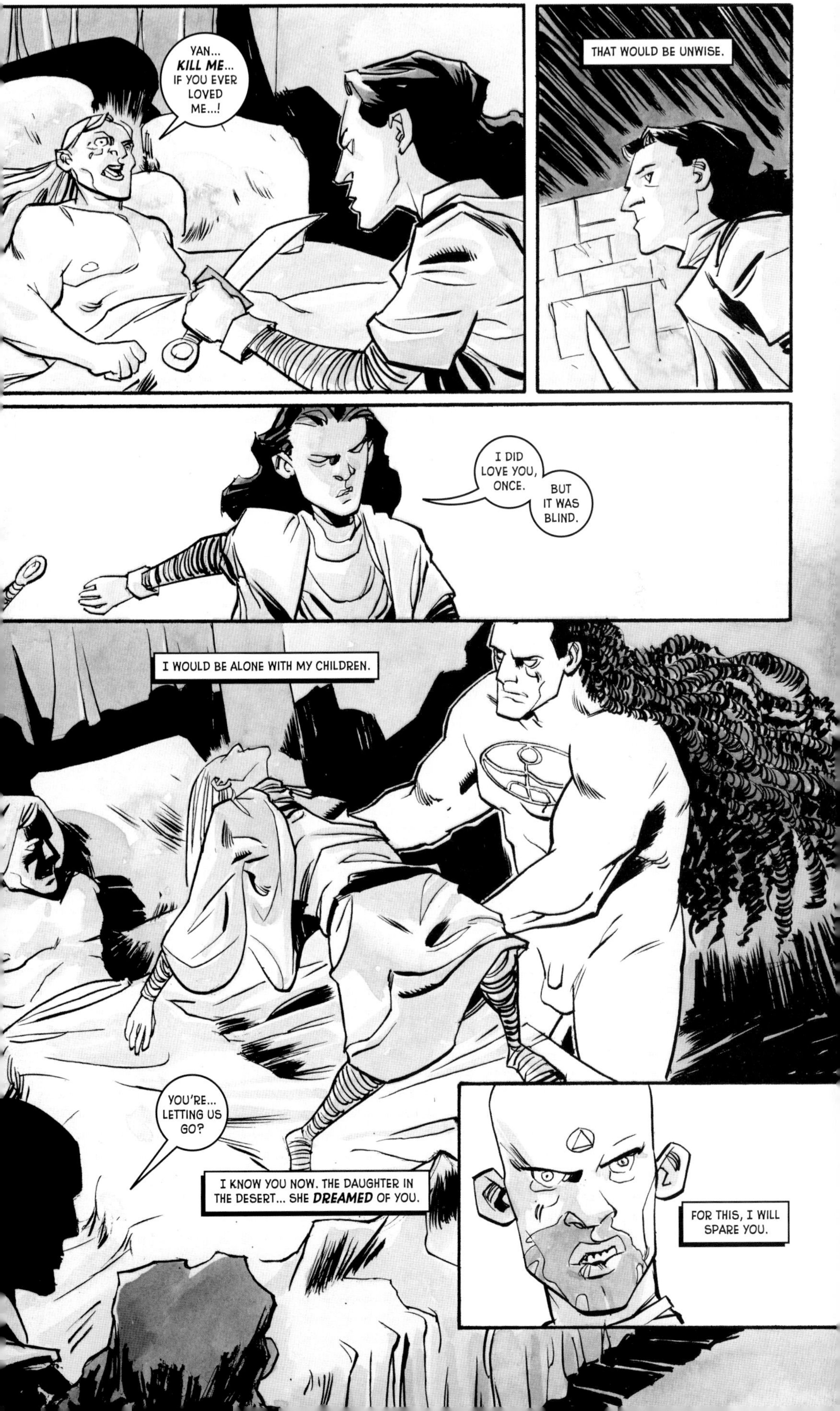
YAN... **KILL ME**... IF YOU EVER LOVED ME...!
THAT WOULD BE UNWISE.
I DID LOVE YOU, ONCE.
BUT IT WAS BLIND.
I WOULD BE ALONE WITH MY CHILDREN.
YOU'RE... LETTING US GO?
I KNOW YOU NOW. THE DAUGHTER IN THE DESERT... SHE **DREAMED** OF YOU.
FOR THIS, I WILL SPARE YOU.

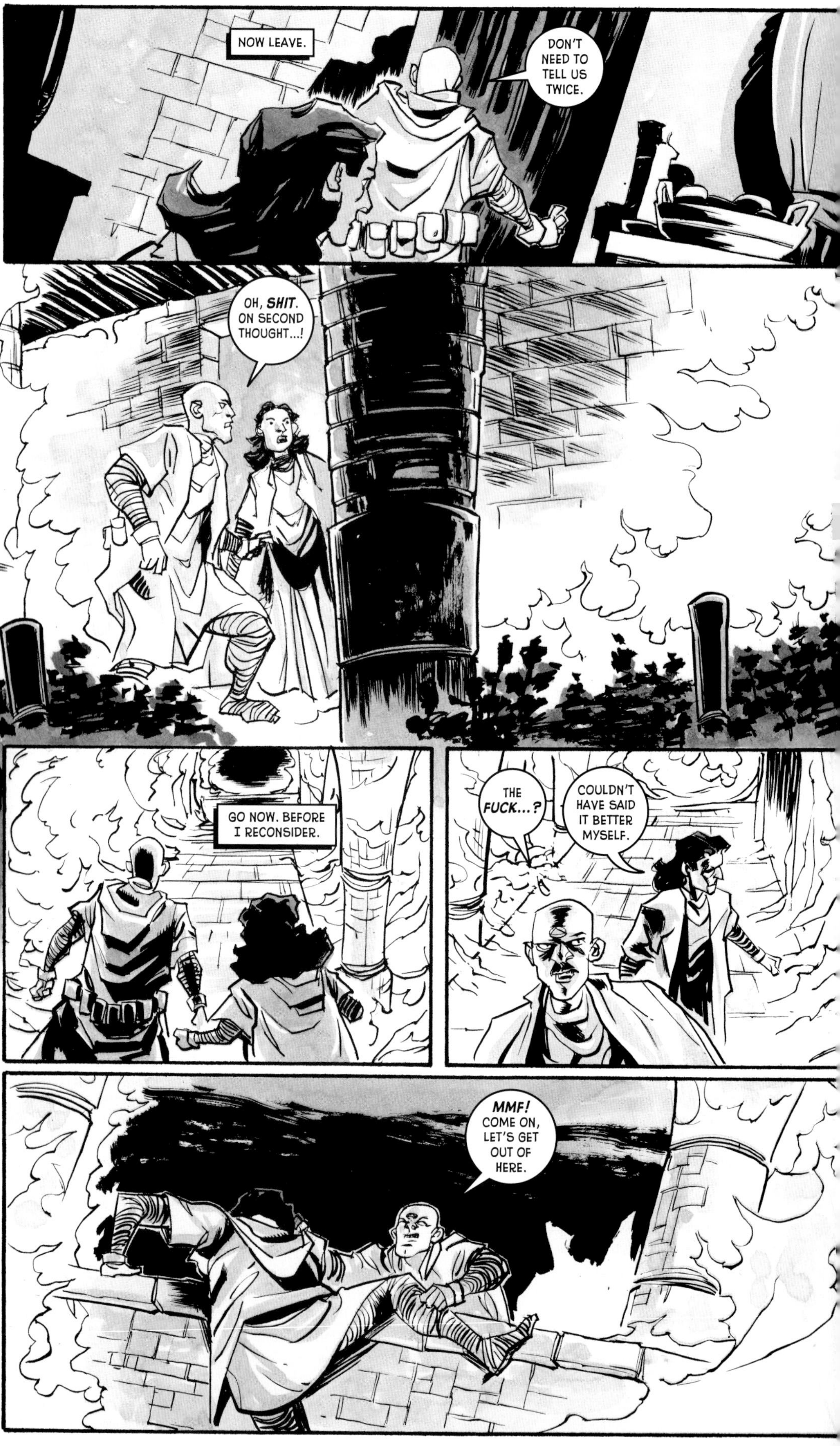
NOW LEAVE.
DON'T NEED TO TELL US TWICE.
OH, SHIT. ON SECOND THOUGHT...!
GO NOW. BEFORE I RECONSIDER.
THE FUCK...?
COULDN'T HAVE SAID IT BETTER MYSELF.
MMF! COME ON, LET'S GET OUT OF HERE.

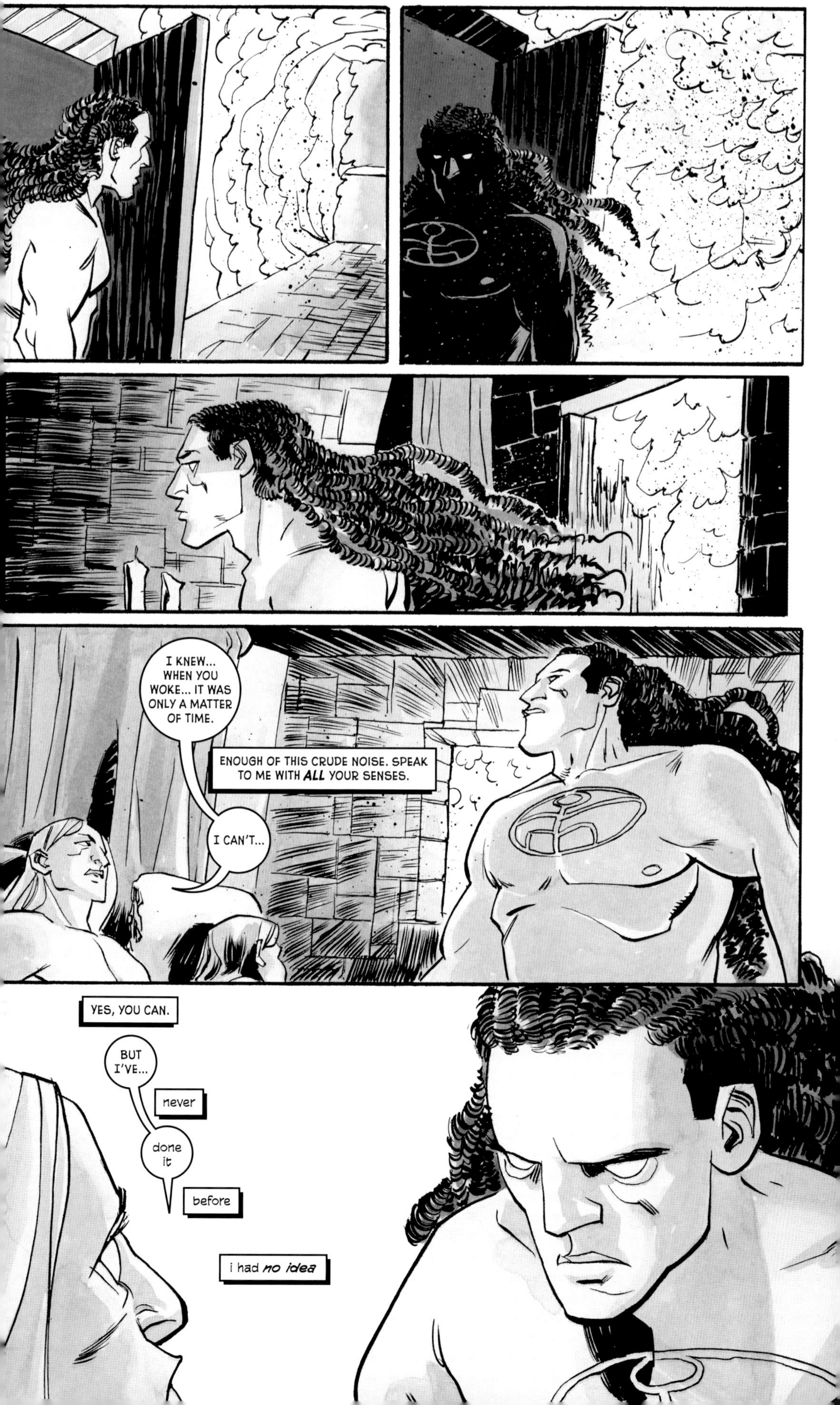
I KNEW... WHEN YOU WOKE... IT WAS ONLY A MATTER OF TIME.
ENOUGH OF THIS CRUDE NOISE. SPEAK TO ME WITH ***ALL*** YOUR SENSES.
I CAN'T...
YES, YOU CAN.
BUT I'VE...
never
done it
before
i had ***no idea***

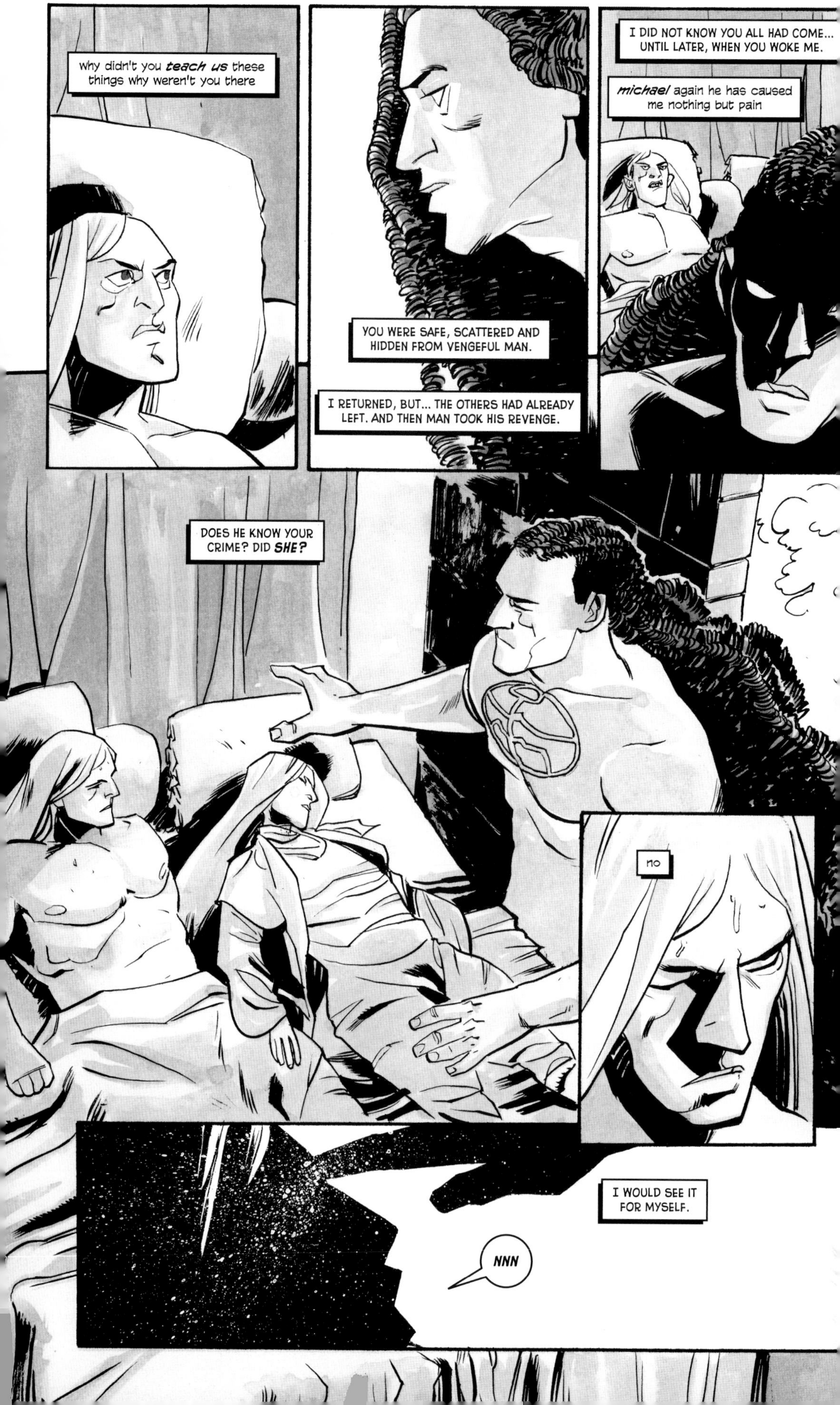
why didn't you ***teach us*** these things why weren't you there
YOU WERE SAFE, SCATTERED AND HIDDEN FROM VENGEFUL MAN.
I RETURNED, BUT... THE OTHERS HAD ALREADY LEFT. AND THEN MAN TOOK HIS REVENGE.
I DID NOT KNOW YOU ALL HAD COME... UNTIL LATER, WHEN YOU WOKE ME.
michael again he has caused me nothing but pain
DOES HE KNOW YOUR CRIME? DID ***SHE?***
no
I WOULD SEE IT FOR MYSELF.
NNN

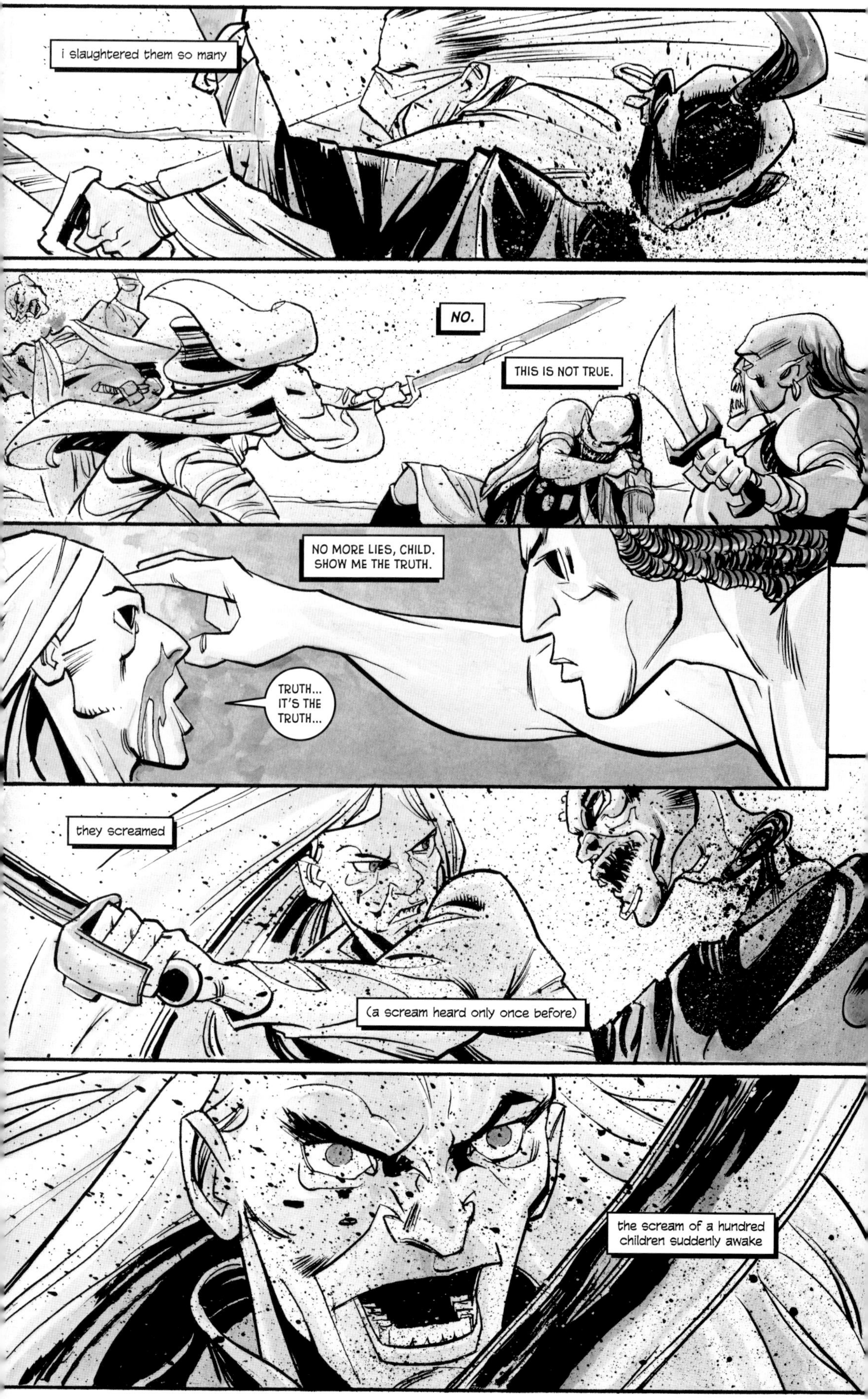
i slaughtered them so many
NO.
THIS IS NOT TRUE.
NO MORE LIES, CHILD. SHOW ME THE TRUTH.
TRUTH... IT'S THE TRUTH...
they screamed
(a scream heard only once before)
the scream of a hundred children suddenly awake

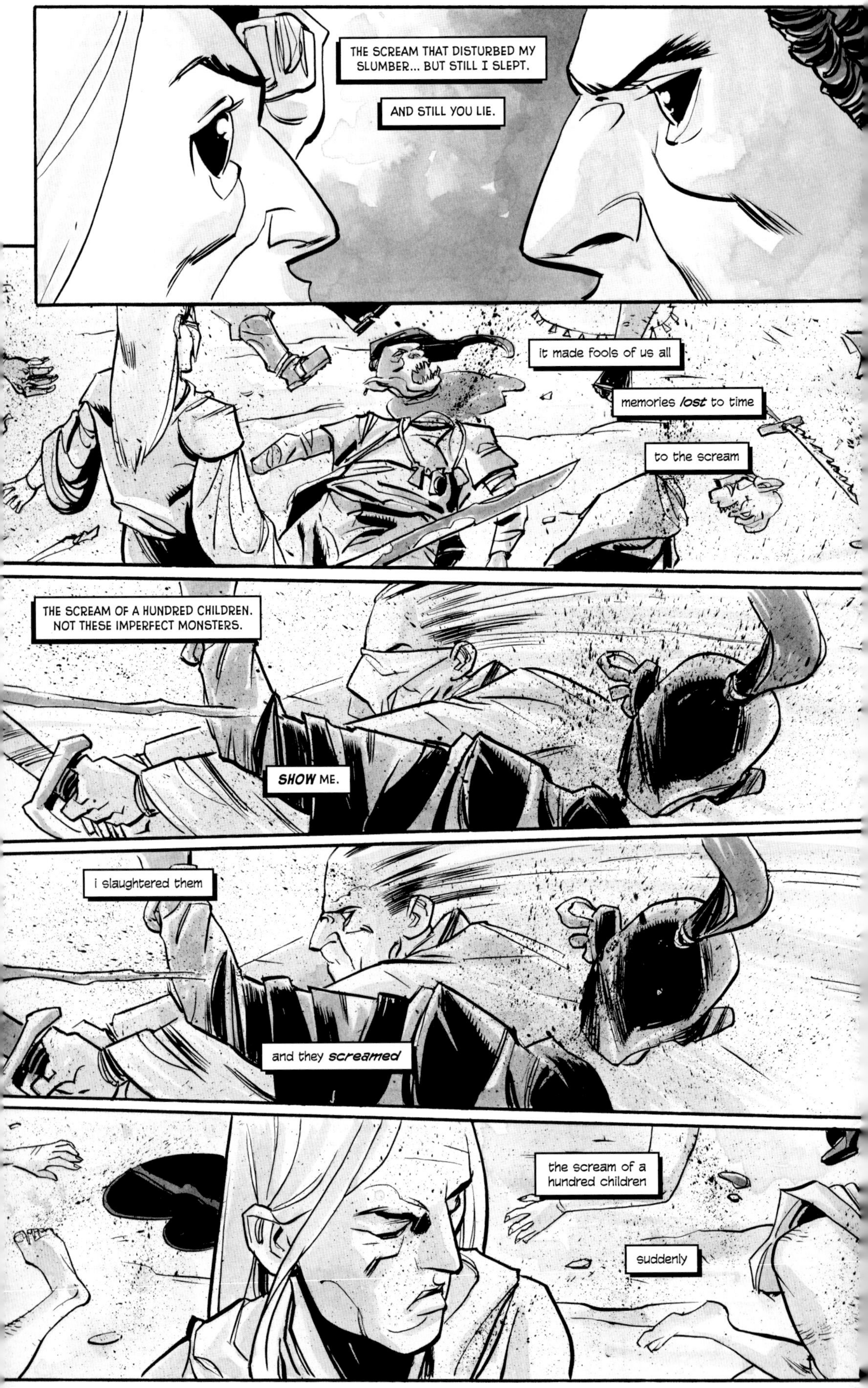
THE SCREAM THAT DISTURBED MY SLUMBER... BUT STILL I SLEPT.
AND STILL YOU LIE.
it made fools of us all
memories *lost* to time
to the scream
THE SCREAM OF A HUNDRED CHILDREN. NOT THESE IMPERFECT MONSTERS.
SHOW ME.
i slaughtered them
and they *screamed*
the scream of a hundred children
suddenly

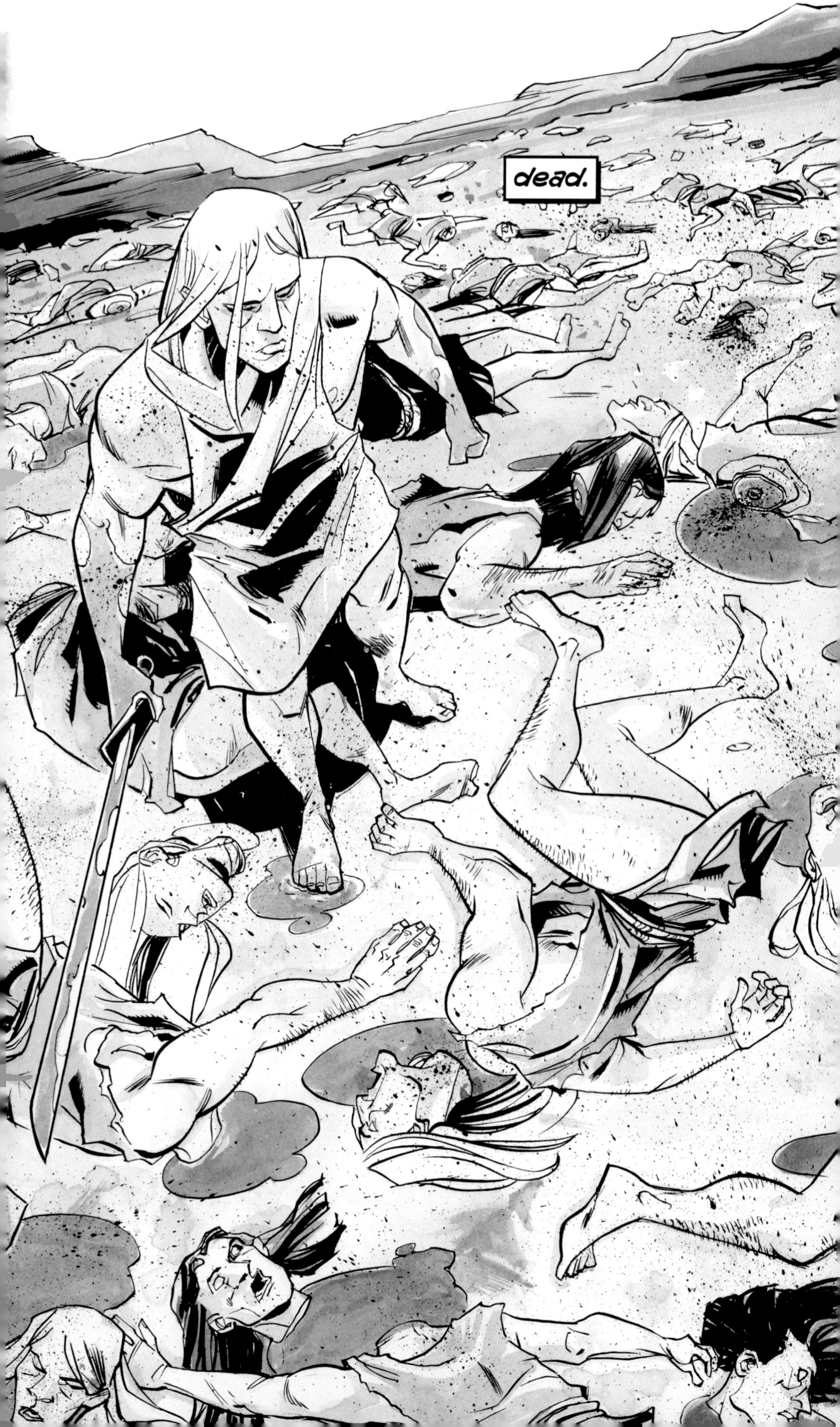
dead.

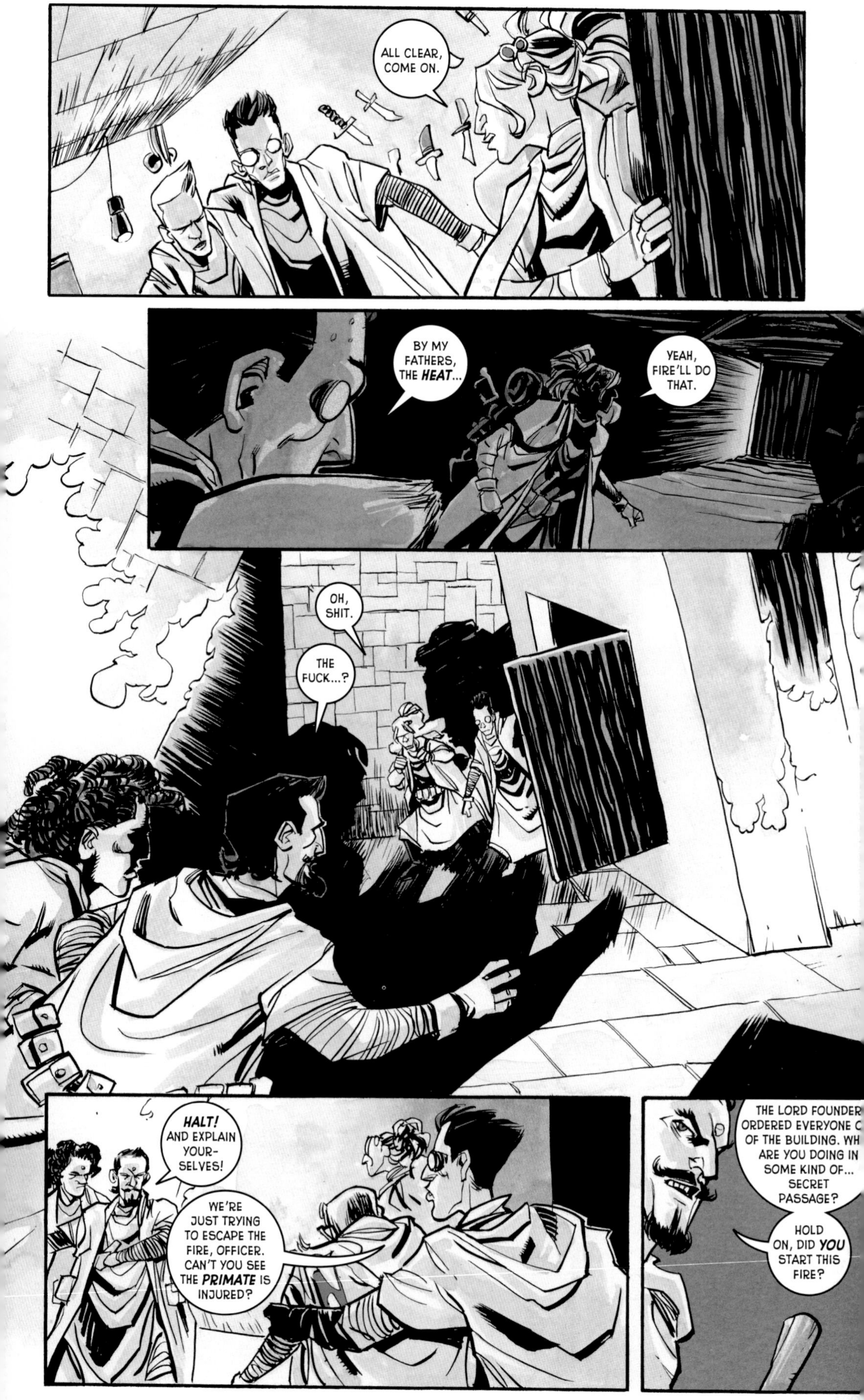
ALL CLEAR, COME ON.
BY MY FATHERS, THE HEAT...
YEAH, FIRE'LL DO THAT.
OH, SHIT.
THE FUCK...?
HALT! AND EXPLAIN YOUR-SELVES!
WE'RE JUST TRYING TO ESCAPE THE FIRE, OFFICER. CAN'T YOU SEE THE PRIMATE IS INJURED?
THE LORD FOUNDER ORDERED EVERYONE O OF THE BUILDING. WH ARE YOU DOING IN SOME KIND OF... SECRET PASSAGE?
HOLD ON, DID YOU START THIS FIRE?

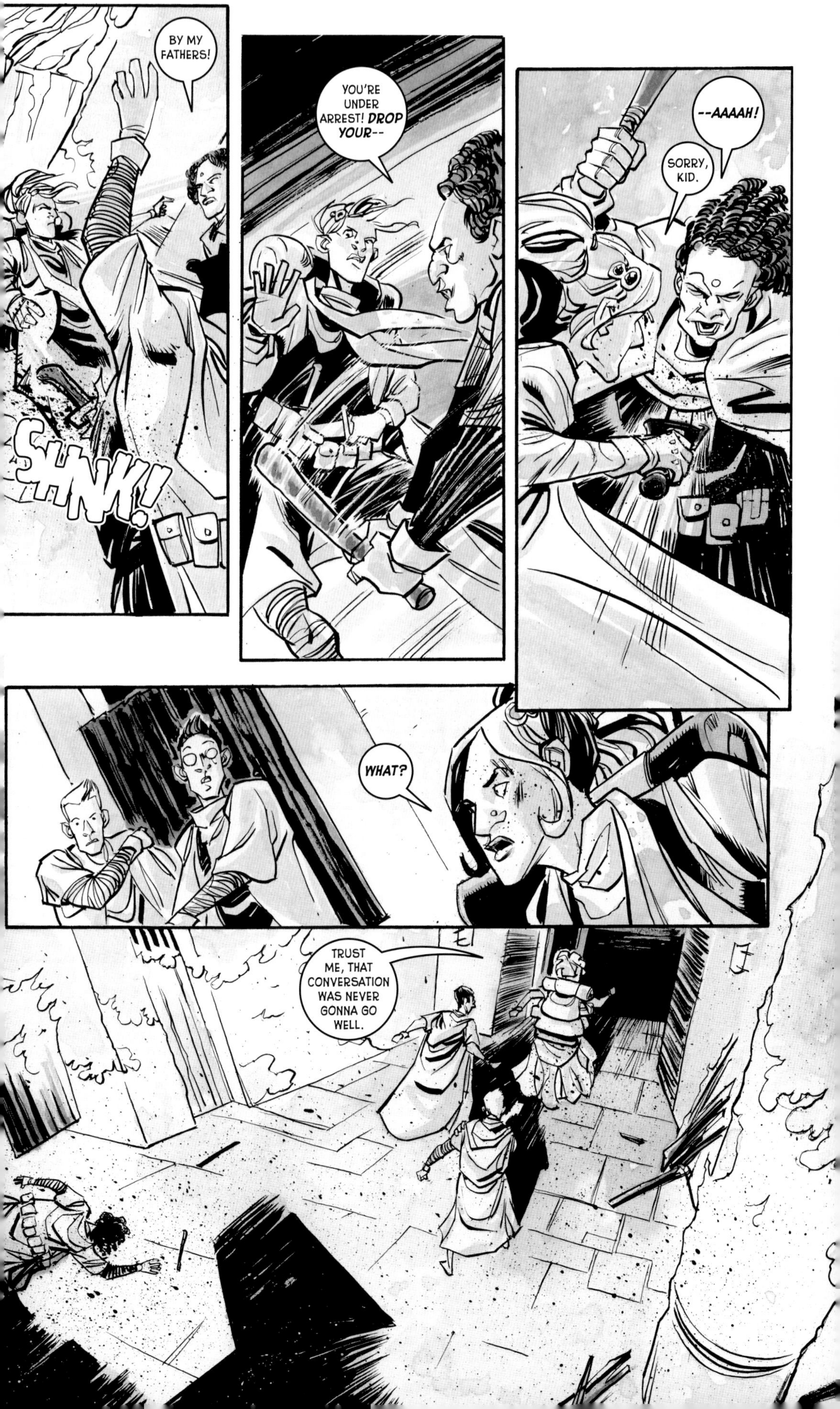
BY MY FATHERS!
SHNK!
YOU'RE UNDER ARREST! DROP YOUR--
--AAAAH!
SORRY, KID.
WHAT?
TRUST ME, THAT CONVERSATION WAS NEVER GONNA GO WELL.

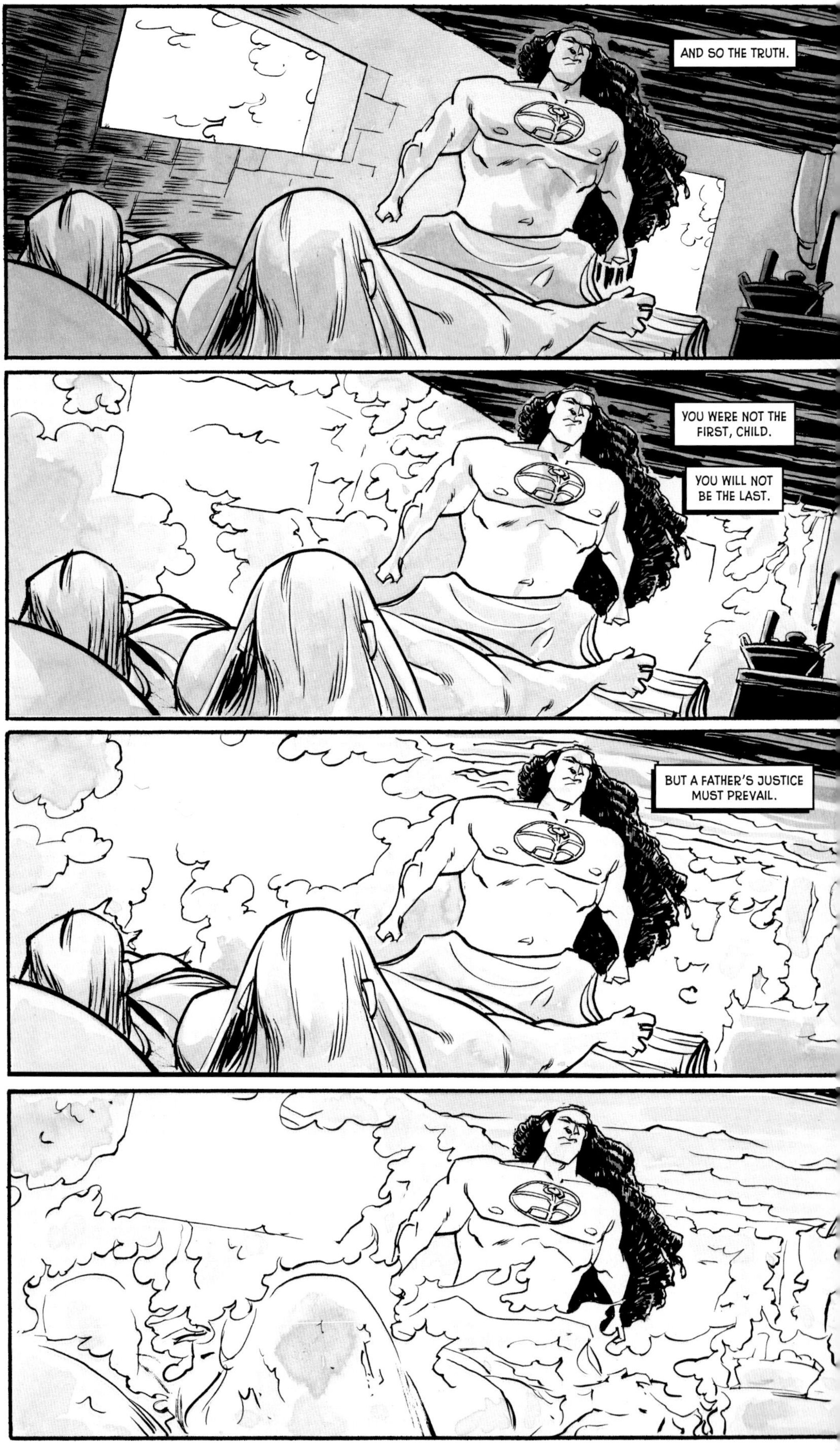
AND SO THE TRUTH.
YOU WERE NOT THE FIRST, CHILD.
YOU WILL NOT BE THE LAST.
BUT A FATHER'S JUSTICE MUST PREVAIL.

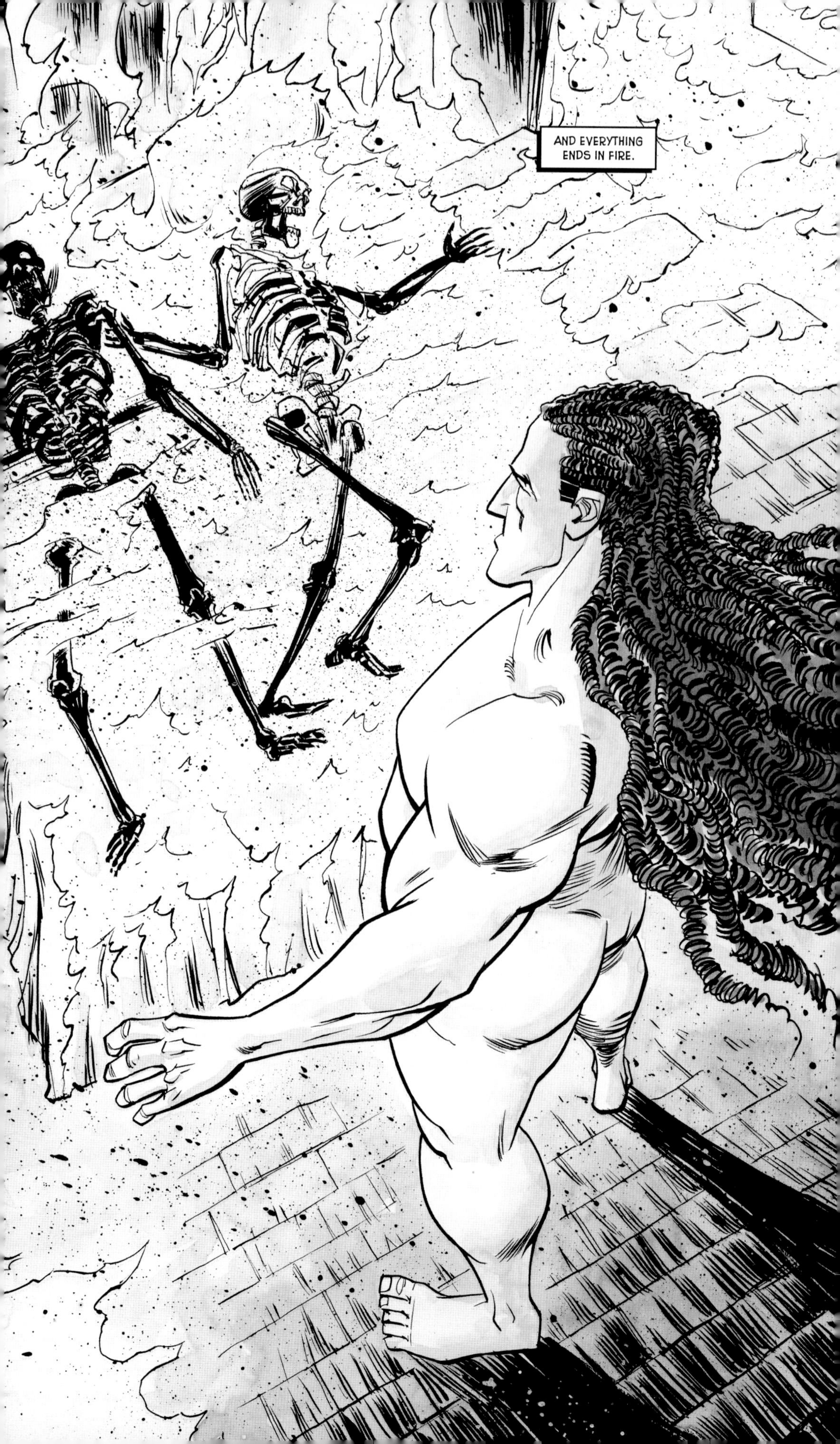
AND EVERYTHING ENDS IN FIRE.

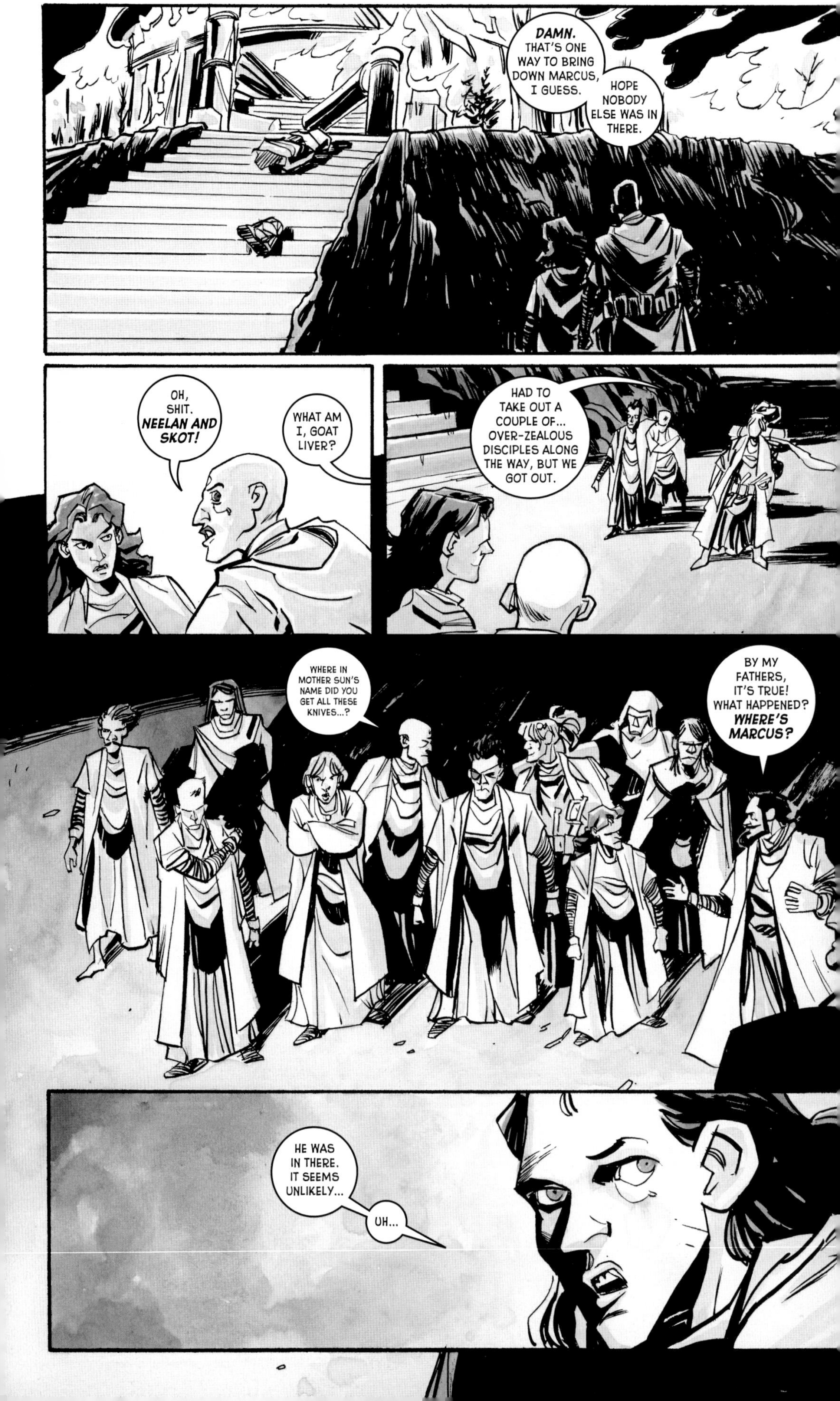
DAMN. THAT'S ONE WAY TO BRING DOWN MARCUS, I GUESS.
HOPE NOBODY ELSE WAS IN THERE.
OH, SHIT. NEELAN AND SKOT!
WHAT AM I, GOAT LIVER?
HAD TO TAKE OUT A COUPLE OF... OVER-ZEALOUS DISCIPLES ALONG THE WAY, BUT WE GOT OUT.
WHERE IN MOTHER SUN'S NAME DID YOU GET ALL THESE KNIVES...?
BY MY FATHERS, IT'S TRUE! WHAT HAPPENED? WHERE'S MARCUS?
HE WAS IN THERE. IT SEEMS UNLIKELY...
UH...

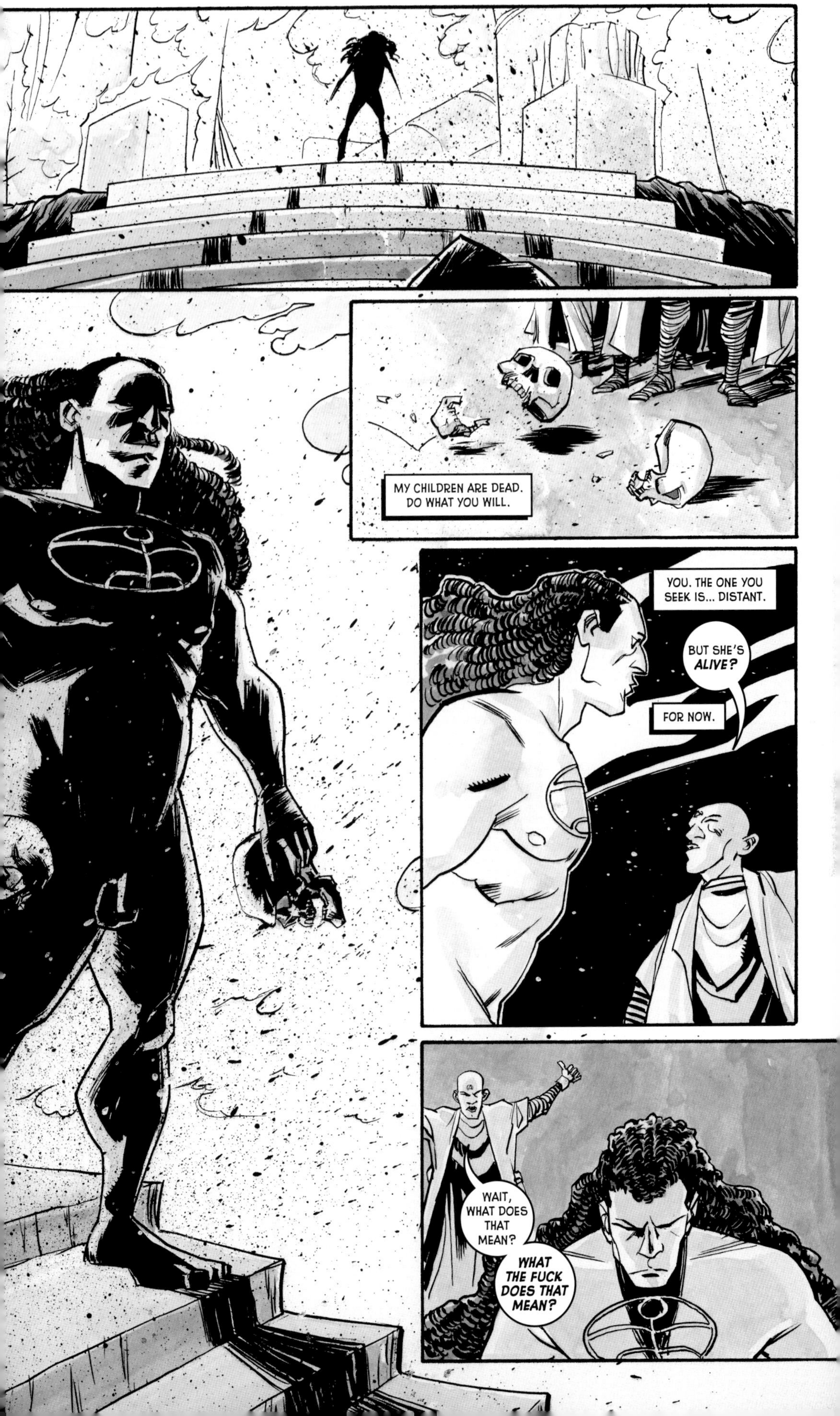
MY CHILDREN ARE DEAD. DO WHAT YOU WILL.
YOU. THE ONE YOU SEEK IS... DISTANT.
BUT SHE'S *ALIVE?*
FOR NOW.
WAIT, WHAT DOES THAT MEAN?
WHAT THE FUCK DOES THAT MEAN?

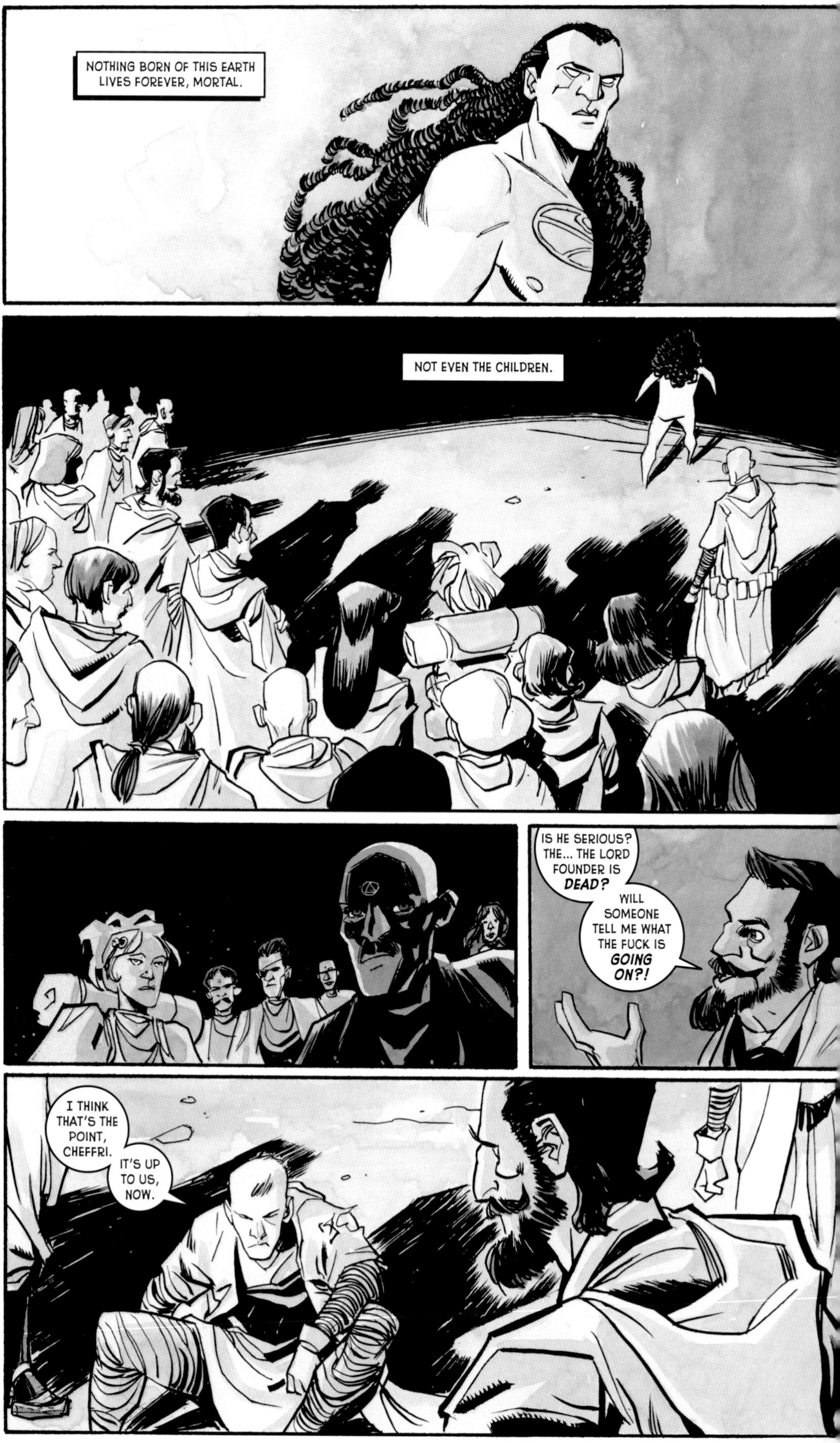
NOTHING BORN OF THIS EARTH LIVES FOREVER, MORTAL.
NOT EVEN THE CHILDREN.
IS HE SERIOUS? THE... THE LORD FOUNDER IS **DEAD?**
WILL SOMEONE TELL ME WHAT THE FUCK IS **GOING ON?!**
I THINK THAT'S THE POINT, CHEFFRI.
IT'S UP TO US, NOW.

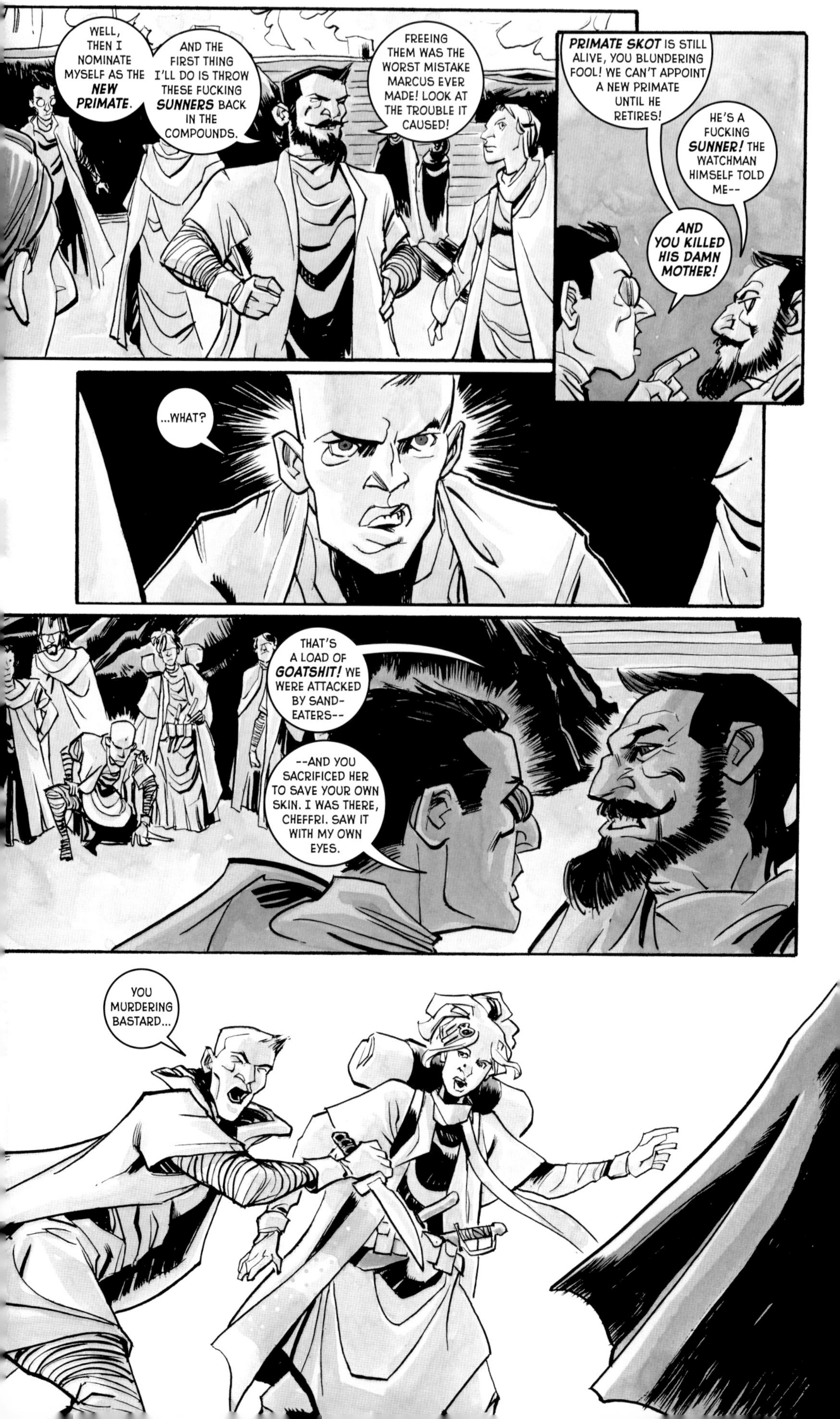
WELL, THEN I NOMINATE MYSELF AS THE NEW PRIMATE.
AND THE FIRST THING I'LL DO IS THROW THESE FUCKING SUNNERS BACK IN THE COMPOUNDS.
FREEING THEM WAS THE WORST MISTAKE MARCUS EVER MADE! LOOK AT THE TROUBLE IT CAUSED!
PRIMATE SKOT IS STILL ALIVE, YOU BLUNDERING FOOL! WE CAN'T APPOINT A NEW PRIMATE UNTIL HE RETIRES!
HE'S A FUCKING SUNNER! THE WATCHMAN HIMSELF TOLD ME--
AND YOU KILLED HIS DAMN MOTHER!
...WHAT?
THAT'S A LOAD OF GOATSHIT! WE WERE ATTACKED BY SAND-EATERS--
--AND YOU SACRIFICED HER TO SAVE YOUR OWN SKIN. I WAS THERE, CHEFFRI. SAW IT WITH MY OWN EYES.
YOU MURDERING BASTARD...

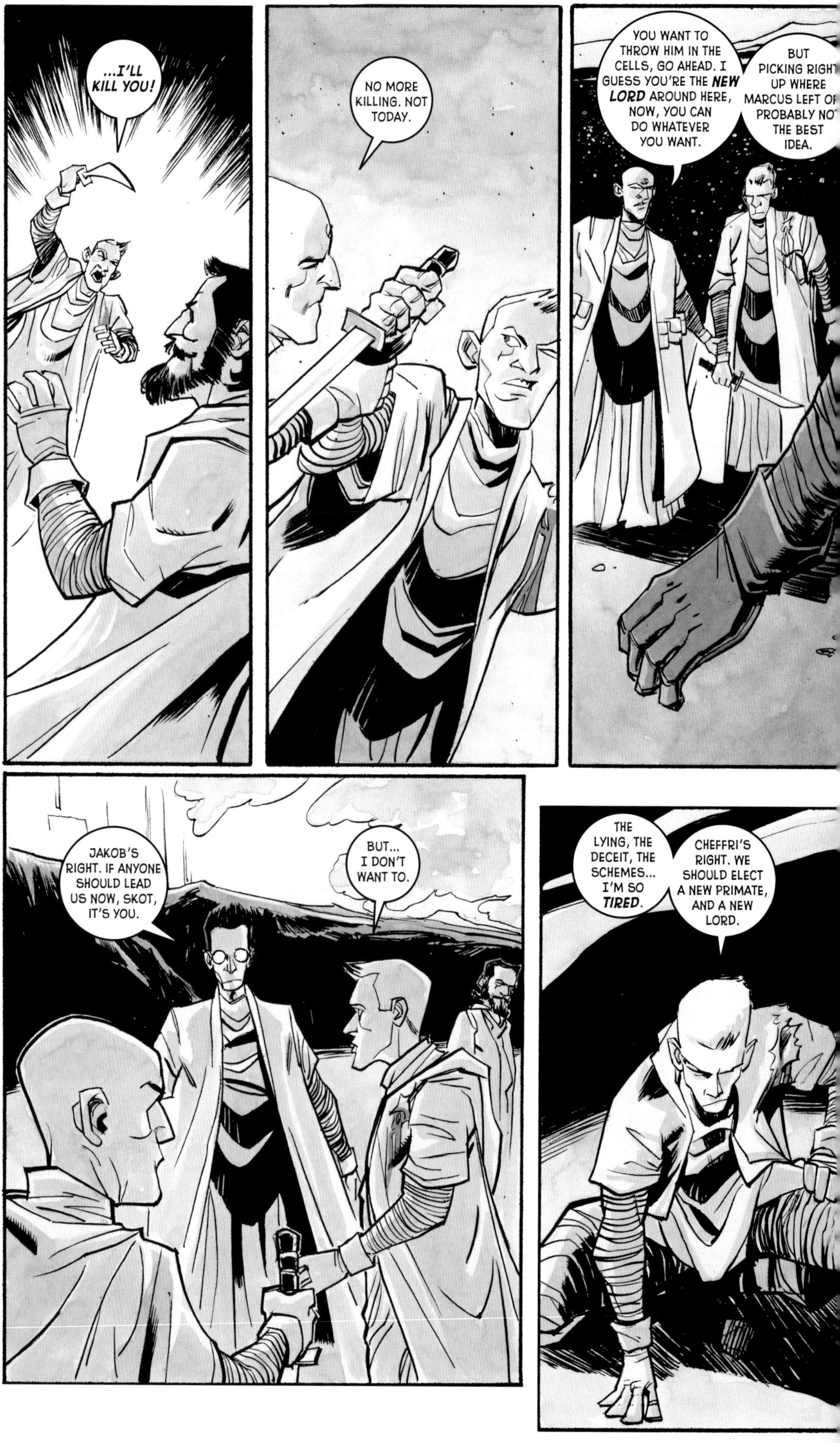
...I'LL KILL YOU!
NO MORE KILLING. NOT TODAY.
YOU WANT TO THROW HIM IN THE CELLS, GO AHEAD. I GUESS YOU'RE THE NEW LORD AROUND HERE, NOW, YOU CAN DO WHATEVER YOU WANT.
BUT PICKING RIGH UP WHERE MARCUS LEFT O PROBABLY NO THE BEST IDEA.
JAKOB'S RIGHT. IF ANYONE SHOULD LEAD US NOW, SKOT, IT'S YOU.
BUT... I DON'T WANT TO.
THE LYING, THE DECEIT, THE SCHEMES... I'M SO TIRED.
CHEFFRI'S RIGHT. WE SHOULD ELECT A NEW PRIMATE, AND A NEW LORD.

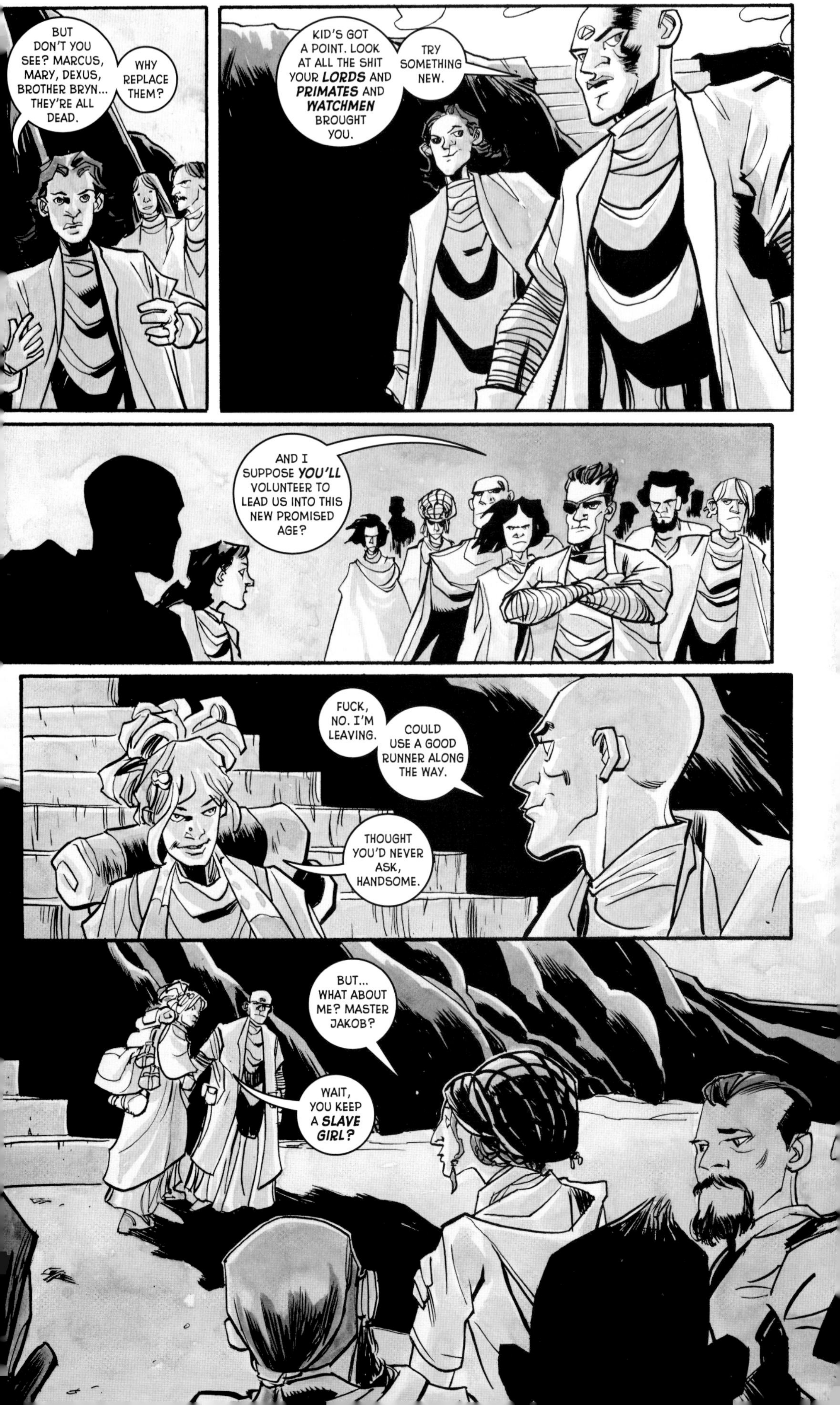
BUT DON'T YOU SEE? MARCUS, MARY, DEXUS, BROTHER BRYN... THEY'RE ALL DEAD.
WHY REPLACE THEM?
KID'S GOT A POINT. LOOK AT ALL THE SHIT YOUR LORDS AND PRIMATES AND WATCHMEN BROUGHT YOU.
TRY SOMETHING NEW.
AND I SUPPOSE YOU'LL VOLUNTEER TO LEAD US INTO THIS NEW PROMISED AGE?
FUCK, NO. I'M LEAVING.
COULD USE A GOOD RUNNER ALONG THE WAY.
THOUGHT YOU'D NEVER ASK, HANDSOME.
BUT... WHAT ABOUT ME? MASTER JAKOB?
WAIT, YOU KEEP A SLAVE GIRL?

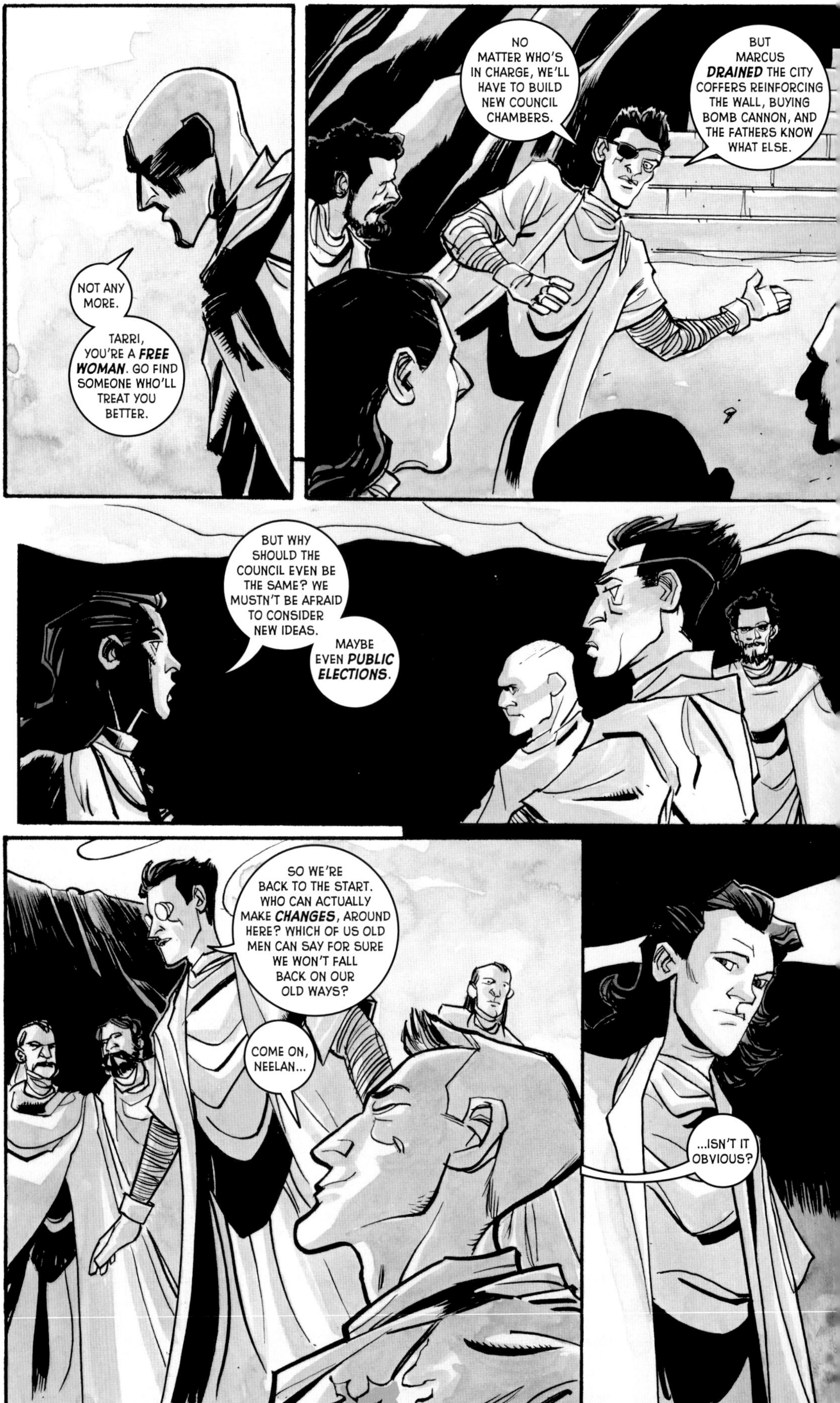
NOT ANY MORE.
TARRI, YOU'RE A FREE WOMAN. GO FIND SOMEONE WHO'LL TREAT YOU BETTER.
NO MATTER WHO'S IN CHARGE, WE'LL HAVE TO BUILD NEW COUNCIL CHAMBERS.
BUT MARCUS DRAINED THE CITY COFFERS REINFORCING THE WALL, BUYING BOMB CANNON, AND THE FATHERS KNOW WHAT ELSE.
BUT WHY SHOULD THE COUNCIL EVEN BE THE SAME? WE MUSTN'T BE AFRAID TO CONSIDER NEW IDEAS.
MAYBE EVEN PUBLIC ELECTIONS.
SO WE'RE BACK TO THE START. WHO CAN ACTUALLY MAKE CHANGES, AROUND HERE? WHICH OF US OLD MEN CAN SAY FOR SURE WE WON'T FALL BACK ON OUR OLD WAYS?
COME ON, NEELAN...
...ISN'T IT OBVIOUS?

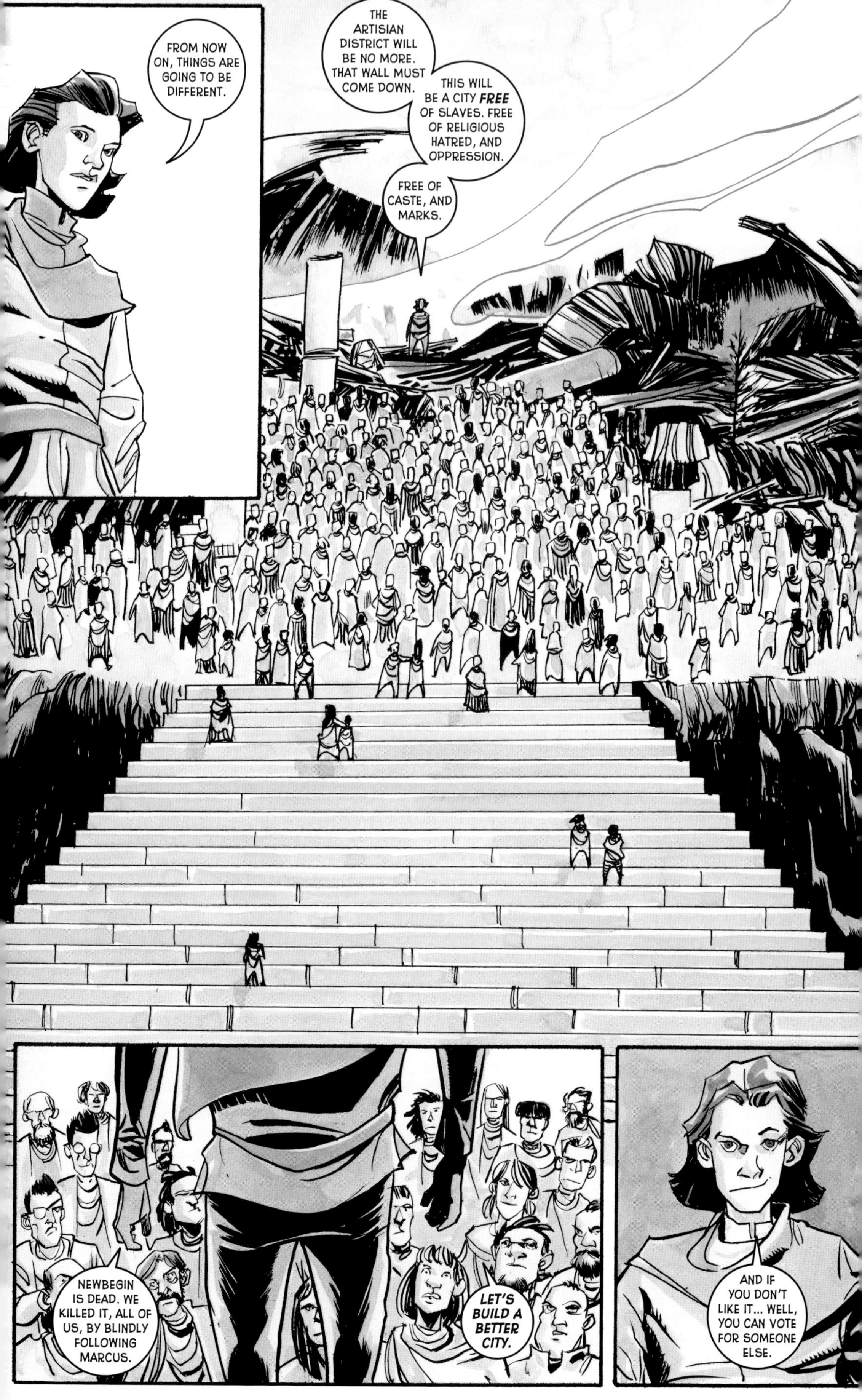
FROM NOW ON, THINGS ARE GOING TO BE DIFFERENT.
THE ARTISIAN DISTRICT WILL BE NO MORE. THAT WALL MUST COME DOWN.
THIS WILL BE A CITY **FREE** OF SLAVES. FREE OF RELIGIOUS HATRED, AND OPPRESSION.
FREE OF CASTE, AND MARKS.
NEWBEGIN IS DEAD. WE KILLED IT, ALL OF US, BY BLINDLY FOLLOWING MARCUS.
LET'S BUILD A BETTER CITY.
AND IF YOU DON'T LIKE IT... WELL, YOU CAN VOTE FOR SOMEONE ELSE.

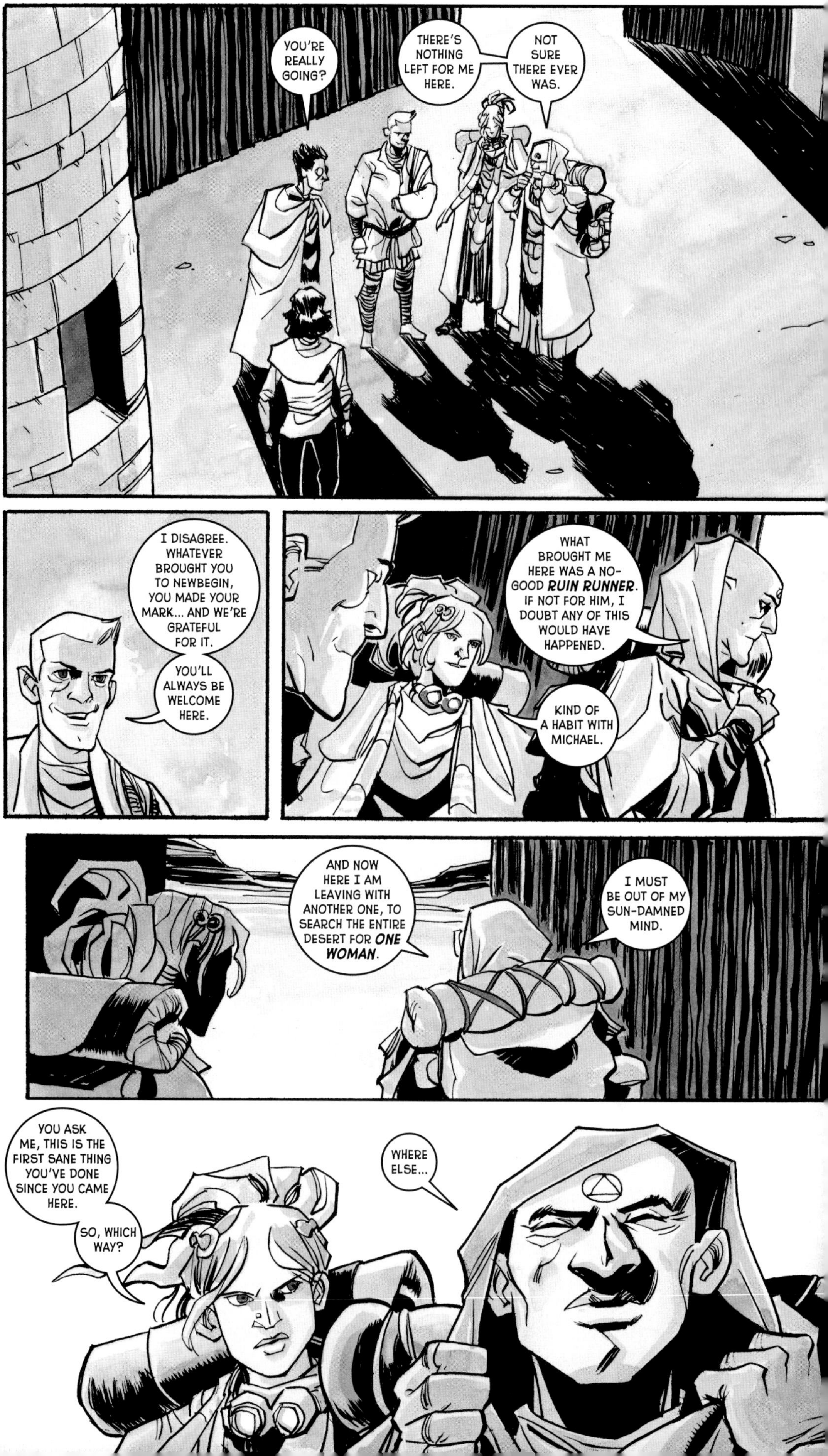
YOU'RE REALLY GOING?
THERE'S NOTHING LEFT FOR ME HERE.
NOT SURE THERE EVER WAS.
I DISAGREE. WHATEVER BROUGHT YOU TO NEWBEGIN, YOU MADE YOUR MARK... AND WE'RE GRATEFUL FOR IT.
YOU'LL ALWAYS BE WELCOME HERE.
WHAT BROUGHT ME HERE WAS A NO-GOOD **RUIN RUNNER**. IF NOT FOR HIM, I DOUBT ANY OF THIS WOULD HAVE HAPPENED.
KIND OF A HABIT WITH MICHAEL.
AND NOW HERE I AM LEAVING WITH ANOTHER ONE, TO SEARCH THE ENTIRE DESERT FOR ***ONE WOMAN***.
I MUST BE OUT OF MY SUN-DAMNED MIND.
YOU ASK ME, THIS IS THE FIRST SANE THING YOU'VE DONE SINCE YOU CAME HERE.
SO, WHICH WAY?
WHERE ELSE...

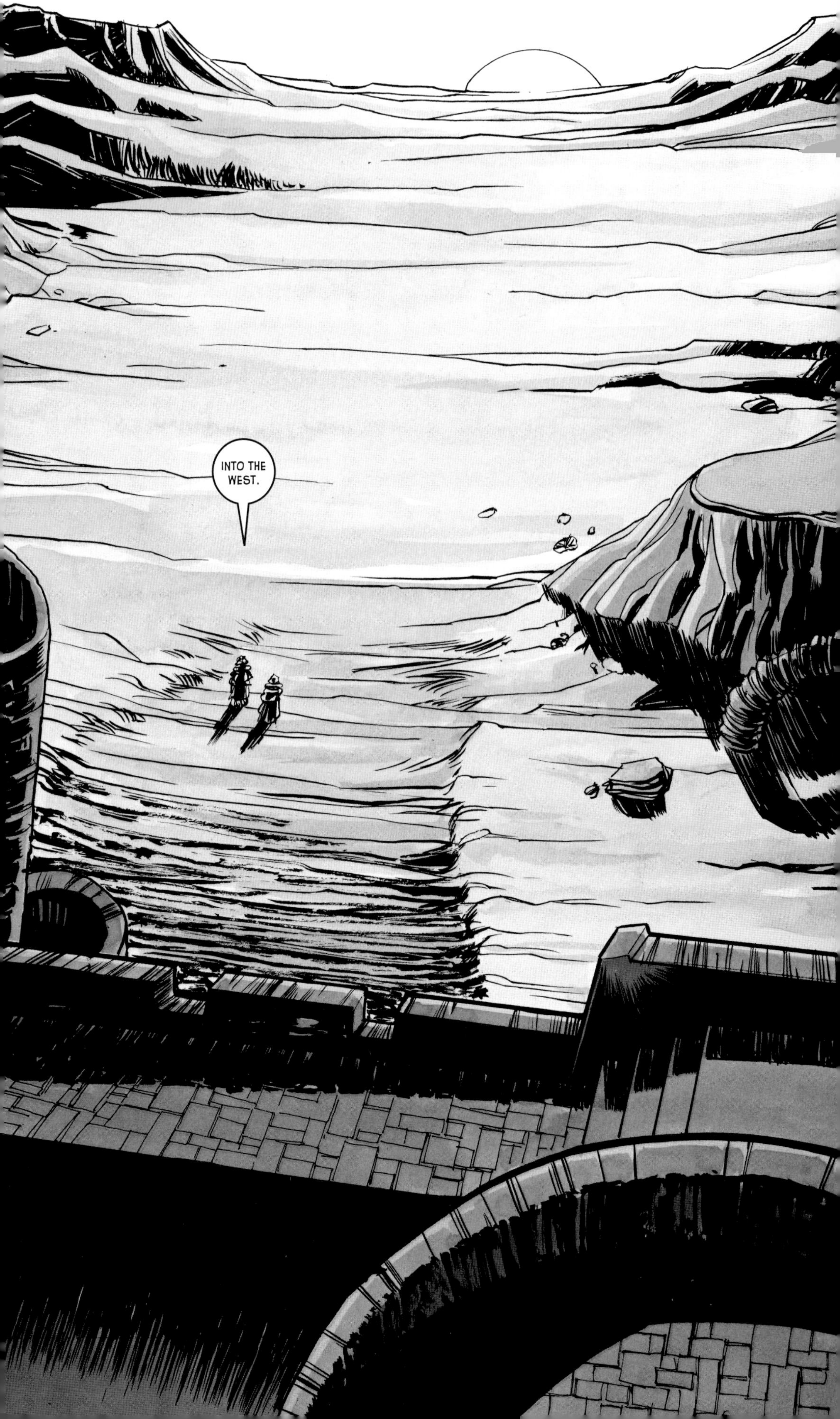
INTO THE WEST.

TO BE **CONTINUED**

ANTONY JOHNSTON

Born and raised in central England, Antony is an award-winning, *New York Times* bestselling author of graphic novels, comics, videogames, and books. He lives in northern England and wears a lot of black.
ANTONYJOHNSTON.COM

Justin hails from the mighty Bay Area, where he still lives and works with his wife and family. When he's not poking around farmer's markets or knee deep in a card game, you'll find him drawing. Justin has illustrated both WASTELAND and RESURRECTION for Oni Press, and has also worked on titles like MASKS AND MOBSTERS, GHOST TOWN, and the anthology CONTINUUM: THE WAR FILES, for other publishers.
JKGREENWOOD.COM

JUSTIN GREENWOOD

WASTELAND: THE APOCALYPTIC EDITION

THE ULTIMATE VERSION OF THE EPIC SAGA

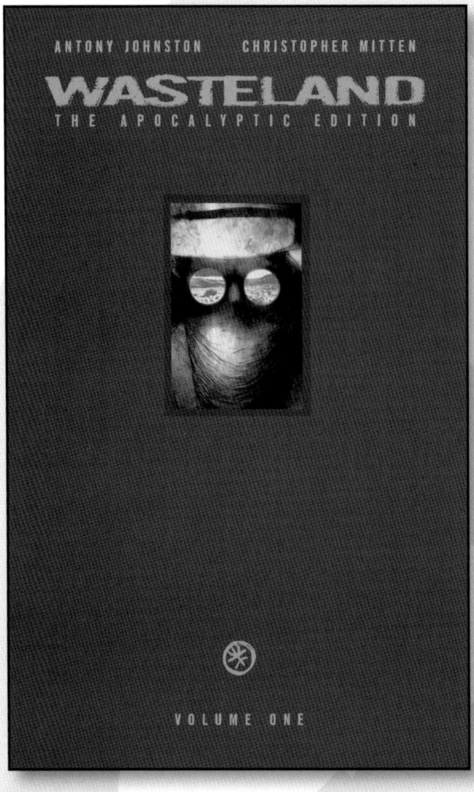

ANTONY JOHNSTON
CHRISTOPHER MITTEN
WASTELAND
THE APOCALYPTIC EDITION
VOLUME ONE

The Apocalyptic Editions contain every issue of Wasteland, plus full-color cover galleries, the 'Walking the Dust' travelogue essays, and new illustrations. They're presented in oversized, cloth-bound hardbacks with gold leaf embossing and superior paper stock.

...Trust us, these things will survive the Big Wet.

THE APOCALYPTIC EDITION, VOLUME 1

JOHNSTON & MITTEN, ET AL
384 PAGES · HARDCOVER
ISBN 978-1-934964-19-4

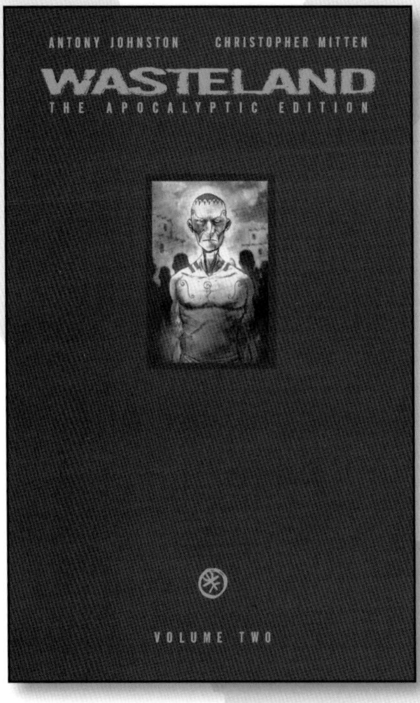

ANTONY JOHNSTON
CHRISTOPHER MITTEN
WASTELAND
THE APOCALYPTIC EDITION
VOLUME TWO

THE APOCALYPTIC EDITION, VOLUME 2

JOHNSTON & MITTEN, ET AL
352 PAGES · HARDCOVER
ISBN 978-1-934964-46-0

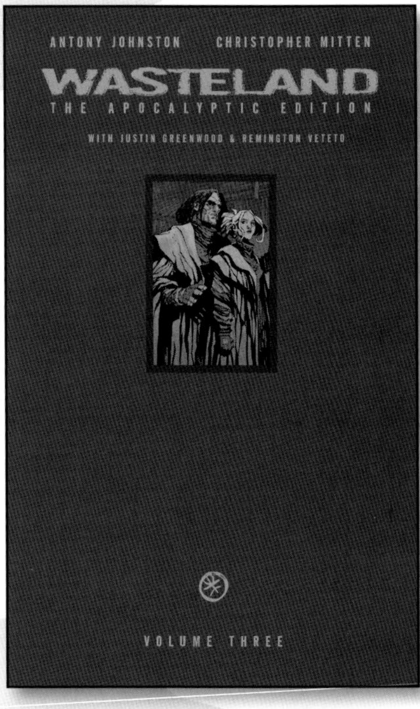

ANTONY JOHNSTON
CHRISTOPHER MITTEN
WASTELAND
THE APOCALYPTIC EDITION
WITH JUSTIN GREENWOOD & REMINGTON VETETO
VOLUME THREE

THE APOCALYPTIC EDITION, VOLUME 3

JOHNSTON & MITTEN, ET AL
394 PAGES · HARDCOVER
ISBN 978-1-62010-093-6

WASTELAND
ANTONY JOHNSTON
CHRISTOPHER MITTEN
BOOK 01
CITIES IN DUST

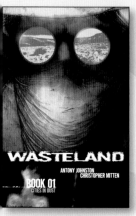

BOOK 01
CITIES IN DUST

JOHNSTON & MITTEN
160 PAGES · PAPERBACK
ISBN 978-1-932664-59-1

"Overflowing with grit, mutants and high-caliber dialogue."
WIZARD
WASTELAND
ANTONY JOHNSTON
CHRISTOPHER MITTEN
BOOK 02
SHADES OF GOD

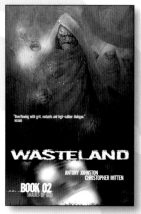

BOOK 02
SHADES OF GOD

JOHNSTON & MITTEN
136 PAGES · PAPERBACK
ISBN 978-1-932664-90-4

WASTELAND
ANTONY JOHNSTON
CHRISTOPHER MITTEN
BOOK 03
BLACK STEEL
IN THE HOUR OF
CHAOS

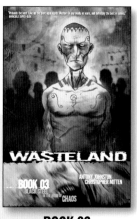

BOOK 03
BLACK STEEL IN THE HOUR OF CHAOS

JOHNSTON & MITTEN
128 PAGES · PAPERBACK
ISBN 978-1-934964-08-8

WASTELAND
ANTONY JOHNSTON
CHRISTOPHER MITTEN
BOOK 04
DOG TRIBE

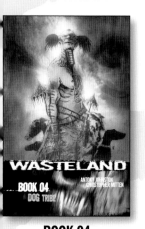

BOOK 04
DOG TRIBE

JOHNSTON & MITTEN
104 PAGES · PAPERBACK
ISBN 978-1-934964-17-0

WASTELAND
ANTONY JOHNSTON
CHRISTOPHER MITTEN
BOOK 05
TALES OF THE UNINVITED
WITH
CARLA SPEED McNEIL
JOE INFURNARI
CHUCK BB

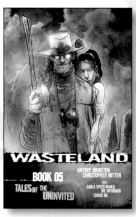

BOOK 05
TALES OF THE UNINVITED

JOHNSTON & MITTEN, ET AL
128 PAGES · PAPERBACK
ISBN 978-1-934964-29-3

WASTELAND
BOOK 06
THE ENEMY WITHIN
ANTONY JOHNSTON
CHRISTOPHER MITTEN

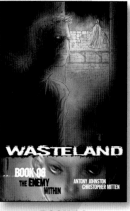

BOOK 06
THE ENEMY WITHIN

JOHNSTON, MITTEN & VETETO
152 PAGES · PAPERBACK
ISBN 978-1-934964-30-9

WASTELAND
BOOK 07
ANTONY JOHNSTON
JUSTIN GREENWOOD
UNDER THE GOD

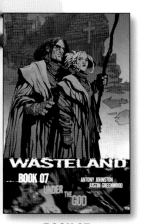

BOOK 07
UNDER THE GOD

JOHNSTON & GREENWOOD
144 PAGES · PAPERBACK
ISBN 978-1-934964-94-1

WASTELAND
BOOK 08
ANTONY JOHNSTON
RUSSEL ROEHLING
LOST IN THE OZONE

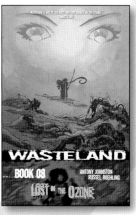

BOOK 08
LOST IN THE OZONE

JOHNSTON & ROEHLING
128 PAGES · PAPERBACK
ISBN 978-1-62010-013-4

AVAILABLE NOW FROM ALL GOOD COMIC AND BOOK STORES

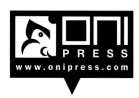

ONI PRESS
www.onipress.com

IPRESS.COM ANTONYJOHNSTON.COM CHRISTOPHERMITTEN.COM JKGREENWOOD.COM RUSSELROEHLING.COM